T0293567

Praise for Tech Startup

If you search for a contemporary definition of the word "tenacity," you will surely find a photo of Jothy Rosenberg. He typifies every aspect of that key entrepreneurial trait.

—Jules Knittel Pieri, founder, CEO, investor, author;
Board Member, XFactor Ventures

As you read the colorful stories and the lessons learned in this book (be sure to read the seven-sentence "haiku" of elevator pitches), you will quickly come to realize what I have come to know from working with him: Jothy is the Patton of startup founders. Smart, experienced, willing to change, supremely confident, and just plain will not give up. Ever.

—Kaigham Gabriel, President and CEO, BioForge; CEO, Draper
Laboratory; Deputy Director, DARPA; co-founder, Chairman, and CTO, Akustica

I joined my first startup at age 50—both an exciting and terrifying experience. I was lucky to have Jothy as my CEO and co-founder. If you're thinking of leading or founding a startup, this book is a must-read.

—Marco Ciaffi, Director Embedded Systems,
Re:Build Fikst; co-founder and VP Engineering,
Dover Microsystems; Senior Engineering Manager, RSA

Founding, building, and running early-stage tech companies is never easy. For anyone who is thinking of founding a company or who already has, read Tech Startup Toolkit. *Jothy has provided a brilliant and straightforward roadmap for everything that you will see on your journey.*

—Patrick Morley, former CEO, Carbon Black;
part of four IPO deals

The people who are crazy enough to think they can change the world are the ones who do.

—Steve Jobs

Get the eBook FREE!

(PDF, ePub, Kindle, and liveBook all included)

We believe that once you buy a book from us, you should be able to read it in any format we have available. To get electronic versions of this book at no additional cost to you, purchase and then register this book at the Manning website.

Go to https://www.manning.com/freebook and follow the instructions to complete your pBook registration.

That's it!
Thanks from Manning!

Tech Startup Toolkit

How to launch strong and exit big

Jothy Rosenberg

Foreword by Vivjan Myrto

MANNING

Shelter Island

Manning Publications Co.
20 Baldwin Road
PO Box 761
Shelter Island, NY 11964

Development editor:	Karen Miller
Review editor:	Isidora Isakov
Production editor:	Kathy Rossland
Copy editor:	Tiffany Taylor
Proofreader:	Jason Everett
Technical proofreader:	Marjukka Niinioja
Typesetter:	Dennis Dalinnik
Cover designer:	Marija Tudor

ISBN: 9781633438422
Printed in the United States of America

To Carole, my anchor

contents

foreword

I will either find a way or make one.

—Hannibal

In a world where everything looks like an overnight success, often glossing over the grinding gears of building companies and, most often, failure, Jothy Rosenberg's story emerges not just as a beacon for aspiring entrepreneurs but as a guidebook that enriches our understanding of the perseverance required to navigate the unpredictable seas of startup culture.

Jothy Rosenberg is not your typical author or entrepreneur. His journey from a two-time cancer survivor who lost a leg and a lung as a teenager and was given "zero chance" of survival, to a powerhouse in the technology entrepreneurship space for over three decades, is a profound testament to human resilience. His life, defined by overcoming seemingly insurmountable odds, imbues every page of this book with deep insights and unstoppable determination.

Tech Startup Toolkit: How to launch strong and exit big does more than recount Jothy's experiences; it offers them as lessons in the guise of stories. Through each chapter, he shares not only the triumphs but also the lessons learned from devastating setbacks. His narrative style—engaging and humor-laced—brings to life the trials and triumphs of his entrepreneurial journey, making the lessons accessible and relatable to anyone facing their own battles, whether in Silicon Valley or beyond.

Jothy doesn't just tell stories; he teaches through his experiences. He offers candid, practical advice on dealing with investors, boards, and the many challenges of leadership. His insights are born from real-life trials and triumphs, providing invaluable guidance to those at the helm of a new venture.

Jothy's ability to articulate the lessons learned from five decades of facing and overcoming adversity is a rare gift. His stories are not just applicable to those dealing with personal health challenges or disabilities; they resonate with anyone navigating the rough waters of life's challenges. His practical advice extends beyond business strategies to fundamental life lessons on resilience, adaptability, and perseverance.

Tech Startup Toolkit is thus more than a business manual; it is a narrative of enduring spirit and relentless pursuit. It inspires potential founders and anyone who dreams of making their mark despite the odds. The book demystifies the entrepreneurial path, offering both inspiration and practical strategies essential for anyone aspiring to innovate and lead.

For aspiring entrepreneurs, this book is a treasure trove of strategies; for seasoned business leaders, it offers new perspectives on familiar challenges; and for the general reader, it presents the awe-inspiring story of a man who continuously redefines the possible. Each chapter builds on the last, culminating in a comprehensive guide that is as informative as it is inspiring.

As you embark on this journey with Jothy Rosenberg, expect to be moved, educated, and inspired to think like a startup founder. This book doesn't merely change the way you approach entrepreneurship—it transforms how you face challenges and seize opportunities in life.

Dive into *Tech Startup Toolkit* and let Jothy's life lessons empower you to navigate your path, whether in business or in overcoming personal challenges. It's more than a book; it's a new way of thinking about resilience and success.

—VIVJAN MYRTO,
Founder and Managing Editor, Hyperplane

Like seams of gold in a goldrush-era mine, many countries now have strong seams of innovation running through them. Sure, one of the motivations for an innovative tech founder is to strike gold with a profitable exit so all the founders and investors get rich beyond their wildest dreams. But most founders I know don't start with the certainty that they can build the next unicorn company—it's not the best premise for a startup. Instead, they start with an idea they believe will change the world, and they want to take that idea and turn it into a new company. Then they want to bring to market a product that implements their world-changing idea. You change a big enough market in a meaningful way, and your wildest dreams will not be nearly wild enough. But, of course, it is not nearly as easy as that sounds.

You may have heard that roughly 8 out of 10 startups fail. If that statement dissuades you, maybe you are not ready for the startup adventure. If instead that statement elicits from you a "Well, mine won't be one of those eight!" response, you have the right attitude. It would be hard to find a human endeavor that is more fraught with mistakes, risk, and outright failure than the entrepreneurial game of startups. It would also be hard to find a human endeavor where the payoff—intellectual, emotional, and financial—is more rewarding.

There is a phenomenon I have observed in myself and in countless other entrepreneurs: armed with that great idea, the individual becomes singularly focused on founding a company, putting most other things in their careers on hold. I relish that moment of focus and clarity, because the goal is set, the tasks are laid out in front of you, progress is rapid, and it is yours to build the way you think is right and good—you are totally in control of your own destiny. I also am well aware that after the IRS has issued your new venture a tax ID, the state has issued its articles of incorporation, and you have deservedly had a celebration of that accomplishment, reality sets in, and you realize that the number of items on your to-do list is positively overwhelming. What should you do first? What can be left for later? Who can help you make this dream a reality?

These, and many other critical questions, are why I wrote this book. In the process of founding and leading nine startups over 35 years, I asked these questions, too—but I had to figure out the answers myself because I couldn't find the book I needed. So, I set out to document the situations I found myself in, the decisions I made, the consequences of those decisions, and what I learned from each. I made a fair number of mistakes, some small and some catastrophic. I believe we all learn the most from our mistakes, not from our great successes. That led me to build this book on a foundation of telling the unvarnished truth.

The first goal I have is to help you avoid my mistakes (go make your own) and have a smoother journey to building a successful business. My second goal is that during moments when you feel overwhelmed, when you are not sleeping, when you have so much coming at you that it feels like you are in the middle of a maelstrom, I can give you a resource to guide you regarding the most critical achievements so you can ignore all the things that can wait and focus sharply and clearly on what really matters. And my stretch goal is to chip away at that 8-out-of-10 failure statistic and turn it around to move closer to 8 out of 10 startups succeeding (for those who read this book, of course).

Okay, who precisely did I write this book for? It is for the prospective founder who has an idea and thinks their idea has the potential to impact a very large market—but they're not sure where to start. It is for the founding team that has already created their startup but realizes they don't know what they don't know and are looking for help. It is for all the CEOs (frequently also founders) of early-stage (Series A or earlier) startups who need to raise money, guide their team to prove product–market fit, and create a go-to-market strategy.

This has been a labor of love. I hope you find it useful.

acknowledgments

I have a lot of people to thank for this book finally coming to fruition, starting with my wife of 43 years, Carole Hohl (affectionately known as "Carole with an 'e'"). Through all these 35 years of startups, including a move away from "safe" North Carolina to earthquake-prone California, she has always been supportive, even during all those sleepless nights and cold sweats. And when one startup ended, and she was sure that was it, Carole remained supportive (tolerant?) while I got the next one going, sometimes with an (understandable) roll of her eyes. Once settled in Boston, I had the incredibly masochistic idea of doing a startup in Portland, Oregon, commuting there from Boston—and she was tolerant (but rolled her eyes even more). As for this book, she watched as I dedicated mornings from 4:00 to 6:00 a.m. to it; and anecdote by anecdote, she asked probing questions that made it much better. She is the love of my life.

Susan and Patrick McCoy have been our best friends since we met at Duke in 1978. Susan is always curious about the next company, the next book, the next challenging sport. I wrote quite a bit of this book while visiting them in pastoral mid-Vermont.

I have known Erin Servais for almost 15 years. My first experience with her was when she worked for the publisher of the first edition of my memoir, *Who Says I Can't*. It reads well and doesn't offend anyone because of her great skills in both development and line editing—and, most importantly, due to her skills at asking me to be more politic in certain areas, even to the point of insisting on major deletions. Since then, she, too, has become an entrepreneur who started her own company called Dot and Dash. She provides her line editing and other types of book development skills as a service. And like a true entrepreneur, when AI became mainstream, she jumped on it and now teaches editors how to use AI to do their jobs better. For this book, even though the publisher provides editing services, I still brought Erin in to apply her skills; she has been fact-checker extraordinaire, did development editing without even meaning to, and applied her line-editing superpower to make this book much better.

My team at Dover is in multiple anecdotes in this book. I am grateful that they are all lifelong friends. A special shout-out goes to Marco Ciaffi, who was officially the VP of engineering but in practice was a model COO. Marco was one of the five cofounders. The others were Steve Milburn, Eli Boling, Greg Sullivan, and Andrew Sutherland. Leslie Barthel was the director of marketing, and I learned an incredible amount from working with her. Leslie provided me with great counsel every step of the way, sometimes with gentle but firm rebukes (accompanied by eye rolling) about things she thought I should be doing differently.

Nicole Perrault is a technical writer with whom I have worked at five companies. We continue to work together and maybe are destined to always do so.

Many thanks also to Vivjan Myrto, who authored the foreword to this book. Vivjan is the rare VC who loves the earliest possible stage for companies building what he calls "hard tech." He got things started for us by committing to lead Dover's seed round. He's always positive, even when things go south. His approach always kept me looking for that next rabbit to pull out of my hat. Vivjan and I also have a special bond based on both of us being surprise survivors of multiple bouts of cancer. Mine took my leg and a lung at ages 16 and 19. His began at age 15 with a cancer diagnosis followed by a year of failed therapy in his home country of Albania, after which he was given a year and a half to live. Then, in a last-ditch effort for treatment and survival, he set his sights on the United States. Through sheer perseverance and determination (I call this grit), he was able to move to the United States to undergo a series of life-saving treatments, culminating in a bone-marrow transplant in 2004 that saved his life.

Michael Stephens, the assistant publisher at Manning, the publisher of this book, was part of my post-pandemic, post-apocalyptic Dover experiences, when I reached out to old friends I'd lost touch with for almost a decade. During our reconnecting Zoom call, we discussed an idea I was exploring about collecting anecdotes I'd been jotting down for a dozen years and compiling them into a book. Immediately after the call ended, with no further discussion about Manning publishing the book, he sent me a DocuSign publishing contract. Being a very busy guy responsible for a steady stream of titles moving through Manning's processes, his interactions with me were infrequent but highly impactful. I am proud to consider him a friend.

The Manning staff were very easy to work with and did a wonderful job. They include India Hackle and Karen Miller, who helped shape the book in the early stages of each anecdote during development editing. Also important to the ultimate product was an incredible cast including Kathy Rossland, Robin Campbell, Aira Dučić, Ana Romac, Tiffany Taylor, Sam Wood, Aleksandar Dragosavljević, Melissa Ice, Rebecca Rinehart, Ivan Martinović, Radmila Ercegovac, Stjepan Jurekovic, Malena Selic,

Christopher Kaufmann, Matko Hrvatin, Goran Ore, Doug Rudder, Eleonor Gardner, Rejhana Markanovic, and Breckyn Ely.

Thank you to review editor Isidora Isakov and to all the reviewers: Abhilash Babu, Aliaksandra Sankova, Andrej Abramušić, Andres Damian Sacco, Chris Allan, Chris Bolyard, Christopher Bailey, Dirk Gómez, Eder Andrés Ávila Niño, Federico Grasso, Heng Zhang, Madiha Khalid, Manzur Mukhitdinov, Matteo Battista, Maxim Volgin, Mikael Dautrey, Nadir Doctor, Noel Llevares, Noreen Dertinger, Oliver Korten, Onofrei George, Peter Morgan, Rohit Poduval, Sashank Dara, Scott Ling, Sebastian Maier, Simon Hewitt, Simone Sguazza, Srikar Vedantam, Sriram Macharla, Steve Prior, Swapneelkumar Deshpande, William Jamir Silva, and Zorodzayi Mukuya. Your suggestions helped make this a better book.

Peter Brumme could be known as Mr. GTM; I learned from him everything I know about how complex and vital to the success of a startup the go-to-market strategy is. He helped me construct the anecdote on that topic in this book.

Miles Arnone was our early landlord and a friendly skeptic of my plans for Dover, and his thoughtful challenges made my plans much better. Now he's the CEO of Re:Build, doing the startup thing himself, and he has built a great company with a model culture.

If I am the father of Dover, Ken Gabriel is arguably its grandfather. He was assistant director at DARPA as my team and I were wrestling with the first cybersecurity concepts that became Dover. He knew of us and how powerful our basic ideas were. Then, when I needed a place to incubate Dover and he was CEO of Draper, he made working there and building the initial team over two years easy and a wonderful experience. All along, he remained our strongest advocate and later became our independent board member. I have always valued his sage advice.

Dave Chen is my friend and cofounder times two of GeoTrust and then Ambric, both in Portland, Oregon, on the other end of exhausting weekly commutes.

Bryan Rosenberg is my brother and an investor in Dover. When things got really difficult, he jumped in with me, and we both loaned the company money. This was the only thing that kept it alive to fight another day, which it keeps doing to this moment.

And finally, what writer can leave out their dog, who lies on the couch next to me whenever I am writing? Harper is my unofficial mental health support Golden Retriever.

about this book

Tech Startup Toolkit is not the typical deeply technical book that Manning normally publishes. This is a business book that I wrote because it is the book I wish I'd had to refer to as I set out to found and run a series of nine startups from 1988 to the present. I'm not sure if I made more mistakes than other founders/CEOs, but it sure seems as though I had a lot of what we euphemistically refer to as "learning experiences."

Over the course of all my startup experiences, I found that there is an incredible amount to know. Perhaps now—but certainly not when I began my run—the entrepreneurial business schools cover some of this. I think we have all found that although what we learn in school is super helpful and useful, it is nothing like what we learn once we get out in the real world. Besides, when someone gets an idea, and they strongly believe it has the potential to be the basis of a new company, this person may not have gone to business school yet or might never want to. But I did not want to write another textbook or even a "Startups for Dummies" type of book. I had really good luck with my memoir *Who Says I Can't* about personal challenges I had in my life; in that book, I related to readers things I learned the hard way that I hoped could help them short-circuit the intermediate steps and get right to the result they needed. I wanted to do the same thing here—but instead of the challenges of dealing with being an amputee cancer survivor, these are the challenges of dealing with being a startup founder and/or CEO.

I decided to write this book as my "business life memoir." That means much of it is in the informal first-person style of storytelling because that is precisely what I am doing here—telling stories about what happened to me in certain startup situations that are common and may provide some guidance for those who follow me and read this book. I call them anecdotes rather than chapters because I had three goals for each one: (1) They stand alone, so you can read them in any order you like, and you can refer back to one when you need that information; (2) they are short—usually six to eight pages; and (3) each is focused on a single very narrow topic or lesson. There is a bit of didactic information in many anecdotes, so to keep the story-telling flow uninterrupted, I put the didactic information in clearly delineated callouts. Each anecdote also ends with a paragraph called a moral that sums up the important learning contained in that anecdote. I believe there may be times when someone skims the book, *only* reading the summary bullets at the beginning, the callouts, and the morals, and that is a fine way to consume the information.

Because all of my startups were technology companies, the experiences in these anecdotes are from technology companies. I do not believe this means the book is only for someone who is or might become a founder or CEO of a tech startup. I know lots of non-technology startups that go through all the same types of formation process, financing, building culture, people issues, board dynamics, and so on. But I do not think this book covers the issues of starting a grocery store, a franchise business, a family business, or lots of other types of startups.

In terms of the knowledge required to understand this book, my goal is not to require any (because I didn't have any when I decided to do my first startup). Having said that, you do need to be interested in starting a new business, either as its leader or as part of the founding team—or perhaps you can do this as an employee of a startup company while you learn what a startup feels like on the way to doing your own at some time in the future. The reader ideally is a current or future founder or a senior person working at a startup. There are anecdotes about raising money, financing terms, and things like cash burn rate, but none of these are handled at the level a CFO would require. Instead, I assume you are not the CFO (well, if you are the CFO, your interest in this book is for a future role where you are no longer the CFO) but that you have an accountant, controller, or even a CFO who does the heavy lifting; you have to know just enough on these topics to make the critical decisions and to know what is important and what can wait until later.

liveBook discussion forum

Purchase of *Tech Startup Toolkit* includes free access to liveBook, Manning's online reading platform. Using liveBook's exclusive discussion features, you can attach comments to the book globally or to specific sections or paragraphs. It's a snap to make notes for yourself, ask and answer technical questions, and receive help from the author and other users. To access the forum, go to https://livebook.manning.com/book/tech-startup-toolkit/discussion. You can also learn more about Manning's forums and the rules of conduct at https://livebook.manning.com/discussion.

Manning's commitment to our readers is to provide a venue where a meaningful dialogue between individual readers and between readers and the author can take place. It is not a commitment to any specific amount of participation on the part of the author, whose contribution to the forum remains voluntary (and unpaid). We suggest you try asking the author some challenging questions lest his interest stray! The forum and the archives of previous discussions will be accessible from the publisher's website as long as the book is in print.

about the author

JOTHY ROSENBERG is truly an incorrigible entrepreneur who has founded and led nine startups, two of which had exits over $100 million. His startups were in a variety of areas, most recently cybersecurity. Jothy led Dover through harrowing times, including when the pandemic caused him to transform it into a Department of Defense business. Recently he transitioned to executive chairman and hired a CEO from a major defense contractor.

Prior to his 10-year journey creating and running Dover, Jothy started and ran startups in the supercomputer, internet infrastructure (Webspective sold for $106 million, or 30× ROI), TV broadcast, web browser security (GeoTrust sold for $125 million, or 8× ROI), and Hollywood special effects markets. In the early 1990s, he ran the most profitable division of Borland International as VP and Business Unit Manager of a $300 million profit-and-loss center where he was responsible for four major products servicing 4 million customers.

Jothy created the Can Do Productions TV production company that created three full episodes of a reality TV show called *Who Says I Can't*, episodes of which are now on YouTube. Jothy founded and runs The Who Says I Can't Foundation, a 501(c)3 charity that focuses on restoring the self-esteem of young people who become disabled by getting them the adaptive equipment they need to participate in their desired high-challenge sport.

Jothy has a PhD in computer science from Duke University and a BA in mathematics from Kalamazoo College. He had a five-year appointment teaching computer science at Duke with a joint appointment at the Microelectronics Center of North Carolina (MCNC), where he was a VP and co-founder. A NASA research project of his at MCNC led him into the entrepreneurial world because he was determined to turn the supercomputer he designed for the Space Shuttle into a new startup in Sunnyvale called MasPar.

Jothy has authored six books: *How Debuggers Work* (Wiley), *Securing Web Services* (SAMS), *Who Says I Can't* (self-published), *The Cloud at Your Service* (Manning), *Adventures on the Can Do Trail* (for ages 4-9, self-published), and this book: *Tech Startup Toolkit: How to launch strong and exit big* (Manning). He has also written chapters for several books, as well as numerous articles and white papers. His weekly podcast on all things startup, is called the Adventures on the Can Do podcast. He is the inventor on four patents, and is a member of the Forbes Technology Council where his articles on a variety of topics appear on Forbes.com.

Jothy lives with his wife, Carole, and his golden retriever, Harper, in Wayland, Massachusetts.

Part 1

First time leading a startup

You are a founder and will be a leader in a new startup. This part of the book includes four anecdotes that will help you navigate these early waters of the brand-new startup you are creating or joining to change the world. The anecdotes in this part are as follows:

1 Scratching the startup itch: How I became an incorrigible entrepreneur
2 What makes you think you are CEO material?
3 A venture-backed turnaround: A dangerous place to be
4 The founding team: Who's in and who's not?

I start with a story of how I became an entrepreneur after having started my career as a computer science professor. Then we take up an important topic: who should be the starting CEO of this new tech startup? The answer may surprise you. I learned an important (and personally expensive) lesson about that the hard way.

It is fairly common for a person's first time leading a company to happen at a company they already work for that needs a new leader. But if it is a venture-backed company, there could be rough water ahead.

This part closes with an anecdote about founders. It's a topic that has proven over and over to be fraught with emotion and egos.

Scratching the startup itch: How I became an incorrigible entrepreneur

- Entrepreneurial itch? Dreaming of launching the next big startup?
- Can you truly evaluate your startup idea soberly and without emotion?
- Who can offer sage advice to steer your promising venture?

What causes the itch to drop everything and create a startup? For me and many others, it is the desire and belief that you can change the world. It might be the recognition of a problem that you see a way to solve (like Fred Smith, who founded FedEx to deliver urgent packages overnight). It might be a product you think fills a niche that no one else has yet figured out (like Spotify, which "fixed" the pirating problem that the sudden ability to stream music created while at the same time preventing the huge financial catastrophe the music industry saw on the horizon as the sales of CDs dried up). It might be an efficient solution to something you recognize as inefficient (like Larry Page and Sergey Brin, who founded Google, used their patented page-rank algorithm to make theirs by far the most efficient search engine, and obliterated all competition). Or it might just be that you have an insatiable desire to do something really challenging where you get to call the shots and it is 100% up to you to succeed or fail.

Many founders want to take their big idea and build a structure around it that allows it to become a product or service sold into very large markets. For that, they are willing to forgo saving for retirement, the stability of a job at a big company, and perhaps a salary for the initial phase of their new startup. None of this would happen, of course, if these sorts of people had not seen founders of successful startups get very rich. That financial reward highly motivates prospective founders to trade security for the risk–reward potential of a large exit. Because they are keenly aware of the tradeoff, they structure their "deal" so that if the startup is successful, they will make up for the years of little pay or savings for retirement and be set for life financially.

1.1   *Discovering the startup "itch"*

I was a professor of computer science at Duke University in Durham, North Carolina, where, in 1983, I had recently completed my PhD in that same department. As a professor, I was expected (and wanted) to do research to support part of my salary and that of some students working with me. I was also expected to teach, and I enjoyed both aspects of my job. But I was not sold on being a lifelong academic. I was surrounded by technology that was advancing incredibly fast, including processor speed, storage capacity, and networking ubiquity, and I watched as new tech companies constantly burst on the scene, building inventions that were changing the world. I couldn't help but wonder what being part of one of those world-changing companies might be like.

I didn't recognize it then, when wading ankle-deep in thousands of tiny processors on a two-foot-square circuit board at my Duke University lab in 1987, but looking back, I realize I had the restlessness—or maybe the "itch"—of someone looking for the opportunity to start my own company. I just had no idea what that could be or how to do it, yet.

My first research project was with a colleague at North Carolina State University, just down the road in Raleigh. We won a NASA research contract to build a single-board, space-flyable, massively parallel supercomputer with more than 1,000 small processor chips on it arranged to function in parallel, making it a supercomputer with unprecedented power.

This was the start of NASA's Space Shuttle era. When in space, the Shuttle collected large volumes of vital telemetry data from onboard sensors, which it had to send down to Earth to be processed into actionable information. This worked fine until the Shuttle and the sun were aligned with the ground station, causing a "sun outage" during which the computers on Earth were blocked from receiving data. The situation was dangerous if the data indicated the Shuttle needed to fire a thruster or the main engine to move out of the way of space debris, but NASA was unable to alert the Shuttle until it moved past the sun.

The solution was to build a supercomputer powerful enough to process the telemetry data and small enough to fit onboard the Space Shuttle. This is where we came in. Our single-board device was a supercomputer of amazing capability. It was built to be especially efficient at processing the types of telemetry data the Shuttle was collecting: by doing this continuously on board, there would never be a sun outage when the shuttle would lose its communication link with the ground station. That meant the Space Shuttle astronauts would be safer, thanks to our computer. This was a fun, fascinating, high-impact project that consumed me and several of my students.

To figure out exactly how this computer we were designing would work and to understand how to write applications for it, I needed to purchase two "real" supercomputers we would use to simulate our single-board computer before we built it. Turns out I was purchasing serial numbers 1 and 2 from a startup called Convex Computer. Each of these machines had a footprint of about 32 square feet and was 6 feet tall. They required a special raised floor, a highly air-conditioned room, and oodles of power. Our simulations of our little single-board, two-square-foot device kept these two giant supercomputers completely consumed. And yet these simulations, entirely done with software, ran about 1,000 times slower than our eventual hardware devices.

My simple observation that our NASA supercomputer-on-a-board could do certain applications faster than the fastest supercomputer in commercial production got me thinking that this device should have incredible value to the commercial world. Eventually, this thinking created in me the germ of an idea that maybe a supercomputer this small could become the basis for a new company doing something that had never been done before. The most powerful supercomputers of that time were giant machines that not only needed special, enclosed computer rooms with massive power requirements, but also required plumbing to provide them with water cooling. What if I could turn our work into a company that filled the need for massive compute power with small, very-low-cost supercomputers that plugged into standard wall current, with no special cooling needed?

How are people positioned to found a new startup?

Before they even bother calling themselves founders of anything, they must see if their idea really has merit. Often, one or more of the founders comes from the startup's target market. They may have very detailed knowledge about a huge, unsolved problem that the market faces and thus also have a good idea for how to solve it. For most tech startups, that means they are building some sort of proof-of-concept product and showing it to prospective customers to get their reactions and feedback.

1.2 Putting the necessary pieces together

When you ask "What if?" like this, that's your itch talking. Building a revolutionary supercomputer that filled an unmet market need was mine.

I had no idea how to go about making this "what if" company a reality. But I started to ask around. I was being bold, and I was also nervous. However, in my brain, a "bit" had flipped, and I was determined to figure this out.

My first step was to find out whether anything like this idea was being done already. Was this going to be duplicative, or was my idea totally unique?

My second step was to use any connections I could think of to try to form a team—ideally with people who had started a company before, so I was not heading into the unknown alone.

I did not get answers to my questions from people around me. It was now 1987, and Research Triangle Park, North Carolina, had no startup culture yet. This meant I was going to have to explore my idea in either Boston or Silicon Valley, places already steeped in startups, venture capitalists, and all the supporting infrastructure new tech companies require.

My wife, Carole, being from Ohio, begged me to choose Boston and not California, since in her mind, California was going to slide right into the Pacific Ocean during the next big earthquake. I complied and went to Boston first to visit an existing supercomputer startup called Thinking Machines, where I knew two people from my university role; they took my calls and invited me for a visit. Thinking Machines was building a machine similar in architecture to what I would end up building based on my NASA contract work. My thought was that if I could join a company already building a machine like what I was building for NASA, I could both enjoy the technical work and also learn how a startup runs in preparation for a future startup of my own.

You've probably seen a Thinking Machine with its giant red blinking lights since it was the computer in the control room of the original *Jurassic Park* movie. Danny Hillis, the founder of Thinking Machines, famously said, "The joke around here is that we want to build a computer that will be proud of us. The fact is we really mean it." I thought that was a bit over the top, but this was an unusual company. They were among the first to have "playrooms" where staff could play with kids' blocks, train sets, and Barbie dolls—because, the thinking went, the interaction might allow employees to let off steam and be more creative. Also, during company-paid, sit-down, hot multicourse lunches served by waiters, Sheryl Handler, the CEO and a trained concert pianist, played her grand piano to soothe the souls of her stressed-out employees. This lunch scene was a shocking waste of money to me, especially for a startup.

As I talked to employees, it sounded like everyone was doing experiments, not building a product for sale. I got the strange feeling that this was more like a computer lab for MIT graduate students than a for-profit company with sales quotas and schedules to meet. Everything seemed inefficient and wasteful. Yes, I had initially gone to Thinking Machines to consider joining, but after seeing its excesses, I realized I did not want to be a part of it—I wanted to build a company that would compete with it.

Seeing this company as the only competition we would be dealing with anytime soon really got my competitive juices flowing. Thinking Machines already proved there was a market for super-powerful computers by selling its crème-de-la-crème version; we could outmaneuver the company by building a workhorse, blue-collar version, make our machine much easier to acquire and manage, undercut them, and outsell them, beating them in the market. I knew if I could get the right team and the right advice about how to do a startup, we could kick this company right in the blinking lights.

My first call in my network was to my cousin Carol Peters. She also happened to be the only person I knew in a high-tech company. Cousin Carol had gone from being an administrative assistant to a senior executive at a company called Digital Equipment Corporation (DEC), which was then a major force in the computer industry. She could not believe what I was asking. When I mentioned the type of machine I had been working on and what I had in mind, the line went quiet. What stunned her into silence was the amazing coincidence I unknowingly revealed: several people from DEC, including her husband, Peter Christy, were discussing launching a startup to build a supercomputer that could take on Thinking Machines. Just like me. Now it was my turn to go silent on the call.

But there was no time to let my stroke of luck sink in. First I needed to know the next steps. Peter called me back later that same day and told me to get my butt on a plane and come talk to his group in Silicon Valley. They were moving fast. If I wanted in on the ground floor, I needed to hurry.

1.3 The ground floor

When I arrived at MasPar (a name conjured from *massively parallel*), I found a group of founders who welcomed me so warmly that it was as if we'd all known each other for years. This was not an interview. They already knew what technology I had been developing, and they were as excited to hear about my work as I was to hear about theirs. We seemed like a good match, and they expressed interest in incorporating my NASA contract results into the machine they were beginning to build.

This was a pretty good way to "start" a company. I was not jumping into being CEO—we had a perfectly adequate one, and besides, I had no clue whatsoever how to be CEO yet. I could watch and learn how the CEO thing worked at a startup and how financing the company was done. (We had cream-of-the-crop investors, including Kleiner Perkins and Sequoia Capital, as our leads. In fact, probably the most famous venture capitalist of all time, John Doerr, was on our board.) I now see this as the best way to do your initial startup: not jumping in as a first-time founder when you've never been part of a startup before, but working as part of the team and learning how a startup works from the inside.

MasPar ended up making a machine that had not 1,000 processors in it, like our NASA board, but 32,768 of them. And yet it was just the size of a four-drawer filing cabinet and needed no special raised floor or cooling like a Thinking Machine. It plugged into standard wall current and could sit in a regular office environment. That was unprecedented. But sadly, it did not have awesome blinking lights like the Thinking Machine.

We developed and sold 100 of our machines in four years, which was also amazing for a supercomputer. We landed customers like American Express, *The New York Times*, and the National Security Agency. Those customers bought it because it could do tasks they needed done that were not possible with any other computer. This type of machine, with a single instruction operating across all the processors in parallel, is extremely good at searching for patterns—which is what American Express and *The New York Times* wanted it for (we were never allowed to know what the NSA wanted it for). American Express and *The New York Times* would load up a lot of credit card records or news articles across all the processors and initiate a search. That search, operating in all processors simultaneously, reported any credit card records or articles that matched the search.

In addition to selling machines to some prestigious accounts, we achieved our goal of beating Thinking Machines in the market. Thinking Machines went out of business early in our reign, and the company never sold more than a few dozen machines. But at least those machines were Danny Hillis' friends.

However, our downfall was the pesky Moore's Law. This "law" means a special, powerful machine won't stay all that special or powerful for long. It wasn't another supercomputer competitor that killed our business—all it took was normal Intel processors following Moore's Law and getting faster and faster.

> **DEFINITION** *Moore's Law* is an observation (not an actual law) that the number of transistors in a computer chip, and its processing power, double every two years or so.

After four years, I knew we had accomplished what I set out to do with my research, I had learned all I could from this startup, and it was time to move on. I never for a minute thought of going back to academia. I had "been there, done that." And I was now addicted to the pace of innovation, the ability to adapt and change on a dime, the strong camaraderie of a startup, the feeling that I was in charge of my own destiny, and the almost total lack of company politics. But before I could go back into the startup world, I knew I had something critical to learn. I wanted to go to whatever company made the highest-quality software on the planet. And every single person I asked agreed that company was Borland.

Is startup life for you?

Creating a startup can be the most satisfying, rewarding, exciting, creative thing you ever do. And it just might be the most lucrative, as well. But sometimes it is none of those things.

Without scaring you, you need to know that most startups fail. I know that because several of my startups did fail. But I keep at it because even in ones that fail, there is something addictive about the ways in which a startup is more powerful than the largest company. Having a small, close-knit team with everyone's incentives completely aligned, all working together to change the world, means

- You can turn on a dime if you need to.
- Decisions get made fast (usually by one person without layer after layer of approvals).

- You get close to customers, which means you can get the product or service exactly right.
- The product development team is free to try radical new things a big company can never do because it's too risky.

Still, starting a company is not for everyone. You need to be bold and willing to take risks—and your family has to be on board. It's the risk part that everyone thinking of starting a company needs to really search deeply about. About 80% of startups fail, and if that happens you need to find something else to do. But if you have the stomach for it, the rewards are abundant. Getting to work as part of a high-energy, high-performing team where 10 people accomplish what it takes 100 to do at a big company. Developing and building a product in a way that big companies just can't because they don't look the same way at the risk of building a brand-new product. And of course, the financial potential of a startup that wins and has a good exit is motivation for everyone at a startup.

1.4 The moral of this anecdote

Creating a startup can be the most satisfying, rewarding, exciting, creative thing you'll ever do. And it just might be the most lucrative, as well. But sometimes it is none of those things.

Most startups fail. Several of mine did. But I also had two that were acquired for over $100 million. I was drawn to entrepreneurship because I wanted to be in control of my own destiny, and I loved the speed with which a startup could move. It was addictive. It was also very hard. But I had gone through years of people telling me "can't" about all things difficult. That had driven me to get my PhD and was now driving me to build companies.

What makes you think you are CEO material?

- Could you really handle being CEO? Better question yourself first.
- How do you formulate the all-important elevator pitch?
- Are you sufficiently resilient to leverage VC rejections as constructive feedback to iterate and improve?

My first taste of startup excitement with MasPar was behind me. Then, after four years of rising through the executive ranks at Borland International in Scotts Valley, California, I had succeeded in my goal of learning how building the highest-quality software in the world is done. Plus I was gaining valuable management experience for my path to becoming a startup CEO without having a deliberate plan to do so.

The journey to becoming a tech startup CEO can be challenging. It is very likely that some investors will strenuously challenge your readiness or ability to be CEO even when you think you are ready. But even if they seem sure you are *not* ready, I learned that such challenges can be misguided. I made a big mistake listening to the doubters too much.

2.1 First crack at being a founder

At Borland, I was responsible for four of the most lucrative products the company sold, and the division I ran was the largest in the company, doing over $300 million in revenue annually. I had responsibility for engineering, marketing, customer documentation, and support. In 1996, the company decided to move my family and me to Boston for a year to acquire a startup there called Open Environment Corporation (OEC). This acquisition was critical to my division's strategy, and going east to integrate this startup into the bigger company was going to continue to scratch the startup itch that I had in no way lost—it had just gone into a brief hibernation. Borland management above me—the senior vice president (SVP) and CEO—seemed desperate for me to go: they paid my wife's full-year salary so she could take a leave of absence from her job, they rented us a house for the year, they had me leave my BMW convertible behind and bought me a Toyota 4Runner for Boston winters, and they signed a deal I insisted on whereby if I left Borland for any reason whatsoever, they owed me a full year's severance. This deal was almost unbelievably good—I was so new to the ranks of large public company senior executives that I did not know this kind of deal was possible. As it turned out, I would exercise the *full year's salary severance* term of our agreement to leave to do my first of eight startups in Boston.

Almost as soon as I arrived in Boston, Borland lost everyone who formed my lifeline of support back to the Borland "mother ship," as I liked to call it. My boss, the SVP, took a huge offer to go to Microsoft, and shortly after that, the board fired the CEO for not making a profit the previous quarter. The startup itch remained very strong in me. Once my family and I decided to stay in Boston, and with the Borland mother ship starting to go down, four of the top engineers from OEC and I decided we had an idea inspired by their work that could add real value to the nascent Web. It was a capability called *load balancing*.

It was 1997, and our new startup's load-balancing concept was based on the simple observation that the Web would not only be used for static marketing content as it had been so far. A few companies were starting to realize this could be a platform for highly interactive applications. Victoria's Secret was one of the first to figure this out, in kind of a bad way: in 1999, the company had a Super Bowl ad that encouraged people watching to go right then to Victoria's Secret website to see a lingerie model. Naturally, all those football fanatics rushed to their computers, and they completely overloaded the *single server* running the Victoria's Secret site, causing it to crash. Our load-balancing solution would automatically and seamlessly balance the workload across a bunch of servers to prevent a single server from crashing as its capacity was exceeded. Turns out Fidelity Investments wanted this too, to allow people to directly interact with their 401(k) accounts; that could mean thousands of customers wanting to be serviced at the same time, and Fidelity Investments definitely did not want to see a repeat of what happened to Victoria's Secret.

This is how Webspective got its start.

Webspective's technology

Webspective's technology grew out of work originally done for distributed computing that was prevalent in the mid-1980s to late 1990s. In particular, the model of having monitors and agents was repurposed to provide a solution called *load balancing* for Web servers on the internet. The idea turned out to be very simple once a particular feature of Web browsers is understood.

Browsers have a redirection capability built in such that if the server at the URL the browser attempts to use wants that browser to instead go to a different URL, the server can use a redirect command built into the HTTP protocol to tell the browser to go to the alternate URL. Redirection is commonly used when information has been moved from its previous location to a new server but users and the web pages they visit have not yet been updated with the change.

One other simple building block is needed to complete the picture: a server needs to be able to tell how heavily loaded it is. That is, it must be able to determine how many Web connections it can handle and how many it is currently handling.

The main URL of a company points to a server (e.g., fidelity.com) that is the monitor that will receive all incoming connection requests. This monitor gets a constant stream of load information from each server it is connected to, which are the agents (e.g., fidelity100.com, fidelity200.com, etc.). As a new connection is made to the monitor, it determines which is the most lightly loaded of all the agents currently available, and it sends the browser making the incoming request an HTTP redirect command to the URL of the most lightly loaded agent. That redirect goes back to the browser, which sends its connection request to the new server (agent) it was just notified about.

As the load on fidelity.com rises over time, new agent servers are added, which the monitor is configured to know about; in this way, an almost infinite number of agents can be handled, and smooth load balancing can be achieved. This technology, delivered to Fidelity Investments (which was also an investor) in 1998, was so successful that it was in continuous operation at fidelity.com for a decade.

2.2 Almost CEO

The team really wanted me to be the CEO. I was honored and nervous, and I had no idea what I would be getting myself into. I did not feel at all qualified to be CEO (yet), especially because I had never so much as touched sales; plus, marketing at Borland was totally different from the kind of marketing a company selling enterprise software to huge corporations like Fidelity Investments was going to need.

CEO or not, first I had to find money to fund this new venture. The OEC team I had joined forces with had seen their founders raise money, so they were plugged into the Boston venture capitalist (VC) community. They knew of a guy who had raised money locally and was now a consultant for startup teams like ours that had no network of VCs they could waltz into and ask money from. This consultant knew all the good VCs in Boston and said he would make those warm introductions for us.

For those introductions, you need a blurb about your company. This is a single paragraph, known as *an elevator pitch*, that can be spoken in 30 seconds and will catch the interest of an investor and excite them enough that they will take the meeting with you.

The seven-sentence elevator pitch to investors (template)

Introduction: I am [your name], the [your position] at [startup name], which provides [product/service brief description].

Problem & Solutions: We help [market, types of customers] solve [problem they experience] by providing [your key benefits].

Competitors: Unlike [your competitors in the target market], our solution [highlight key differentiators].

Market Opportunity: This is a $[market size] opportunity in [region/country] alone, and now is the best time for [your goal] because [why now].

Business Model: We make money by [revenue streams].

Achievements: We have already achieved [your accomplishments].

Request: We currently need [amount you are raising] to achieve [your next milestones and timeframe].

Avoid the temptation to add more sentences—remember, this is only about getting a "yes" to a meeting request. You get to say all those extra cool things when you are in the meeting room with the investors, presenting your full pitch deck.

Our consultant also had experience creating and pitching a PowerPoint deck that tells the startup's story. (You can read all about what goes into this pitch deck in anecdote 7, "The art of pitching to institutional investors.") He taught me how to create a reasonable deck, and he made introductions to a list of local VCs who would take a meeting with me.

> **TIP**   Please always remember that no VC will respond to a cold call, so never bother trying that. Even if their website has a link to upload a business plan, don't bother. Those things are auto-deleted. They will only take a meeting if someone they know, trust, and respect makes a warm introduction.

My first pitch to raise money to get Webspective started (so far, the team was living off our savings and working out of the CTO's basement) was going to be at a VC firm named Commonwealth Capital Ventures, where I would be meeting with the firm's patriarch, who was named Mike Fitzgerald. I was pitching about the future of the Web and how the way the Web was currently working would not cut it any longer. Companies like Fidelity Investments wanted to support interactive applications right through people's browsers, and we had proven technology that we had adapted to solve this problem. Plus, we could deliver it to the market in a matter of months.

Before I got very far into that story, Fitzgerald leaned forward with an intense look that sliced right through me and said, "What makes you think you are CEO material?"

With that, he dug straight into my biggest insecurity. I didn't have a heart attack, but I did feel like crawling under the table. I was suffering from *imposter syndrome.*

He kept going and went right for the jugular, adding, "You have zero sales and marketing background, and that is unacceptable. You *can't* be the CEO."

After that meeting, I told my cofounders that I could not be the CEO but would continue to raise the financing and then be an advisor. But I now was on a mission to get a role where I could learn sales and marketing skills that Fitzgerald and I both knew I sorely lacked. What hit even harder was that someone had just said *can't* to me (see my book *Who Says I Can't*), so I had to go do whatever it took to be CEO-ready (in the eyes of investors who thought like Fitzgerald). At least my cofounders had convinced me they thought I had what it took to be a CEO. That helped make me optimistic that I'd be one someday.

Why be a startup CEO?

Be a startup CEO for the same reason you should consider moving up from individual contributor to manager, to director, to vice president in a large company: you have a vision of a major problem that exists in the market, and you think you know how to build a solution for it. You think you know how you want to sell it and to whom. You also think you know the right messaging to use to get people to understand all that. But you will need a team to build that solution, a team to sell it, a team to market it, and all the other people to make a company work. You are viewed as a leader because of your experience and what you know. But you cannot possibly do all that is needed by yourself. You need a team, and they need you to be CEO to lead them.

The next VC I met with was Ted Dintersmith of Charles River Ventures (CRV). My cofounders had gotten to him first, and he was hell-bent on stopping me from dropping out as the Webspective CEO. He tried very hard, and he came close to convincing me. The problem was that everything Fitzgerald said was haunting me, adding fuel to my fires of self-doubt, and nothing Ted could say was going to counteract that. Many years later, I realized that Ted had been right and Mike was wrong. A tech startup needs a tech CEO at first, especially when that CEO is a passionate founder; prior experience is secondary.

2.3 *Avoiding four-legged sales calls with a technical CEO*

Right out of the gate, the CEO of a highly technical and disruptive startup needs to be highly technical themselves so they can credibly explain how this works, why this works, why it's disruptive, and how it's defensible. This is the person who has the most passion about the problem and the company's solution and who usually conveys that passion best. And that CEO needs to be able to do that without taking the CTO with them on every sales call or investor meeting. I call those *four-legged sales calls*. And face it, they are prohibitively expensive.

I know a lot about four-legged sales calls from many years later when I was CTO and working with a CEO who was not technically trained. He would ask me to accompany him to every critical customer or investor meeting where he would operate as the salesperson but defer to me for all technical questions. But after that, when I was CEO, I had literally hundreds of meetings where I was able to field all questions, both business and technical. The dramatic difference in efficiency of a technical CEO who is able to fully represent the company is hard to overstate.

Ted realized the value of a technical CEO. He was very frustrated with me and tried one more time, but to no avail. I was already reaching out to all the investors I had met through the Webspective financing campaign to see if they had a portfolio company with a role as CTO that would allow me to have a technical leadership position while spending most of my time working closely with the CEO to learn the sales and marketing I believed the CEO job required.

The idea of shadowing the CEO during the normal course of their day came initially from Fitzgerald, and it made sense to me. I thought then, and still think, that if you are someone with a strong technical background, easing into the CEO role via this type of shadowing will set you up for a greater likelihood of success and reduce the likelihood of your investors shortening your tenure by looking for someone new with strong sales DNA. But the alternative view, espoused by people like Ted Dintersmith, is that a highly disruptive company with groundbreaking technology like Webspective may have a short rocket-ship trajectory in which the technical CEO is the most desirable choice. If Webspective had taken five years instead of two to reach a profitable exit, I have no doubt the investors would have pushed me out in favor of a salesy CEO. You will have to determine which scenario you are staring at when you decide whether to take that first CEO role, even if you feel like a CTO.

Meanwhile, Fidelity Ventures and CRV ended up being the investors in Webspective, and they found a CEO shortly after the initial round closed. Webspective's product was as groundbreaking as we had hoped; Fidelity became our biggest customer and used the product for over a decade. After just two years and doing only $2 million in revenue, Webspective was acquired by a company called Inktomi for $106 million during the height of the dot-com bubble. (Shortly after that, Inktomi was acquired to become the search engine for Yahoo.) With a sale of $106 million, the startup CEO typically owning 10% of the stock, and very little *dilution* having occurred, somewhere around $10 million went to the CEO. Because I did not listen to Ted and did not stay as CEO, my stake was one-tenth of that. That put a cold, hard dollar value on my very bad decision.

> **DEFINITION** *Dilution* is the reduction in the ownership percentage of current investors, founders, and employees caused by the issuance of new shares.

2.4   *The moral of this anecdote*

Technology startups need technical founders/CEOs to lead them for the initial phase of entry into the market because the technical CEO can explain the value proposition and the product better than anyone. But investors frequently push aside these CEOs later when the company is ready to scale if they do not have strong sales experience. To get that sales experience and to learn how startups function, joining a startup that has strong salespeople in the CEO and/or VP Sales roles is a wise way to begin your startup journey. However, if you have an inventive, disruptive idea and a team that backs you, go for the CEO role and don't step out of the company. Even if you are pushed aside later, your stake in the company will remain, and the success of the company will still reward you handsomely.

A venture-backed turnaround: A dangerous place to be

- Do you know when investor priorities might clash with yours as CEO?
- Is your startup's path aligned with your investors' 10-year time limit?
- Are you ready to say no when an investor asks you to take on a venture-backed turnaround?

There can be a lot of benefits in joining an existing startup with a great CEO to learn from on the way to being ready to be CEO yourself. But it has to be the right thing for you, not just for investors, who are not looking out for your interests first; they are looking out for theirs first. I also want to point out the danger inherent in being the leader of a venture-backed startup that requires a turnaround. In fact, the concept of a venture-backed turnaround is an oxymoron because VCs want their companies to build, grow, and exit—the last thing they want to spend a lot of effort on is a portfolio company that is failing and needs remedial action to even survive. And if you are new to the CEO role, you never want to be thrust into the CEO role of a turnaround. I unfortunately learned several of these lessons the hardest way possible.

The next step on my way to becoming a CEO was taking a CTO role at NovaSoft, where I could work closely alongside the CEO and learn from his considerable sales and marketing prowess. Investors, who had reinforced my insecurities, insisted that this was exactly what I needed to do to fill my sales and marketing knowledge gap and truly be CEO-ready. But when I had been on the job less than six months, the CEO who hired me was fired, and I was far from feeling I had learned how to be a great CEO from him, much less how to be good at sales.

3.1   *Thrown into the deep end*

What did the CEO do to get fired? He established a plan to do $21 million in his first year, and then he spent accordingly, including opening offices in London, Paris, Munich, and Tokyo.

He overcommunicated. He overspent. He micromanaged.

Micromanaging a team backfires because senior, experienced people expect to be given goals and the resources they need to meet those goals. Then they expect to be trusted to get the job done and to communicate when challenges occur. Instead, he told his salespeople which customers they should call each day, and he told engineering the current highest-priority bug they needed to fix each day. He constantly sent emails and texts—probably 50 messages to each of his team members during regular work hours and then 5 to 10 more from 5:00 to 10:00 p.m. It got so extreme that we started holding secret off-sites at the home of our head of human resources to share stories and come up with strategies to constrain him so we could get our jobs done.

In addition, he used sales techniques that had worked in his previous role but were not going to work with this product or these customers. He thought it was possible to pressure customers by offering them special deals for end of month, end of quarter, and end of year. That only works for commodity products where you can deliver them and walk away, not for complex, business-to-business (B2B) software products that take weeks of training, customization, and installation.

NovaSoft ended up doing revenues of $11 million, not $21 million, but with expenses commensurate with revenues of $21 million. That emptied the coffers completely. This large a loss for a VC-funded startup was staggering. The board was angry.

Right after news of this big loss came down, I got a strange email from the chairman of the board, Brian Jacobs, asking if I would like to join him for dinner at a place of my choosing. This was weird. I'd never gotten any emails from any board members, much less been asked to have dinner with one—and the chairman, no less. I was immediately suspicious. I picked my favorite (and kind of expensive) Italian restaurant in Newton Centre. Brian tried to make this seem like something that happened all the time: the chairman having a quiet dinner with the CTO. I let the small talk and eating happen for a bit and then decided to break the ice.

"So, Brian," I said, "why are we here?"

This gave him permission to get to the point. The CEO (he insisted on just using his title, not his name) had totally missed the mark on revenues and had way overspent, and now he had to go. Ok, wow, Brian was telling me they planned to fire my boss, the CEO, before he even knew it himself.

Brian was very direct now. "Given our financial performance, we are in no position to hire a CEO from outside. We want you to be CEO."

He let that sink in for a minute. Clearly the CEO had really run this thing into the ground. The investors had an albatross around their necks … and now they wanted me to fly it.

I took a few quick sips of my wine. The wine was very good, but it didn't alleviate the shock that had set my heart racing.

Then I responded, "The whole idea was supposed to be that I needed to learn how to run sales and marketing from the CEO. But with only six months to have learned from him, I don't feel ready."

He switched off the nice, friendly tone and slid into bluntness. Calmly but seriously, he said, "If you won't accept becoming CEO tonight, we are going to shut down NovaSoft tomorrow."

Shut it down? All I could think of were the 45 employees (and their families) whose livelihood might end the next day. Then I considered the huge customers like Abbott Laboratories, Pfizer, Merck, and BMW that I had started to get to know and how they would all be abandoned. Plus we had offices in four countries.

Of course, none of this should have been my problem. But I made it my problem. First mistake.

"You and the board really think I am ready? You think I can do this?" I asked.

"Of course we do. It's not rocket science," he said.

Strange comment, given that all this time everyone had been making the job out to be my moon shot.

"You can do this. And the board will help you. Oh, and by the way, the CEO spent so much money that you will need to lay off about half the company and immediately raise a new round of financing," he said, with what I remember as a totally straight face.

I absolutely should have refused and walked away that instant. Second mistake.

I let emotions inject themselves into my thinking. I liked the team. I thought the technology had potential. I thought I could reposition the company in the market. But I mistakenly was putting too much faith in these investors. And most of all, I did not understand the dynamics of startups and investors well enough to make a smart decision.

I said, "Yes, I'll do it."

Red flags to look for when offered your first CEO position

If any of these red flags exist, think about walking away:

- The startup is a turnaround or restart.
  There is a time limit on how long the investors will remain involved. A turnaround can easily bump into that limit, at which point the investors will simply give up, shut down the company, and write off their investment.

(continued)

- The startup is declining in the market.

  It makes no sense to take on those headwinds when there are so many other opportunities to consider.
- The startup's financing rounds have gone past round B.

  This means it has raised series A and series B but is still not growing. This is not a good omen for you as a freshman CEO to be able to improve the company's prospects.
- The startup's board is large.

  If the company has raised several financing rounds, with new investors coming in on each round, the board can become quite large. It can expand to include not just full board members but also board observers (more on this in anecdote 27, "Board observers—observe only, please"). A large board is extremely challenging for an experienced CEO to manage, and it is way more than a freshman should be expected to handle.
- The startup's investors' funds have been investing for too long.

  Whether you're a freshman or an experienced CEO, take note of how long the current, active set of investors' funds have been investing. If they are closing in on 10 years before you exit and no new investors have come in, you could be at risk of the investors wanting to shut down the company and walk away. Not all funds have the 10-year cliff; some funds only go 7 years. Whatever the right number is, try to find out where you are relative to that cliff—if it is only two years away, that's not a good place to be.
- You have not been offered a very good compensation package.

  It was very early in my journey, and I was naïve, so I did not push for what anyone in this situation should absolutely demand: a very good compensation package with kickers if the investors shut down the company.

Led by the inside investors, most of whom were on the board and were leading the way for the rest of the investors, I managed to raise a round F on an emergency timescale. Such an emergency timescale, in fact, that I ended up raising it using a pay phone in the basement of a skiing lodge while on a long-planned vacation.

This was to be a small round of financing. It was sized to be just enough to cover the losses the previous CEO caused so as little dilution as possible would affect the existing investors. *Dilution* happens when the company creates new shares for each new set of investors to buy, which then provides the company cash in exchange for these shares. The new shares are essentially created out of thin air—a board resolution with concurrence of a majority of existing shareholders makes the new shares suddenly exist. Because the number of shares totaling 100% of the company has increased, each of the shares that existed before the new ones now represents a smaller percentage ownership of the company. These previous shares are *diluted*.

NovaSoft's board, dominated by the largest investors, also wanted me on a short leash. I got that. How could they really believe I would walk in as CEO and work magic? I was a little unsure of myself, so the short leash was also a safety valve that made sure I didn't go down a wrong path for very long. That's why they provided just enough cash for me to try something, anything, to make the company have some minimal value so they could sell it and have a return on their investment, even if it was pennies on the dollar.

3.2 Turning NovaSoft around

I got to work fast. My mission was to move NovaSoft out of the document management industry, where we were fourth in a market that was declining. I had to quickly get NovaSoft into a new market that was growing fast, or at least growing somewhat. And I had to do it with the team and technology we already had. I wanted to make changes that were bold, that would excite the employees, and that would get existing customers and new ones interested in what we were doing. First I changed the company's name to Factpoint, with attention-getting, blinding orange as our signature color. Changing the name of a languishing, not-well-known company versus a large successful company with millions of customers is like the difference between an Oscar for foreign animated short film versus the Oscar for best actor—in the case of the former, no one really cares. Here I was trying to clear the air and allow everyone new to the company to not be distracted by negative perceptions of NovaSoft. Rod Hodgman, my VP of marketing, was brilliant and had an idea for how to get us into content management, which was growing by leaps and bounds. (The essential difference between document management and content management is that *content* refers to the text on websites, and *documents* refers to electronic files, such as Word documents, spreadsheets, diagrams, and PDFs.) We could do this with the same team and technology and with relatively little new development needed. Of course, the *market* was vastly different.

We repurposed our pharmaceutical manufacturing-process-management software to this new concept of content management for the Web, which was still young. Morale rose rapidly. We landed 3M, GM, and Fiat as our first three customers that did evaluations and signed letters of intent to purchase the system. This level of sales activity in such a hot new market got front-page (back when these things had physical pages) coverage in the printed *InfoWorld Magazine*—probably the most influential IT publication of its day.

We had proof that this new idea "had legs," and my whole team was the most bullish they had been in many years. But we did not yet have enough revenues coming in to be cash-flow positive, which meant we needed yet more cash from investors. We needed a round G: a small one of only $2 million.

I was excited and optimistic. When the board saw the transformation I had made in this company in just six months and the very promising progress in acquiring new customers, I felt confident that they would get behind me and support our new direction. It was Halloween, and in that infamous board meeting, I offered several options, including one to raise the $2 million and—just to be complete—one to shut down the company. Of course, I knew they would never choose shutdown.

After my presentation, the board asked me and the senior executives I brought to the meeting to leave the room. We were outside for 30 minutes—5 minutes would have been sufficient for them to take a quick vote. Something was wrong. It looked like we were about to get a trick, not a treat.

We were invited back in, and there was Paul Maeder looking at me while Chairman Brian looked at his shoes.

Paul was the one to speak for the whole board. "While we love the new name, the new direction, and the amazing progress you have made in the market in such a short time, we have decided the course of action we want to take is to shut it down and fire all the employees tomorrow morning."

And the reason? Not because they were unhappy with our market progress. It was because this company had been part of these VC firms' investments for almost 10 years. And the limited partners (their investors) in those 10-year-old funds either want a return in that time or want to write it off as a loss. They don't want to be stuck with illiquid and hard-to-transfer holdings when they are trying to wrap up the fund, and a write-off is better financially because they can get some tax benefits. This is the brutal aspect of the venture investing business where all thought is on the investment returns and not on the impact on people. It's essential that the CEO can put themselves into that mindset, too, and not push past this 10-year goalpost without a plan for an exit.

The 10-year venture fund goalpost

Turnarounds are hard. Something is wrong at the company, and you must figure out what it is and how to fix it. Venture-backed turnarounds are much harder because there is a built-in time limit on getting the company turned around, growing, and succeeding. Neither is a good situation for a freshman CEO who has enough challenges figuring out the CEO job. Freshman or experienced, the CEO must make careful note of where their company is in the VC lifecycle. Venture capital funds are typically structured under the assumption that fund managers will invest in new companies over a period of 2 to 3 years, deploy all (or nearly all) of the capital in a fund within 5 years, and return capital to investors within 10 years. When it goes beyond that time horizon, the limited partners may put pressure on the fund managers to write off that investment and move on to other things.

As the CEO, you must always be thinking of when the exit (sale or IPO) might occur. On the other hand, if things are going well and you raise successive rounds of financing and bring in at least one new investor on each round, you get to "reset the clock." That's because a new investor, by definition, is just starting with you, so the 10-year clock is just starting for them. What happens to the older investors for whom that clock may run out? They may decide to write off an old investment, but it no longer affects you because they can't shut you down. And if your company is raising new rounds with new investors, things must be going well. Older investors always seem to find a way to make exceptions for a positive situation.

3.3   *The human cost of VC investments*

Regardless of how dispassionate investors want to be about their fund's 10-year limit, there is a human cost. Paul and the other original VCs expressed zero compassion to my team and me when describing their limited partners as being "tired," as if they had just bench-pressed too much weight as opposed to making a decision that affected 45 employees' families' livelihoods—not to mention the very hard work that I (whom they begged to do this) and my team had done for six months to save this company that was, in my mind, being cavalierly thrown away. But this decision was final. They did not want to keep this investment on the books, regardless of progress made or impact on the people, and they had no willingness to debate it.

I stomped out of the room with full-on tears in my eyes. Were they from sadness? Or anger? Or disappointment? Yes, yes, and yes. And fear, too—fear of laying off people who'd worked so hard, and fear of what kind of reaction they would have. Eventually I would also get around to my fear of not having a next thing lined up. No paycheck always put me on edge.

3.4   *The moral of this anecdote*

Experienced CEOs can find good opportunities for themselves doing turnarounds. They can be very lucrative, as the investors of a company in distress want help from an experienced CEO and are willing to pay for it. Plus, there can be great satisfaction in succeeding in a turnaround situation. The risk, besides the fact that sometimes best efforts don't succeed at healing a distressed company, is that the investors may prioritize the 10-year limit their limited partners impose on them above achieving successful milestones in a turnaround.

The inexperienced CEO, and especially the freshman CEO, should be extremely cautious about taking on a venture-backed turnaround. Be sure you understand the VC business model and the lifecycle of the funds in the startup. If they are two years or less from the end of the fund's lifecycle, the red warning flags should be at full staff. This is the essence of the Sisyphean task of trying to do a turnaround in a venture-backed startup. Either walk away or, with eyes wide open, negotiate a very beneficial compensation package that protects you if they pull the plug early.

The founding team:
Who's in and who's not?

- What is the role of a startup founder?
- Who gets the founder badge, and when should it be awarded?
- Crafting founder equity—what's the best way to structure it?

In the nine startups I either founded or ran, or both, I have had one, two, three, five, and six founders. How that is determined is not a science but a very important art that sets the stage for how the company culture will materialize.

I came into my first startup, MasPar, as employee number 12; but because of my research at Duke, they made me honorary founder number 6, which had no substance to it, such as stock or title. Four key leaders from Open Environment and I became the five founders of Webspective. At FactPoint, the Chief Marketing Officer and I were the two founders (also meaningless because this was a turnaround). At GeoTrust, the CEO and I (the COO) were a founding team of two. Later, almost the same group of four from Webspective recruited me to be a cofounder with them of Service Integrity. Aguru had a founding team of three. Mogility had a founding team of two. Ambric also had two formal founders, but they added me later as a founder in name only of the software division. At Dover, I recruited a core team of a VP of Engineering, a CTO, Chief Scientist, and two senior engineers to join me, and the six of us became the founding team. My nonprofit, The Who Says I Can't Foundation, is the sole example of me being a solitary founder.

However many founders there are, they have a strong leadership role and therefore a culture definition role. This anecdote is important to present you with ways to work with the founding team, whether you are one of them or not. You will learn how to compensate founders who really are founders at the time of formation—not the kind who get the title long after the company was formed. And as surprising as it may seem, sometimes founders can turn into a negative force within the startup—something I have had to deal with twice—so I present some ways to deal with that unfortunate situation.

4.1 What is the role of a founder in a startup?

Founders present at formation were there at the start and in most cases are the creators of the product and the vision for the company. They are naturally going to be leaders of the company. They also tend to have critical operational roles, such as Chief Executive Officer (CEO), Chief Technology Officer (CTO), or Chief Marketing Officer (CMO), which further cements their leadership roles. When problems need to be solved—whether they are in the product, in the messaging, in anything strategic—the CEO and the board, and even the investors, will naturally want to hear what the founders think about the situation. They also have another role that is nonoperational: they provide trust and stability. These are the people who should be the last to lose faith, because this company is "their baby." None of them should leave early. If the company starts to struggle, it is the founders who get together to figure out what needs to change and then lead the rest of the company in effecting that change perhaps doing some sort of pivot.

4.2 How and when do people get the title "founder"?

These early days, when it is just the team "in the garage," are when there will be a lot of discussion about who the founders of this new enterprise will be. For example, if there is a group of very senior, experienced people and a group of very junior people joining them, will the junior folks also be founders? Tough decision. This decision matters a lot financially. When you formally file the founding documents and legally create the company, you will have to declare who the founders are because they are treated differently, with, among other things, special stock.

> **NOTE** *Cofounder* is used a lot when there is one *initial* founder and a core group wants to be part of the founding team and would be demotivated without the cofounder moniker. In other cases, when there is not one central founder, everyone in the initial founding group uses *cofounder* and no one is simply founder.

You would think the group of founders would be well-established right when the company is formally formed and would be cast in stone, as in "once a founder, always a founder," and that no one could be added as a founder at some later time. But the title is so desirable that I have seen people come in years later, demanding to be anointed as founders. One wants to slip them a piece of paper ripped out of a dictionary where the word *founder* is defined, but I'm afraid that in these situations, non-subtlety would be lost. Sometimes I have thought, "*Why not just make every single person in the company a founder and be done with this pettiness?*"

This happened at GeoTrust. The company was four years old and still had not found its niche, so I brought in a guy with great ideas who really wanted to run a company. The fit seemed perfect, and I hired him as CEO and stepped to the side and became CTO. But he and some others he brought in decided they were to be called founders. Because I was no longer CEO, I couldn't overrule that decision. From then on, we had a founder (just me, because my cofounder departed) and several Johnny-come-lately founders.

The Dover founders' story is a good case study in *founderism*—a new term I just made up to mean "*the art of naming a founding team.*" I decided that the six who formed the core team of Dover were all to be considered founders. This many founders raises eyebrows with investors because it means this founder group holds a very large percentage of the company's stock spread across many people, leaving less for other leaders. It also means each individual founder holds less than if they were part of a one- or two-person founding team. Investors want to make sure the most senior people are well-incentivized, and with six founders, that incentive is somewhat diluted.

Incentive stock options vs. founder shares

On day one of company formation, the founders collectively own 100% of the company. Everyone else owns options, which are promises of future stock after the options vest and the owner exercises them. Vesting is the process of turning this promise into ownership, typically defined as "X shares vest per month to become shares you may exercise to make them shares you own." Exercise is the process of paying a price called a strike price to buy options you have vested and now own. Almost certainly the price employees will have to pay to exercise their vested options will be orders of magnitude higher than what founders paid for their stock.

Non-founders have what are called incentive stock options (ISO). Most technology startups have a policy that every employee has some because they are considered a powerful incentive to stay with the company. When they are exercised and become shares, they can be sold if there is a buyer. If the shares are held for less than a year, the profit (amount they are sold for minus the amount they were exercised for) is treated as income by the IRS and therefore is taxable at a high rate: 24%, 32%, 35%, and a top bracket of 37% for typical employees working at technology companies. It is important to note that the incentive in their name is because not only does the employee have to stay at the company month after month to vest more shares, but if they leave, they only have a small number of days (usually 90) to exercise any options they've vested.

Founder shares, as opposed to employee options, are shares owned outright by the founder, purchased at an incredibly cheap price. This means if they get 500,000 founder shares, they might pay only $50 total. Chances are that the shares will be held at least a year before the founder can sell them. Holding the shares for a year avoids the profits of that sale being treated as income; instead, they are capital gains. The tax rate on net capital gain is no higher than 15% for most people. Even with founder shares, there is a strong incentive to remain with the company because they reverse vest. Reverse vesting for four years means if the founder were to leave after two years, they would only have reverse vested in half their shares; the company would buy back the other half.

Founders win on the price of their shares, on the amount they get, and on the tax they have to pay on their gains. No wonder so many entrepreneurs want to get the moniker founder.

DEFINITION   *Vesting* means the time at which a right to purchase stock becomes unconditional. Over a period of time, an employee earns rights to receive stock as a result of their employment, but until the rights are earned, they are not able to claim ownership. If they leave the company, unvested shares are forfeited.

4.3   Determining who is in the "in" group and the "out" group

Did all six of our group need to be founders? Perhaps not. But then, who should have been left out? All had made significant contributions prior to forming Dover. In such a situation, the one or two who get left out could become demotivated and angry and might not be willing to continue with the rest of the group. That would, at best, be a great loss. At worst, it could severely hamper the new company's ability to build the product the team has envisioned. This is a very tough decision for the leader to make.

Who is a founder, and who is not? The way you answer this question can potentially break your company. But suppose the initial group who worked (maybe with little or no salary) for weeks, months, or even longer is eight people. Are they all founders? If not, what are the criteria for those who are in and those who are out? The answer depends on 1) what you are building, 2) the experience level of the members of the group, and 3) who you consider to be essential. For example, because Dover was building a hardware/software product that was very complex with several subsystems, some hardware and some software, it required a founder to be the leader of each technical group, and the loss of any one of them would have made building the desired product much more difficult.

Dover's group of six founders was a challenging size, and not just because a large amount of stock was handed out to the founders. It was also challenging because the "exclusive club" was much more noticeable to the rest of the company, and because of the sheer burden of managing this many people who believed they had "elite" status. The last point deserves a bit of a deeper dive.

When this many smart, strong-willed people who feel they are the leaders of the company are thrown together into a group, meetings can get contentious. Managing this group so that it does not career out of control and spill into the rest of the company, scaring other employees and ruining the company's culture, can be (and was for Dover) a real nightmare. On the other hand, if I had left, say, two of them out of the founders group, they probably would not have stayed with the company—and that would have meant we would not have developed the incredible product or the valuable patents we did. That tradeoff is always going to be there and is why the CEO has such a tough job.

Without the pressure to open up the group so it becomes that big, two or three founders, such as CEO, CTO, and CMO, is the ideal size, in my opinion. But if you are going to lose critical people if you decide they are in the "out" group, it may be better to err on the side of inclusion, within reason, so you keep the team together.

4.4   *The moral of this anecdote*

Founder is neither an organizational nor an operational title. It is a preface to one of those. Nevertheless, it is considered one of the most prestigious, and yet contentious, titles in the life of a startup (and the CEO who runs it). Founders get special stock, which, if the company is a rocket ship, upon exit will make them vastly richer than almost anyone else in the company. This is why the title is so coveted. It is also coveted because it conveys an elite status to the rest of the employees and company observers on the outside. Determining who is and who is not a founder is a critical step the CEO must take, but it cannot be handled lightly because not conveying the title on someone who's certain they deserve it may cause that person to leave and the company to not gain their contributions. Conveying it on too many can cause conflicts that bleed over into the rest of the company and its culture. There is no certain right answer to who should be and who should not be a founder. Ultimately, my advice is simply to be very thoughtful and careful, to make your decision, and to communicate that decision clearly and strongly.

Part 2

Raising money

Y̲ou and your team have officially formed and launched the new company. You may be able to self-fund, but most startups can't and need to raise money. There is a lot to know when it comes to having a smooth financing round. I've laid out the most crucial things you need to know, along with stories to explain the consequences of critical decisions along the way. The anecdotes in this part are as follows:

5 Friends and family, angels, venture capital, or strategic?
6 Angels: Your bridge financing solution
7 The art of pitching to institutional investors
8 Investors aren't your friends
9 Understand the VC business model: Raise money faster
10 Seed: The first priced round
11 Term sheets: An institutional investor wants to invest in you
12 Due diligence: An exam you must pass

On day one, you may need some money to get a place for your team to meet (even if you are going to operate with everyone remote, and even if that meeting place is a shared-office location). A great way to get a small amount of working capital is from friends and family. I contrast that with having the first raise be from angel investors, venture capitalists, or strategic (corporate) investors.

Angel investors and how to pitch and succeed with them are such big and important topics that I dedicate an anecdote to them. It's a different process with institutional investors such as venture capital firms, so that's its own anecdote as well. Then it is time for a very important lesson: that investors are not your friends, and their first priority is always what is best for them and their limited partner investors, not you. To be successful in raising from the right VCs for you, it's essential to understand their business model, which is what drives their choices.

Seed is the first round where your company will have an official value because it sets a price on your stock. Then it is time to understand the huge number of terms that will be legally binding for an investment in your new startup. I go through them term by term and offer the simplest explanation I can of what each term means to you and what you need to watch out for.

The final anecdote in this section addresses a major work product you will need to put in place before that first term sheet is presented to you: your data room. A data room supports the due diligence process that investors go through so they know everything about you and your business before they pull the trigger on an investment.

Friends and family, angels, venture capital, or strategic?

- What are the prime funding sources for your brand-spanking-new startup?
- When attempting to raise from friends and family, will it be smooth sailing or choppy waters?
- Do you know when it makes sense to call on angel investors?
- Strategic investors can be a good source or not. Are you clear on their ups and downs?

On a major Defense Advanced Research Projects Agency (DARPA) program called CRASH, I co-led a large program where we invented technology that blocked virtually all cyberattacks. Then, in 2015, after four and a half years of research, I took two of the most central people behind it with me to a laboratory where we could "incubate" these ideas into a brand-new startup.

> **DEFINITION** *Incubation* is about creating a *safe* space in which all the work necessary to create a new company can be done carefully *before* the company has to face the real world of customers and investors. *Safe* in this context mostly has to do with money.

The lab where I chose to do this incubation was the Charles Stark Draper Laboratory, better known just as Draper. The lab put the initial group of us on salary and let me hire the rest of my team and pay them, as well. Half of that salary money was going to be a loan that the spin-out would have to pay back to the lab using equity (ownership), and the other half would be considered the lab's investment in its own ability to use the technology we developed for its customers. We incubated inside this lab for exactly two years, building technology, doing market research, talking to prospective customers, landing a lighthouse customer, and trying to prove to ourselves and others that we were viable as a new company ready to head out into the big bad world, ready to take on competition, ready to sell something people would buy, and close to financeable at the seed financing level. I named the company Dover.

> **DEFINITION** *Lighthouse customers* are called that because they serve as a "beacon of light" for the rest of your future customer base to follow. This is why getting a critical mass of them is essential to a successful product launch. They may not guarantee that the product they approve of will reflect precisely what the early and late majority customers want, but without them, you will never even have any early or late majority customers—you will not have crossed the chasm.[1]

When I was sure we were ready, the founder group (now six people) made the leap—all deep cybersecurity expert engineers except me. Upon our departure, the CEO of the lab and I decided we would add a few hundred thousand dollars more to the loan the lab was making so I had some initial cash to do basic formation tasks like finding office space, opening a bank account, setting up payroll, and hiring critical support functions like finance, legal, and IT. My team loved to tease me about this final bit of cash from the lab's CEO, calling it my "dowry." This $300,000 dowry was nowhere near enough to fund us as we added essential team members in areas like sales and marketing or to even fund us long enough for me to raise the first round of seed financing we would need to take us out for a year or more. But it was the absolute maximum amount Draper could offer. I was confident in my ability to raise more money fast enough to keep the team paid; I had a short-term financing plan in mind.

If your founder group can work for maybe six months with no salary while you prove a few things about the market need, your solution fit, your value proposition, what your minimum viable product might look like, who your competition will be, and what your differentiation will be, that's an ideal way to start without raising capital right away. Even better is if you and some of the other founders are very well off so you can self-fund even longer. If so, you are the lucky ones. Sometimes, however, the team includes more than just the founders, or the founders can't afford to live off their savings from day one. This means most founders, including us at the brand-new Dover, need a small initial infusion of capital right at the get-go.

---

[1] Jay Fuchs, "4 Ways Lighthouse Customers Can Predict a Product's Future," HubSpot Blog, September 4, 2020, updated June 15, 2021, https://blog.hubspot.com/service/lighthouse-customer.

NOTE   Prior to getting institutional investors involved in a startup, the most likely initial sources of funding are friends and family, angels, and a seed round. Seed is a priced round, and although a decade and more ago it was typically the purview of angel groups, it is increasingly being done by venture capital investors. What most people consider major financing rounds from venture capitalists are typically labeled starting at A. Each successive round is typically led by a brand-new investor, and each gets bigger because the company is supposed to be getting more and more successful in the markets in which it operates. Rounds D and E are usually quite large and go beyond what venture capital firms typically do; this becomes the realm of private equity. In fact, I used to joke about whether VCs could even say the alphabet that high because one rarely hears about venture capital rounds past C.

5.1   Friends and family stage

At formation, it's frequently too early to get a seed financing round from VCs because they are looking for revenue or at least confidence that you are close to revenue. So where do you go for an even smaller, earlier round than seed? One option to consider is what is called *friends and family*. I'm not even talking about people who invest as individuals professionally, called *angels*. I am talking about having all the founders reach out to every single person in their contact list who is a friend or family member. And I am talking about asking for individual investments as small as $1,000. If the team has friends and family who can afford to take the risk on your startup, it is a really workable way to raise a small amount of cash that, at your low initial burn rate (how much net cash you spend each month), should be sufficient to get you to where you can raise a seed round from early-stage VCs.

Friends and family know you, they want to support you, and many get very excited to vicariously be a part of your journey. It's the closest they can be to joining your startup. Asking for money from family and friends can be a very scary proposition, however. These are people who like you and believe you will—maybe more than you realize—make this company succeed so that your friends and family make some money, or at least don't lose any money. But the Securities and Exchange Commission (SEC) does not consider them to be "sophisticated." Not sophisticated mostly means they may not assess risk very accurately. One becomes sophisticated, according to the SEC, by having made many investments, having invested over $1 million, having a large income, and a few other SEC metrics.

Many a relationship has been forever ruined by an investment gone bad. The stress of having a family member at risk of losing their money may be too much to be worth it for you. I didn't even offer the potential to invest in my most recent startup to any of my family members except one, and the one I did offer it to (my little brother) invested a lot but could tolerate the risk of losing it. Still, I didn't want him (or any of my friends and family) to lose *anything* because I would be seeing them for the rest of my life, which meant there was a constant tiny version of my little brother standing on my shoulder asking why I was doing that thing, and shouldn't I be considering this other thing?

When doing a friends and family raise, using SAFEs is a wise way to do it.

DEFINITION *Simple agreement for future equity* (SAFE), in legal parlance, is a convertible note that gives the bearer a discount on the price of equity institutional investors pay at the next round. In normal English, these are *simple* financial debt instruments that promise *equity* (that means stock, also known as *shares*) in your company at a lower price than a VC pays. These early investors earn interest on their money invested. Friends and family who invest in your new venture give you their cash investment in return for this note that promises them a future ownership stake.

SAFE notes have terms about what happens if there is financing by an institutional investor like a VC, if there is never any investment by an outside new investor, or if the company goes under and there is no money to pay SAFE note holders. But as the first letter in SAFE says, they are simple. East Coast entrepreneurs tend not to use them as much because they are more conservative and want much more protection from downside risk; but in California, SAFEs are used extensively precisely because they are simple, they are fast, and they favor the entrepreneur. There are many more terms and protections for investors in a more traditional convertible note than in a SAFE. But from the company's standpoint, SAFEs are simpler and more company-friendly. If you are in the East, push to use them anyway because they seem to be gaining acceptance; as with many things startup-related, California tends to lead the way, and other geographies follow a bit later.

In my most recent use of them, the SAFE documents came together in about 2 days, and within 10 days of distributing them to people with a short blurb explaining what our company was going to do, I was getting commitments that ultimately grew to $675,000. That gave our small team of 12 about six months of breathing room before I had to raise a much more substantial seed round from institutional investors. That next round would include both angels and VCs and ultimately was sized at $4 million. Every one of those friends and family investors then became a seed-round shareholder because their SAFEs converted into equity when the seed round closed.

5.2 Seed stage

Seed is the first *priced round* and is done when the company has defined what problem it is solving and for what market(s) but does not yet have a product for sale and is therefore pre-revenue. Many venture capital firms specialize in seed rounds, but larger firms are also delving into seeds to gain access to more early-stage companies. Most seed rounds are in the range of $1 million to $2 million, but you will find some as large as $5 million.

DEFINITION A *priced round* is a new round of financing led by a new investor who proposes a new price per share that they are willing to offer the company in exchange for equity (shares).

DEFINITION   *Angels* are usually high-net-worth individuals who invest their own money directly in emerging businesses. Many angels are current or former entrepreneurs themselves. They primarily invest prior to venture capital financing.

Some angels operate as loners and are not part of any organized group, but most tend to join one of the over 400 groups that have formed across the United States, consisting of about 15,000 investors. Most of these angel groups are loose affiliations of individual investors, and each person makes their own decisions about which new ventures to invest in. The purpose of the group is to organize those individuals and have structured meetings where new companies come to pitch their stories. Some more established and sophisticated angel groups have created funds that aggregate investment dollars from many members and have paid professional managers for the funds. That model starts to feel like a large VC firm but with lots of tiny, limited partners. In this case, the group establishes a process whereby a decision is made about whether the fund will invest in a particular new company. These fund-based angel groups may on occasion participate in—or even lead—a priced round.

Whether investing as an individual, as part of a group that shares perspectives on each new opportunity presented, or through a named fund, angels don't have the resources a venture capital firm has to thoroughly evaluate a startup. And most VC firms focus on a small number of markets to further build their expertise so they can make better decisions on what to invest in. Table 5.1 shows the different formal rounds of financing up through Series C and the who, what, and when of how those rounds are financed.

Table 5.1   The who, what, and when of the various stages of venture capital financing rounds

Round	Pre-seed	Seed	Series A	Series B	Series C
Form	Cash or debt	Equity	Preferred "A" equity	Preferred "B" equity	Preferred "C" equity
Who	Founders Friends and family	Venture capitalists Angels	Venture capitalists Corporate	Venture capitalists Private equity Corporate	Private equity Corporate
What	Early working capital to get to first financing	First formal financing round after formation from investors focused on early-stage investing	First significant financing round in which one or more VCs become involved in a company previously financed by founders, seed VCs, and/or angels	Scaling round when the company has proven it is able to grow fast	Management and investors are contemplating an exit and need to prepare and raise the value of the company in preparation.

Table 5.1   The who, what, and when of the various stages of venture capital financing rounds *(continued)*

Round	Pre-seed	Seed	Series A	Series B	Series C
When	Immediately upon formation	When they agree with and buy into your "story" of opportunity	Once proof of product-market fit is shown (typically three paying customers)	When sales and marketing are what is needed to grow	When the company is contemplating an exit
Size	$100,000 to $750,000	$1 million to $2 million	$2 million to $10 million	$10 million to $25 million	$25 million and up

There is a common pattern of progression where seed investors succeed and get bigger, their funds get bigger, and the VC business model (see anecdote 9, "Understand the VC business model—raise money faster") move them away from doing seed to doing later and later, larger and larger investments, but a new crop of seed firms has appeared on the scene that specialize in and really like the early stage of seed investing. One such firm in Boston, which led Dover's seed round, is Hyperplane Venture Capital.

There is a conundrum with some seed-stage investors: they tend to be inexperienced, they have no brand yet, and they may even be confused about what they are. Many want to hurry up and get to the point that they can raise a bigger fund and become a later-stage VC. Hyperplane, however, knew what it liked and became well-known and well-respected for it. Hyperplane likes what is called hard tech: hard as in difficult. Hyperplane and a few other hard-tech seed investors are attracted to startups whose technology is complex, probably patentable, usually defensible, and likely disruptive. I was attracted to the firm because it operates as a true partnership of equals, plus the people are friendly and not unreasonably demanding of the entrepreneur. Hyperplane became our lead investor and later continued its strong support even when we hit some speed bumps.

Incubators can be a good option to get an early-stage company started. One of the most famous in this category is Y Combinator (https://ycombinator.com). Started in 2005 concurrently in Cambridge, Massachusetts, and Mountain View, California, it is now consolidated at a Silicon Valley locale. It selects two batches of companies per year, each of which receives a total of $500,000 in seed money as well as advice and connections. The $500,000 in funding using a SAFE note is in return for a 7% equity stake.

Strategic investors rarely invest at the seed stage because so little is known about how the market will react to the new company.

> **DEFINITION**   *Strategic investors* or just *strategics* are corporate investors: large companies that invest in new ventures usually because what the new venture is doing is strategically important to the large company.

Strategics are a mixed bag. They are slow-moving in all their processes. Most strategics want one of their business units to be your customer or to plan to become so, and they utilize that business unit to evaluate the technology of the prospective investment.

To create Dover's seed round, I got one seed firm (Hyperplane), an angel group (HUB Angels Investment Group), and a strategic investor (Qualcomm Ventures) to invest a total of $4 million, giving us over a year of runway before we would need more cash. Qualcomm's very presence in Dover's seed raised eyebrows and gave us instant credibility.

If you are considering a strategic investor in one of your rounds, don't give them a board seat; offer them special access to the senior team, a detailed briefing after every board meeting, or, if necessary, an observer seat (meaning they attend board meeting but do not have a vote and are supposed to just watch, listen, and report back to their constituents). This can help avoid scaring off their competitors from buying your product. The strategic who invests has a narrow set of aims for their investment (they want their parent company to buy you or at least buy from you), whereas your other investors have much broader aims about a return on investment for their constituents over the long haul. With all that, having such a name-brand investor in early helped us and opened many doors.

5.3   The moral of this anecdote

Each startup is different, but you must get cracking right away to find capital on which to run the company. That could come from a rich founder, but most of the time it comes from investors. You have lots of options about which types of investors to seek. Friends and family can be a helpful option early on if you feel comfortable asking. They know and like you and want to help, but they may not assess risk very accurately. Angel groups are a lot of effort because they require you to work with each individual member of their group to get them comfortable investing. But you can raise significant amounts from an organized angel group. Specialized early-stage investors are called the *seed stage* and have the advantage of being professional and sophisticated investors who will stay with you for the long haul. In some situations, you may even be able to attract a corporate investor, which can be advantageous in terms of the help they can provide, such as connections to possible partners and customers, ability to help recruit the right kind of talent, advice about appropriate business models, and how to compete against entrenched competitors in your specific market.

Angels: Your bridge financing solution

6

- Raising large amounts from angel investors—impossible or totally doable?
- If you are between rounds, are angels a good way to bridge to the next round?
- Can you think of it as a numbers game and apply it to lots of angel groups at the same time?

At several points in my entrepreneurial journey, I found my company not ready to raise money from professional institutional investors—the VCs who come in after seed-stage financings—and seeing the end of our cash looming kept me awake at night. Typically, this was because we had not proven product–market fit (see anecdote 15, "Product–market fit: making sure the dogs will eat your dog food") and were still too far from landing customers. This was the situation when I had raised about as much as I could ($8 million in two installments) from our initial seed-stage investors. To bridge the gap, I needed what is aptly named *bridge financing*. As the name implies, this is funding that bridges the company from one kind of financing to the next. In this case, it was between Series Seed and Series A.

6.1 Angel investors

Who do you turn to for this kind of financing? One good option is angels. Angels are individuals: not necessarily wealthy people but ones who have cash and are willing to take risks with it by investing in early-stage startups. For most angels I interacted with, their sweet spot was to invest $25,000 in each company they decided to support. They like to get in very early and be the first financing a company gets. Because you have not yet raised a lot of money, even a small angel investor can get a meaningful percentage of the company, which is attractive to them. Plus, in theory the follow-on round will be an equity round, so bridge financings usually offer angels a discount of around 20% off the price the VCs will pay in the next round, which makes these bridges doubly attractive. From your perspective, an angel's process for deciding to invest is not nearly as involved or lengthy as that of VCs. Many angels who are or were entrepreneurs themselves have been in your shoes and so are great cheerleaders for what you are doing.

It may not seem obvious, but you can raise real money from angels. It's realistic to get 15 angels from a single large angel group to each invest $25,000. That's $375,000. Get that from three angel groups, and you have over $1 million: sufficient capital to run a company of five with a monthly burn rate of, say, $75,000 for perhaps 15 months. That's a great start.

Angels are perfect for raising $1 million to $2 million just prior to the Series A when you may be raising $5 million to $10 million from VCs. The angel round of financing can come in a couple of different forms. It can be a *priced round*, or it can be a debt round based on *convertible notes*. A priced round from angels is not common, but it does occasionally happen, especially if there is a wealthy individual, a well-organized angel group with a fund, or a *family office* willing to lead this round.

> **DEFINITION** A *priced round*, also known as a preferred stock financing or priced equity round, is when a financial investment is exchanged for stock in a company based on a negotiated valuation of that company.

> **DEFINITION** A *convertible note* is a type of debt that is converted into equity when the next round takes place. It is not a loan to be paid back with interest.

> **DEFINITION** A *family office* is typically a very wealthy person interested in angel investing who can hire a staff to manage their investing.

A lead investor is needed to establish the price they are willing to offer for shares in your company. (There could be more than one investor vying to lead, in which case they will each submit a bid, and you get to choose among them.) This lead angel or group will likely be the largest investor in this round. To be clear, this will not be a $25,000 type of angel—more likely, it will be $100,000 or even larger investment. The price they are offering and other terms they want to establish will be written down in a *term sheet* and presented to you. Once you accept it, that set of terms is shared with all other prospective investors, who then decide if they like those terms and whether to sign on to join the round. A good example of a term sheet used by angels and VCs is freely downloadable (in return for an email address) from venturecapitaldealterms.com.

DEFINITION *A term sheet* is a bullet-point document outlining the material terms and conditions of a potential business agreement, establishing the basis for future negotiations between a seller and buyer. It is usually the first documented evidence of a possible financing or acquisition. It will later be turned into formal, legal documentation of the investment, but it is much easier to negotiate off of this simpler form.

A convertible-note round is the more common way for angels to come in. Typically, they are expecting—as are you—that soon you will be raising a Series A round from institutional VCs, and they want to be part of that round. They can't be directly in that round because the VCs in the Series A won't let them in—but the VCs will have no choice but to let them in if the angels are already holders of convertible notes.

If angels invest in a bridge round via a convertible note, that note is designed to convert into equity at the next financing round. The VCs defining the new round accept the convertible notes because the angels' money helped the company along. They also accept the offered *discount* of 10% to 20% off the price set for Series A shares because it is small compared to the amount the VCs are investing.

6.2   *What VCs think of angels*

Most VCs do not want angels to invest alongside them. That does not mean they don't want to have angels in the rounds previous to them. VCs don't want angels to invest alongside them because angels are not experts in the field in which the company operates (except by accident) and therefore do not offer the company much in the way of assistance for business progress. VCs and entrepreneurs commonly use the term dumb money to describe angels, family offices, and even some VCs. It means these investors offer money, sometimes lots of it, but don't help the company get new business connections, form useful partnerships, or find potential acquirers. If these types of investors are given seats on the board, VCs become alarmed; even if they are just observers who attend board meetings with no voting potential, they are a distraction and a time sink for the entrepreneurs and their management team.

Because they individually invest small amounts, angels add complexity—because of their sheer numbers—to the capitalization table of the company. I try to jokingly diffuse that argument by saying, "Well, that is why spreadsheets can add more rows so easily." But there is more to it than that. They must receive all investor communication, have their questions answered, and get a shareholder vote when certain actions the company proposes require approval. Having said all this, the other side of the coin is that VCs like the fact that angels take risks by investing in early-stage companies—risks the VCs try to avoid. If such a company succeeds, the VCs have the angels to thank for helping it reach the next stage.

6.3   *Finding and pitching to angels*

For either a priced round or a convertible-note round, there is a process you will need to follow to put together a financing legally and thoroughly.

The list of financing legal documents that lawyers will need to create

All of the following documents, as well as many others, are available for free from the National Venture Capital Association website: https://nvca.org/model-legal-documents.

- *Stock purchase agreement*—The definitive agreement between the company and each investor in this financing round, describing how stock is authorized, sold, and issued and specifying closing dates and stock certificate delivery, representations and warranties of the company and of the investors, and conditions to investors' obligations to close and the company's obligations to close.
- *Disclosure schedule*—A comprehensive listing of everything that (your lawyers deem) needs to be disclosed to the investors so there can be no misunderstandings about what the company has done, such as previous investments in the company, stock owned by founders, etc.
- *Investors' rights agreement*—Documentation describing rights to maintain proportional ownership, covenants of the company, restrictions on transfer of stock, right of first refusal, secondary refusal right, co-sale, drag-along rights, and voting.
- *Board consent*—A signed document capturing the board's approval of the financing at a required official board meeting.
- *Stockholder consent*—The formal approval of the financing by existing stockholders (i.e., founders).
- *Stock incentive plan amendment*—The plan for providing options to employees, which will now require modification to account for the additional shares this financing caused and to expand the option pool to enable additional hiring to take place.
- *Amendments to bylaws*—Changes to bylaws, which may or may not be required.
- *Amendments to restricted stock agreements*—Changes to the founders' stock agreement (e.g., the stipulation to change of control protection) that the founders may need to approve.
- *Indemnification agreements*—Agreements that may be required because experienced people have become more reluctant to serve corporations as directors or officers or in other capacities unless they are provided with adequate protection through insurance or adequate indemnification. This document (one for each person being indemnified) accomplishes that.
- *Management rights letters*—Agreements that major investors may require to ensure their board of directors or observer seats as a condition of their investment.

As you start researching angel groups, note this recent development I am seeing: some angel groups state that they are not interested in having prerevenue companies apply. This is bizarre. Don't bother with these groups—this attitude is ridiculous and antithetical to the role angels play in the startup financing ecosystem, which is to be early investors before VCs are ready to even consider a startup and, in most cases, before the startup is generating revenue.

Go to the website of every angel group you can find, driven by lots of Google searches. If you or anyone in your immediate circle has a connection to anyone who is an angel in that group, take full advantage of the connection and mention it in the section of the website application form for identifying such a referral. These referrals help a lot to get your application noticed and perhaps even put at the top of the stack for consideration.

When you apply to an angel group, it will ask if you already have an account at the service it uses to organize its potential investments. In most cases, it will be the dominant platform for the private securities market: Gust (http://gust.com). You say yes on the angel group application form, and it populates the group's site using the Gust information you have provided. Applications done this way take about five minutes instead of the hours required when each angel group created its own set of questions you had to answer. I have found that even if a particular angel group does not work with Gust, it still asks basically the same questions, so the thoughtfulness you used in setting Gust up will still speed up the process of applying to non-Gust using groups.

Information angel groups need in order to consider you for a pitch session

Here are the typical pieces of information you are required to fill in on Gust. Be sure to carefully answer all the questions. Although entering this information on Gust takes hours, as I mentioned, applying to each new angel group will only take an additional five minutes as its application sucks in all this information. Interestingly, the reason it takes many hours to carefully answer Gust's questions is that Gust severely and strictly limits the length of each answer. (The character count is listed in parentheses next to the name of each item below. I repeat, that is the number of characters including spaces!) As the French philosopher and mathematician Blaise Pascal famously wrote, "I would have written a shorter letter, but I did not have the time." The following Gust questions are current as of this writing (in the appendix, I offer my answers to these questions for my startup, Dover):

- *Company summary (450)*—This overview helps investors evaluate your startup. You may want to include your business model, structure, and products/services.
- *Management team (450)*—Who are the members of your management team, and how will their experience aid in your success?
- *Customer problem (450)*—What customer problem does your product and/or service solve?
- *Products and services (450)*—Describe the product or service you will sell and how it solves the customer problem, listing the main value proposition for each product/service.
- *Target market (450)*—Define the important geographic, demographic, and/or psychographic characteristics of the market within which your customer segments exist.
- *Business model (450)*—What strategy will you employ to build, deliver, and retain company value (e.g., profits)?

- *Customer segments (450)*—Outline your targeted customer segments. These are the specific subsets of your target market that you will focus on to gain traction.
- *Sales and marketing strategy (450)*—What is your customer acquisition and retention strategy? Detail how you will promote, sell, and create customer loyalty for your products and services.
- *Competitors (450)*—Describe the competitive landscape and your competitors' strengths and weaknesses. If direct competitors don't exist, describe the existing alternatives.
- *Competitive advantage (450)*—What is your company's competitive or unfair advantage? This can include patents, first-mover advantage, unique expertise, or proprietary processes/technology.
- *Pitch deck*—Upload a PowerPoint file.
- *Financials*—Upload a spreadsheet with your company financials, including, at a minimum, revenues and expenses.
- *Documents*—Business plan (most don't bother with this because your PowerPoint is considered a substitute these days).
- *Financial projections*—Upload an Excel spreadsheet.
- *Supplemental documents*—For example, white papers.

Keep at it, applying to lots of groups. You want the chance to pitch to as many groups as you can at their regularly scheduled (usually monthly) pitch meetings. Get that pitch deck and your presentation tight. Groups have strict time limits you must abide by. Write out your voice track in the notes section of PowerPoint or whatever you use to present, and practice and time the presentation. If you are presenting remotely, you can set it up so you can see your notes. But be sure you know the voice track, so you don't have to read the presentation and sound natural. The written-out voice track is to make sure you stick to the time limit.

Some groups want an 8-minute presentation. Some want 10 minutes. Some go as high as 15 minutes. The shortest I have experienced is 7 minutes. You will know ahead of time what the limit is, but they all tend to be strict. And even though most warn you when you are getting close so you can jump to a conclusion or call for action, if you do run over, they will cut you off before you get to some final point. This kept happening to me. In some cases I expected to be able to see my voice track, but their setup did not allow that. Or I was not fully following my voice track and spent too much time on one slide. Eventually, I followed my own advice and got good at fitting into whatever time limit they set. In most cases, you will have a couple of weeks to prepare for your pitch.

Because many pitches are now done over video, it's worth pointing out the importance of having good headphones, a microphone, and a camera to avoid technical glitches ruining your chance of success.

6.4 Preparing for your pitch

You can memorize even an 18-minute voice track and sound completely natural, not like you are reading. I learned how to do this for a TEDx talk, all of which are exactly 18 minutes long and do not allow notes. Here is what I learned from that experience:

- Write out the entire text you want to memorize. In fact, before you construct your deck, start with your voice track. It is your story, and you want your slides to follow your story, not the other way around.
- Resist the urge to begin memorizing from the front to the back. The correct way to memorize is from the back to the front. Doing it this way means you spend more time learning the later material, so you learn that material better than the material that comes before it. Then if you are forced to jump ahead because you're running out of time, you know the later information the best, allowing you to jump ahead smoothly.
- Because memorization involves reading some lines and then reciting them over and over, you may tend to close your eyes to avoid reading the paper or screen in front of you. To make sure you don't close your eyes when presenting, once you are confident of your material, practice reciting while walking in the woods, in a nearby park, or around your block. You sure won't close your eyes there. Also scan your eyes back and forth as you walk and recite, which is what you will want to do when presenting to the group to stay fully engaged with them as you assess their body language.

Remember, by definition, angels come early in the life of a new company. Compared to the details and progress you can tout later, when you are ready for VCs, angels know there is a lot you have not figured out yet, such as product–market fit (see anecdote 15) or even what the final business model will be. That, plus the much shorter length of pitch that angels allow, means you'll have different content in this pitch to angels compared to your pitch to VCs. I cover the angel pitch deck content next.

6.5 The pitch

Here's what to include in your pitch to angels (no matter the pitch length):

- *Passion and drive*—Your passion and drive need to come through loud and clear and right away. What's driving you? Inject a bit of your personal story so they can include the human aspect in their investment decision. Be honest and authentic, because if they detect a false persona, they will not like you. They are investing their own money, not money from a fund they are managing for others. In the end, they have to like you, trust you, believe in you, and want you to succeed, or they will not invest. Investors are humans and like to be guided by their gut instincts. If you can get that going in them, you have probably won.
- *Business purpose*—Be clear about the purpose of your business. What gave you the idea in the first place? Are you already an expert in this market, and have you discovered a big problem that you are uniquely qualified to solve? What is

that big problem you are solving? And how are you solving it? (Please, no jargon!) Who are you going to help (i.e., your customer)?

- *Business opportunity*—Next, get into the business opportunity, which is what will excite them, especially if you can show any traction at all. This is where discussion of value comes in—value to customers and then value to investors. Describe the commercial opportunity, and size it according to the size of the serviceable addressable market (SAM). Are market trends creating this opportunity? That can be a large force for change that makes an opportunity for the right company—yours—to exploit. This is where you talk about the competition. For goodness' sake, never say there is *no* competition, even if the only competition is some antiquated manual process. If you say there is no competition, they will reply, "Then how can there really be an opportunity?" Talk about how you stand up against the competition. This section is where you get to look smart because you know this area, and you can educate them about it.

DEFINITION *Serviceable addressable market (SAM)* is computed by asking what the total annual revenues would be if every possible customer within a market segment who could buy your product, or a product that contains your technology, buys it.

- *Market traction*—Can you demonstrate *market traction*, proof that someone wants to buy your product or service? An idea is one thing, but proof of traction validates that idea. This does not mean you must have a fully fleshed-out product in the market—they know it is too early to expect that. But you must show evidence that people want what you are offering. You would not be passionate about this if that were not true. You can talk about meetings you have had, about social followers or email subscribers, about a pilot or successful demo and the reactions you got, and any customers you have (even if they have not paid a cent).

- *Return on investment*—Time to convince them that they will get a great return on their investment. Be sure to have your numbers supporting this. They will want to see a good multiple on their investment—10 times, 20 times, or even more. Can you show them how that is possible? To answer this, you will have to think about potential acquirers and what they might pay. Here, you can try to find comparables, just like in real estate, that give credence to your estimate of eventual sale price. Can you talk about how much it will cost to acquire a customer? What is the lifetime value of that customer to your business (i.e., can you sell more than one thing to a given customer)? And what is the projected revenue from all your customers?

- *Personalize*—Remember to research each angel group and personalize part of your pitch to who they are and what they like. For instance, some groups are dominated by finance people, and some are filled with technology wizards. And don't forget to treat this as a story. Humans love stories, so a story pulls them in, and telling a story is easier for you to remember and to tell with obvious passion.

Once you have all the legal documents ready and you have researched and applied to as many angel groups as you can find, you can expect an invitation to a formal pitch session from many of those angels. There is usually a process of filtering applicants down to the number they can reasonably hear from in a single meeting. Some only hear from 3 prospects, and some set that number at 10. Even for someone who has pitched a lot, a room full of 20, 30, or even 40 angels can be a bit daunting. They give you a time to arrive (in person or on a controlled Zoom session), and they put you in a waiting area.

No matter how hard the pitch session organizers try (in the real world, not Zoom), they cannot keep "competitors" from seeing each other. We are competitors in the truest sense of the word: as part of a group larger than can be supported by the resource being sought (money), you must convince the provider (angels) that you are one of the ones who should get that resource. You cannot help scrutinizing those competitors in this situation to "size them up" and decide if they or you are destined to be the winner. As I did this, everyone was very polite and professional to the others in the waiting area. In a few situations, I saw someone I had seen before, proving that the community of entrepreneurs and sources of capital is very small. In some situations, the presentation room was not cordoned off, and I could see the presenter ahead of me and even see their slides. I immediately wondered if their slides or mine were better. Of course, these thoughts may be natural, but they are poison to the need to be relaxed but confident as you head into such a stressful situation.

You will clearly see that the angel group is on a tight schedule and moving all the candidates quickly through the initial steps. When your turn comes, you are led in, and you must set up your laptop and its connection to their video projection system very fast because they count that time as part of your allocation. Be sure to practice this, too! I had a glitch at one meeting where the laptop would not talk to the projector, and I lost two minutes out of the eight they allocated. You guessed it: I got six minutes to present and was cut off abruptly before I reached the conclusion. As you can imagine, I never heard back from them. Be sure to begin with no small talk, as you may naturally want to do, because that also counts against your time.

There are also situations in which you simply must go with the flow. This was the scene when I was pitching to HUB Angels in Cambridge, Massachusetts, for my most recent company. I knew no one in the room. I had only had some email exchanges with the managing partner, David Verrill. I dove right in. But there was a woman in the room who, after her first question, I could tell was going to be the thorn in my side. She wanted me to hurry up and get to the product discussion. I wanted to present the problem and the opportunity first, but she would not have it and kept interrupting me until I gave in and moved ahead in my presentation to the product discussion. However, another person did not understand the product discussion and wanted to know more about the business model and the opportunity, and another wanted to hear about our market traction so far. Pretty soon my time ran out, and it felt like a bad outcome. But my willingness to go with their flow worked to my advantage in the end. Afterward, a group of them, including the managing partner, gathered on the sidewalk outside, and they said positive things about my presentation. I had misread their actions during the meeting. The managing partner said the larger group asked him to start a due diligence process on us, which meant they liked what they heard enough that more than half the attendees said they might invest if the due diligence checked out.

Some even loosely affiliated angel groups can have a big impact. Take Harvard Business School Alumni Angels of New York, the winner in the longest acronym contest: HBSAANY. They all invest strictly as individuals, and they are well-organized, very smart people. There are Harvard Alumni Angels affiliates and investors all over the world, including Tokyo, London, Toronto, Silicon Valley, Boston, Chicago, and, of course, New York. They have a way to syndicate from one branch to everyone at once for truly global participation. Ultimately, I pitched to the global community of branches. Starting in New York, I got 32 global members of the Harvard Business School Alumni Angels to invest an average of $34,000 apiece.

There is another way to gain access to both angel groups and *family offices*. A few organizations have popped up that create a forum where the audience is angels and family office staff, and the presenters are entrepreneurs looking for financing. These organizations typically charge the entrepreneur a fee. One I tried to use charged $5,000 to give an eight-minute presentation. I went to a meeting and did not get a single follow-up or expression of interest. Waste of time and money—but it's good to try some different tactics to see if they might work. Groups that charge entrepreneurs just for creating a venue to meet potential funders are very controversial and have raised the ire of many entrepreneurs (including me). A very organized group providing much higher value is The Keiretsu Forum, a conglomeration of angels that charges $3,000 annually plus $475 per member. The exposure from Keiretsu Forum Northwest is extensive, and it has a rigorous due diligence process that instills confidence that the group does a good job for the investors and the companies. I used Keiretsu Forum Mid-Atlantic and got a solid family office involved, which became a strong repeat investor for us.

Angels are an accessible and effective first step after potentially self-funding or doing a friends and family raise and before you are ready for a first round from VCs. Angels operate as individuals, but they are usually affiliated with a group, so you can find them and get leverage from the group to access dozens of individual angels simultaneously. It's important to work hard to prepare your pitch to the angel group, but fortunately, Gust makes it easy to apply to dozens of angel groups in very short order. The hard part is telling an honest, passionate, coherent, and compelling story in the limited time angels typically allocate. With a compelling story and an effective presentation of that story, you will prevail, and your first round can be filled quickly. That allows you to get back to the real business you and they want you to be doing: *building your company*.

6.6   *The moral of this anecdote*

Angels should be seriously considered as part of a startup's financing strategy. The return on your time investment is quite high because raising from angels does not take nearly the level of effort or time required to close a VC round. Not only can angels be the first organized investment in your startup, but they can fill in later when other investors will not play—in particular, when you need a bridge financing because you are running low on cash but your progress is not sufficient to go after the next round of financing.

The art of pitching to institutional investors

- Will you be in tune with the VC pitch meeting vibe to maximize your chance of success?
- Do you have a great VC pitch deck? Suggestions on how to structure it.
- Surviving VC shark tank drama. Are you ready for nasty curveballs?

Different types of investors require different types of pitches. In anecdote 6, "Angels: Your bridge financing solution," I discussed how to pitch to individual angels, who, even if they are part of a group with organized meetings, ultimately invest about $25,000 per person. In this anecdote, I'll cover pitching to *institutional investors*, which means venture capitalists, highly organized fund-based angel groups, private equity firms, and corporate or strategic investors.

> **DEFINITION** *An institutional investor* is a legally organized partnership or corporation whose sole business activity is investing to make a profit consistent with their corporate structure (for shareholders, limited partners, or a parent company). These are the investors you will get to once you have market traction, have proven product-market fit, or later, when you are ready to scale the company.

There are naturally a lot of common topics between the pitch to angels and the pitch to institutional investors. In both, you need to highlight the problem, your solution, the opportunity, your business model, the competition, and so forth. But as discussed in anecdote 6, the angel pitch is on the order of 10 minutes or less, and the institutional investor pitch is at least 30 if not 60 minutes in length. So even if the outline is similar, the amount of depth you go into is vastly different.

7.1   *The pitch*

The relative informality that works with angels won't work with serious, professional investors. It may seem surprising, but the only way to get an audience with these investors is via word of mouth. This means you must get a warm introduction from someone who knows you and knows the investor, and the individual at the firm must know the introducer and like and trust them enough to accept this meeting. You are starting with a positive—do everything you can to build on it.

You need to tell the story of why, out of the thousand companies whose pitches this partner has seen, yours is worth listening to and is something they will want to invest in.

> **ASK YOURSELF**   Does your idea fit this firm's investment thesis and, more importantly, this partner's investment thesis? If not, you may be wasting precious time.

Most recently, I was pitching a startup whose business model was licensing a hardware design that would be built into a silicon chip. Many, many VCs got burned in the early 2000s: investing when semiconductors was hot and lucrative, but as Japan became dominant in semiconductors, the US market consolidated, openings for small companies vanished, and a lot of money was lost. I got a nice warm introduction to this partner, but my introducer did not realize these VCs now had an almost allergic reaction to investing in semiconductors. At firm after firm, the partner I was presenting to would begin to act strangely by my third or fourth slide, at which point it was best if I politely closed my laptop, stood up, and walked out. I didn't do that, but there was no point in continuing the discussion. That partner had already made up their mind that they were not investing, and a little dance of social politeness ensued; they did not want to kick me out, and I did not want to pick up and walk out, but both of us knew this was a nonstarter. This startup was a real challenge, and after a couple of years of meeting with VCs—I kept track of each of them and their one-line closing statements to me—I had met with over 100 firms.

Investors can be lemmings, and many (except those whose thesis is not to follow any trends) tend to follow the same trends. Recently, trends like Software as a Service (SaaS), artificial intelligence (AI), blockchain or crypto-currency, and consumer-facing products or services have all been very hot, so many investors are focused on those areas. If you do something in one of those categories, great, as long as you are very clearly different and better than anything else in your same, overly crowded category. My part-hardware, part-software cybersecurity company was about as far as you can get from SaaS, AI, and consumer-facing products, but one investor said to me, "Can you do something SaaS in your solution? If so, I might be interested."

Most investors will listen and actively engage while you present. But it was not a rare occurrence to have a partner bring an associate into the room and then—as the associate dutifully takes notes and asks a few questions—look at their phone the entire time. The rudest example of this happened at the biggest, most famous Silicon Valley firm, Andreessen Horowitz.

That first critical, one-on-one meeting with the individual partner who is screening your deal for the full partnership to consider should be a crisp, 30-minute pitch that allows ample time for questions. If you do not wow them, you do not get to pass GO!

The big challenge is that you must fight investors' short attention spans by getting them very excited and interested within the first six slides (or fewer). In fairness, it is not just the short attention spans but also pitch deck fatigue. Don't make it easy for them to lose interest—make your story and your presentation of that story compelling. Remember, engage them with a story, and keep your slides sparse, simple, and easy on the eyes. No matter what, never lead with or focus too much time on technology. That is the cardinal mistake of technical founders time and time again.

7.2 The deck (aka your business plan)

Table 7.1 lists the major elements to include in your pitch deck.

Table 7.1   Major elements of the pitch deck

The big problem	Explain the big problem that motivates you and that you solve. Use no jargon. Be sure to explain how it is not being solved today.
Your solution	Describe your great solution and how it is ideally suited to solve the just-mentioned big problem. This is where you fit in a brief explanation of how your thing works. Don't go deep. If they like this and you, they will have an expert spend time digging in, so no need to do that now.
Big opportunity	Now that they understand there is a big problem and you have a real solution, you want to appeal to greed and tell them how big this opportunity is. Use serviceable addressable market (SAM), never total addressable market (TAM), or they will roll their eyes.
Business model	How do you make money? Are you SaaS, enterprise software, consumer-focused, IP licensing, pure services, or a mix of products and services? Will you have multiple revenue streams? That is ideal if true. Even better is if, as in SaaS, you can point to annually recurring revenue (ARR); if you have that, the VC will be eating out of your hand because nothing excites them more than predictable future revenue.
Go-to-market (GTM)	How are you going to market? This is where you describe the vertical market segments you are starting with. Geoffrey Moore famously called this the bowling pin: he argues that you need a single, narrowly defined vertical market (the bowling pin) that is your solitary focus. What about partnerships? They are a critical aspect of your GTM, so talk a bit about how you will leverage partners to expand sales.

Table 7.1   Major elements of the pitch deck *(continued)*

The big problem	Explain the big problem that motivates you and that you solve. Use no jargon. Be sure to explain how it is not being solved today.
Proof points	If you are pre-Series Seed, you probably do not have customers or revenue to speak of yet, but you have certainly been talking to prospective customers to understand the potential for your product/service. Include what those people said.
	If you are going after an A round or later, you have customers and need to demonstrate product–market fit. This means at least three large customers, except in high-volume consumer applications such as the next Kayak, Airbnb, or even a hardware consumer product like Nest, in which case they want to see large numbers and monthly growth rates. Also include any awards, impressive press, articles, and so forth here.
Competition	Never say there is no competition, even if you are unique. They will discount what you are saying at best and not want to proceed with you at worst. If you are unique, focus on where the money for your product will come from. Assume customers cannot just create new money out of thin air, which means to buy your product, they will probably stop buying something else. That something else, at a minimum, is your competition. This is also where you talk about how you defend yourself against those inevitable competitors.
	Do you have a patent "moat" that protects you from encroachers, like the protective water troughs surrounding medieval castles? Do you have a plan to become dominant in a market niche fast and expand from there, making it hard to challenge you? Is there something else about the product that makes it highly defensible?
Team	Some argue that you should discuss this up front, but they forget that VCs have areas they strongly shy away from. So no, I do not think this goes up front. If you get past the first six slides and still have their attention, you are good, and they will reach this point and want to find out how strong your team is. Some like to include the board and advisors. I think that is rarely valuable unless your advisors are truly a key part of your value proposition or they fill an important expertise gap.
Use of funds	Talk about the raise you are asking for. Describe what you plan to spend the funds on, how long it will last, your burn rate, and your "ask." You should be asking for enough cash to last 18 to 24 months.

That was nice and short, wasn't it? Resist the urge to add a lot more. You will get many chances to go deeper in key areas, so don't load up your first pitch.

You will get whipsawed by investors who provide post-presentation feedback or advisors who offer services that help entrepreneurs craft their pitch decks, saying, "Put the big opportunity up front," "more on product," "less on technology," "team is the most important thing," and so on. You should listen and consider their ideas, but my experience says the outline in table 7.1 is generally the best. It has all the requisite bits, and you can reorder elements based on the feedback.

Another common challenge is a prospective investor who wants you to send the pitch deck to them ahead of time. The problem is that a great presentation in person and one that can be read ahead are not the same thing. In person, you will follow good presentation rules like three (maybe five, if pushed) lines of text on a slide, maximum; lots of good visuals; and your voice track, which guides the listener through the slide, adding useful details. (And, of course, in person, you can be sensitive to confusion or a questioning look from the investor.) But if you send this type of deck ahead of your presentation, they won't hear your voice track, so they will look at your slides and not get your key messages. Do you make multiple decks? Sounds like a good idea until you try it. Because the pitch deck tends to change almost continuously, you then have to make those changes in two decks . . . continuously. Alternatively, you veer off best practice and put more text on a slide. That is a slippery slope, to the point that you could end up with the kinds of slides common in the Department of Defense (DoD) world: an encyclopedia on each slide.

I always end up with appealing slides that have the least text possible but still enough to make the point. It is worth having a talented visual communications expert with graphics skills by your side because excellent pictures are worth . . . you guessed it, a thousand words. I had the very good fortune to have a five-star general of a visual communications expert as my director of marketing: her decks were sendable while being even better when presented in person, so we did not have to maintain two separate decks.

Some gotchas to be aware of

To be blunt here, sexism, ageism, homophobia, racism, and other types of discrimination are issues with more investors than you would imagine. Just be sensitive to the vibe, and if you are getting a strong negative in one of these areas, then be polite, make your exit, and cross that investor off your list. I have seen this kind of discrimination, and unfortunately it is not that rare.

I was doing some early-stage investing in the early 2000s and had a very interesting concept I wanted to take to a partner I knew well at one of the top Boston VC firms, to get them to lead the next round. I was the temporary CEO while we incubated the concept and got it ready for an institutional investor. The permanent CEO was to be a very experienced sales executive who was passionate about the concept this new startup was bringing to market. He was ready to be CEO. I wanted to promote him in that role, and I was very excited for him to be successful at it. He deserved it. I only mention this next fact because it's highly relevant to this story: my friend is Black.

The meeting was set. My friend was super ready with his pitch about him and about the company. The partner greeted us, and we sat in a large, all-glass conference room. There were a minute or two of social pleasantries, and then we were encouraged to begin. My friend got to slide two, and the partner said he needed to excuse himself, telling us he had to go to his office for an important call. He promised to come back in no more than 15 minutes.

My friend and I sat people-watching through the floor-to-ceiling window wall separating us from the comings and goings of the office.

At the 25-minute mark, he said, "He won't be coming back."

(continued)

"Don't be silly, of course he will," I reassured him. "His call just went long. He's a friend."

He started packing up his computer bag. "You've missed the signals that people who look like me learn to read very carefully, and he is not coming back," he said. And just like that, we were out in the parking lot.

"Jothy, you don't see this day in and day out like I do. That partner is racist, and he will not be investing in a company I'm running."

It's ugly, but it's true. Just be aware.

Somewhere along the way during my 35-year entrepreneurial career, investors and entrepreneurs have all but dropped the written business plan for early-stage (seed and Series A) companies; instead, your "business plan" is the pitch deck. Having said that, the exercise of writing a detailed business plan, even if no one ever asks for it, is invaluable (see anecdote 17, "A formal business plan in 10 steps"). Thinking of your pitch deck as your business plan this way will put you in the right frame of mind about how serious an endeavor it is to create your deck and deliver it to perfection. Serious, professional investors see literally thousands of entrepreneurs pitching, so the content, as well as the delivery, better be different, compelling, exciting, and convincing. And you must grab them in six slides, before you get a chance to tell the rest of your story. Everyone has their idea of the perfect outline for a pitch deck. Ultimately, your story, your personality, and your style will determine what the actual outline should be. Once you have that, practice, practice, practice so you are smooth and confident during that initial meeting—the one that opens the gate to continue with that firm.

7.3   *The moral of this anecdote*

These days, investors don't request business plans very often. Certainly not for early-stage companies. Instead, everything hangs on the pitch deck and those 30 to 60 minutes you get with a partner at a VC firm. This is why the content and organization of the pitch deck and your performance are so critical: you only get one chance to make that first impression. If you get a no, you will never know exactly why. Usually they will simply say "Not a fit for us," which could mean it's not a fit or could mean the partner did not find your pitch compelling. So, work very, very hard on your pitch, and practice it a lot, especially in front of friendlies who will give you honest feedback. And seek out expert coaching. Put in the time!

Investors aren't your friends

- Are you decoding investor friendliness correctly? Be clear: it's all business.
- Will you be clear on investor motivations when they provide you with their advice?
- When it comes to a "good" exit, do startup and investor definitions match?

This is a hard but extremely important lesson to learn. You see, venture capitalists, and investors in general, are very personable and friendly, traits that are essential for them to be successful. When you are in their offices meeting them, everyone is extremely nice. When the partner you're working with interacts with you early on, they are so friendly that you will naturally be inclined to think, *this is someone I could be friends with.* That would be a mistake. To them, you are the key to their next payoff, period. You and your company are an investment, not a genuine source of social interaction. Proof of this happens if, say, things start to go awry after they have invested. Then it will be abundantly clear they are not your friend. And if things go wrong for long, they will get rid of you—snap!—just like that. And they will never look back or contact you again.

I was looking to pad my CEO skills by first being CTO at a new company where I could soak up sales and CEO DNA. *Who would know better about such an opportunity than VCs?* I asked myself. What could possibly go wrong?

8.1   *The investor's singular focus: Their investment*

During the Webspective financing campaign, when I was visiting with as many VCs as I had good warm introductions to, I met with Highland Capital Partners, Matrix Partners, and a half-dozen others. I went back to the partners at these firms to see if they had a portfolio company that was a good fit for my new plan on how to become a CEO. It was Paul Maeder, arguably the most highly respected VC in all of Boston, at Highland Capital, who "took me under his wing" and offered two portfolio companies where he was on the board, both of which needed a strong CTO. One was Avid Technology, and the other was NovaSoft.

Avid is a public company that makes software that movie and television production companies use to edit their films into finished movies or TV shows. In the credits for most movies, you will see Avid mentioned by name. By the time I interviewed there in 1998, it had already captured over 90% of the market—which is a big problem. Once you are that dominant in a market and have crushed all competition, you are the one everyone wants to try to beat. The only way to sustain yourself, much less grow at the rate you grew on the way to 90% share, is to find a new market (and hold on to what you have). And if you don't grow, your value to investors diminishes rapidly, and you can crash and burn. To find a new market and grow, Avid decided to go *down market* to small video producers. There were plenty of these, as evidenced by how many videos were being put up on YouTube and later Facebook. Avid considered itself a high-end, very sophisticated (and expensive) editing tool. But Apple had a product for the low end, called Final Cut Pro, and it was moving up market, where Apple would be encroaching on Avid's core business. This was what I was walking into.

From reading the press, I knew Avid's stock was way down, and Paul was saying it had to reinvent itself, embrace Apple's hardware, stop making its own custom hardware, and probably even cannibalize its own business to survive the expected onslaught from Apple. The interview for the CTO role went fine, but I was worried this might not be the best place to learn to be a great CEO. The Avid CTO would lead the effort to build new lower-end products *and* the effort to embrace the Apple hardware, all while weaning the company off custom-made hardware. It would be an all-consuming job, leaving me no time to learn sales. Further, I learned during the interview with the CEO that he did not come from a pure sales background, so he might not be the ideal person to learn sales from; the VP of Sales might be better, but he was not on offer to partner with.

NovaSoft was still a private company in the document-management space, which meant its software managed a process of creating, approving, and storing critical documents for large enterprises. In NovaSoft's case, they were big pharmaceutical companies, and the documents were the recipes for how drugs were created in a production line. The NovaSoft software was really a collaboration tool that everyone involved in the creation and approval of these recipe documents used in what is called a *workflow*. That's a jargony term for an enforced process of well-defined steps and the people who are responsible for each step.

NovaSoft may still have been a private company, but it had already raised rounds A, B, C, D, and E. It was not doing well, and these were not large private equity rounds; they were venture rounds, and mostly they involved the same investors who had already invested. Sales had stalled, the product was considered buggy, and morale was low. The crucial bit of information about NovaSoft that Paul emphasized before I went in was that a brand-new CEO was taking over for the founder, who was being pushed aside. This new CEO was a firebrand former VP of Sales whom the board was pinning all their hopes on to save the company. It seemed to be a good situation in which to learn, because who better to learn about sales from than a former and very successful VP of Sales whom the board believed was going to be a very successful CEO? Two vital skill sets for me to learn on the job, and from the same person, no less. That interview went fantastically: the CEO was super-high-energy, he loved to talk, especially about sales, he appreciated what I would bring to the table as CTO, and he loved to teach, so he was fired up about me joining his company.

But I wanted to ask Paul which of the two opportunities I should take.

Without hesitation, Paul said, "NovaSoft will be best for you."

I was naive and assumed Paul was truly thinking of what was best for *me* when he said it would "be best for you." But what Paul meant—I realized later—was it would "be best for Paul." See, Paul's investment in Avid had already given him great returns when it went public (called an *initial public offering* or IPO), and his firm was probably not holding many, if any, of those shares anymore. That's because when an investor's holding has an *exit* (sale or IPO), they want to sell off the shares they own from their investment in the startup so they can reap the benefits of that investment and share those with the limited partners who gave them the money to invest. But there had been no return on NovaSoft, and it looked like a good exit was unlikely: its performance was far from what would qualify it for an IPO, and no one was buying document-management companies because it was not a very exciting market. What Paul wanted was my help at NovaSoft, trying to make it at least do well enough that Paul's VC firm, and all the other investors as well, could sell it to someone and maybe not lose all the money they had invested.

Types of startup exits

Entrepreneurs need to always be thinking of the ultimate exit because investors get no return on their investment until there is a *liquidity event* and because entrepreneurs also want a financial return for their hard work and sacrifices, and they may not enjoy the later stages of a company once it is no longer a startup. There are five potential liquidity events to think about when planning your exit strategy, plus one I've included that is an exit but is not a liquidity event:

(continued)

1 *Merger and acquisition (M&A)*—This involves merging with a similar company or being bought by a larger company. It's a great way to scale when related companies have complementary skills and can save resources by combining. For bigger companies, it's a more efficient and quicker way to grow revenue than creating new products organically. The investors are looking to be acquired by a larger company eventually so there is cash flowing to them.

2 *Initial public offering (IPO)*—A portion of a company's stock is listed on the stock exchange so the public can purchase it. It used to be the preferred exit and the quick way to riches. But since the internet bubble burst in the year 2000, the IPO rate has declined every year and is now at about 10%. This is a tough road for startups these days. Shareholders are demanding, and liability concerns are high.

3 *Selling to a friendly individual*—This is not an M&A because it does not combine two entities into one. This is a way to "cash out" so you can pay investors and pay yourself. The ideal buyer is someone who has more skills and interest on the operational side of the business and can scale it. It is not the kind of outcome investors are hoping for.

4 *Management and employee buyout (MBO)*—In management buyouts, those already working in the business can transition into more senior roles to fill the gap in leadership. The management team is already familiar with your business, so they should be well-equipped to manage the company.

5 *Selling to a private equity firm*—Increasingly, private equity (PE) firms are buying companies that they then work on to put them in a better position to be purchased by a larger firm. The PE firm typically tries to "fix it up" in two years and get a good return. This works well for the PE firm, but it also can work well for the management team if the PE firm decides to leave them in place.

6 *Acquihires*—Acquihires is a business exit strategy where a company is bought solely to acquire its talent. This type of acquisition can be very beneficial to skilled employees, as you can be confident they will be well looked after once the business itself is sold, but it is not beneficial to investors.

I took Paul's advice and joined NovaSoft because I thought he really was looking out for me and telling me what was going to be best for me.

Avid went on to find a way to expand its business despite Apple's serious challenge while also remaining the high-end choice for all types of video production. Its stock shot up and split several times. NovaSoft was an unmitigated disaster. The amazing CEO was fired before I had even been there six months. I learned nothing positive from him, and it felt like I had totally wasted my time.

8.2   *The moral of this anecdote*

Investors are some of the friendliest, nicest people you will ever meet (most are, anyway), but never ever confuse them for someone who could be your friend. When they suggest having dinner with spouses, going out to a show, going skiing, or going sailing, politely decline. You can't mix worlds when they have so much power over you; they have the money you need for future financing rounds, and if they occupy a board seat, they are also officially your boss. Further, what drives them and what drives you are not aligned. Return the politeness, but—trust me on this—don't become friends with them, or when your company hits the inevitable speed bump, it will hurt even more. Later, when you are not part of a startup and they are not your investor, you can be friends with them, even join their firm and become one of them. All that is fine. But now is not the time for friendship.

Understand the VC business model: Raise money faster

- Who are the key players in the VC firm, and whom should you focus on?
- Do you get the financial motives that make the VC tick?
- Do you understand the VC math that drives when and how they invest?

To succeed in the startup world, you must learn what makes venture capitalists (VCs) tick. Of course, the answer is money, but the way they make their money is through their business model. Understanding their business model is the key to understanding the VC specimen and how to most effectively work with them.

The VC's business model affects which companies they invest in, how much they invest, and who they want running these companies. It determines how they influence the strategy of their portfolio companies so they conform to their metrics of success. It affects whether you and they are at all compatible and if you should even be talking to them.

If you lose sight of their business model, you will lose sight of how they see the world and how they make decisions. This could at best surprise you and at worst mean your startup fails because there is not a lot of room for error.

Before I fully understood all this, I ran afoul of each point. I pitched to VCs when my company was not a good fit for what their fund was trying to do. I pitched to VCs who needed to invest $20 million when all I needed was $2 million. I pitched to VCs when they only wanted to invest in Software-as-a-Service companies but I was building hardware. In many cases, these were VCs who had changed their model since I last knew them; even though we knew each other well, that did not trump making sure I matched my strategy and metrics to what they cared about now. I came to realize that I needed to fully understand the inner workings of the VC business model to avoid these mistakes and raise money faster and more easily.

9.1   The venture capital people

Let's start with the people. Here are a couple of definitions you'll need to know.

> **DEFINITION**　*Venture* means a business enterprise, usually a startup or an early-stage company, that involves a high degree of risk. A *venture capitalist* is a type of investor who funds startups that demonstrate potential for long-term growth.

The big risk for them is, of course, that the venture fails and they lose all their investment. Or the venture could sell, but not for a profit, which is not consistent with their model of *making* money. Early-stage VCs are dealing with ventures where 1 or 2 out of 10 of their investments are successful and the rest fail. They are risk-takers, but only up to a point; they are far from careless. VCs are expected to bring managerial and technical expertise, as well as capital, to their investments, so the risk is balanced by experience and diligence.

> **DEFINITION**　A v*enture capital fund* is a pooled investment vehicle—in the United States, often a limited partnership (LP) or limited liability corporation (LLC)—that primarily invests the financial capital of third-party investors (the limited partners) in high-risk enterprises that standard capital markets or banks won't consider. A venture capital firm typically manages these funds and employs individuals with technology backgrounds (scientists, researchers), business training, and/or deep industry experience.

VCs are by and large very socially adept and gracious people—a helpful trait for someone who is trying to get as much information as they can from you so they can quickly figure out if you have something that could make them and their investors a lot of money. I always liked having these meetings because these people are usually really friendly, and they have incredibly nice offices with an Apple TV for every conference room to make it easy for the entrepreneur to present with no wires to connect or dongles to search for in your bag. When I walked into most of these offices in Boston, they were high up, looking over the ocean; they had delicious coffee, bowls of peanut M&Ms, and very helpful and friendly admins who set me up in the conference room, ready for the partner to arrive for our pitch session.

When you look at the team page on a VC firm's website, you will see a lot of different titles. Here are definitions for the most common investment staff titles. I have sorted this list in order of importance to you, the entrepreneur:

- *Partner*—People in this role run the venture capital firm and make the investment decisions on behalf of the fund. This title may have *Managing* or *General* as prefix as a way to show seniority among all partners. General partners typically put in personal capital, usually 1% to 3% of the VC fund size, to show their commitment to the limited partners. This instills greater confidence in the fund.

- *Venture partner*—This type of partner is expected to source potential investment opportunities ("bring in deals") and is compensated only for those deals with which they are involved. These are frequently entrepreneurs who exited their previous company, are bringing their expertise to a VC firm, and are perhaps looking for their next opportunity (including moving into a partner role). Your goal with a venture partner should be to get them excited enough about you and your firm that they pull in a partner. Keep in mind, they are no substitute for a partner because they don't make investment decisions.

- *Principal*—This is a midlevel investment professional position and is often considered a "partner-track" position. Principals have been promoted from a senior associate position or have commensurate experience in another field, such as investment banking, management consulting, or a market of particular interest to the strategy of the VC firm.

- *Senior associate*—Senior associates do deal sourcing and market research and generally support the partners in all the steps toward making an investment.

- *Associate*—This is typically the most junior apprentice position in a venture capital firm. After a few successful years, an associate may move up to the senior associate position and potentially principal and beyond. Associates often have worked for one or two years in another field, such as investment banking or management consulting.

- *Limited partner (LP)*—This is an investor who is backing the VC firm and who put up the capital. They do not participate in the management of the partnership. The LP's liability cannot exceed the amount that they have invested in the business. LPs in a VC fund are typically entities such as university endowments, pension funds, and, occasionally, very wealthy individuals. The compensation structure is roughly that LPs pay the partnership an annual management fee of 1 to 3% of the fund's size and the partnership has a *carried interest* typically representing up to 20% of the partnership's profits. The remaining 80% of the profits go to the LPs proportionally to the size of their investment in the fund.

- *Entrepreneur-in-residence (EIR)*—This is an expert in a particular industry sector who performs due diligence on potential deals. An EIR (who is usually already known to a partner at the firm) is hired by venture capital firms (usually at a minimal salary like $10,000 per year) temporarily (6 to 18 months) and is expected to develop and pitch startup ideas to their host firm, although neither party is contractually agreeing to make the investment on the firm side or be the CEO on the EIR side. But because they went to the firm to help create a winning startup, most EIRs move on to executive positions within a portfolio company.

DEFINITION   *Carried interest*, often referred to as *carry*, is the primary way VCs receive a share of the fund's profits. Normally, carried interest is set at 20% of the fund's profits after returning the initial investment and repaying management fees to the general partners. This means 20% of the profits generated by the fund's investments go to the general partners of the VC firm as their compensation. The remaining 80% of the profits is distributed to the LPs as their share.

To avoid doubt, you should focus on someone with the title general partner or managing partner, not associate or principle or even venture partner. Having said that, I got the most interest in what my new startup was doing from a venture partner at General Catalyst. But he had no sway over one of the senior partners; senior partners are the only ones who can decide to move something forward. The venture partner is there because they probably had a good exit from one of the VC firm's portfolio companies and are looking for an opportunity to invest alongside the VC firm and potentially join the team of a company the firm is investing in. But keep in mind, venture partners are usually not experienced investors, so they will not be looked to for major decisions.

Venture partners, senior associates, and even associates are all people who may be the initial face of the VC firm to you. You will want to provide all the information these more junior people ask for and at the same time work toward speaking directly to a partner. This is one reason for getting a warm introduction to a firm: that intro will be to a partner.

How to become a VC in three simple injections

I have known several people before they became VCs and saw dramatic changes in them between before and after. So I jokingly came up with an observation of how this happened, based on a series of vaccination shots they would take as a rite of passage into VC-dom:

1 The first shot makes them hyperactive so they become incapable of focusing and end up with the seven-second memory of a goldfish.
2 The second shot instills in them the ability to obtain a perfect assessment of people within 10 seconds of meeting them, which they never feel the need to correct.
3 The third shot makes them forget any operational knowledge they ever had when they were an entrepreneur.

When I describe this to other entrepreneurs, they express strong recognition. And although I am joking, there is some helpful truth in this for you. VCs are constantly juggling many balls rapidly, context-switching from one thing to the next as they try to evaluate many potential deals to find the gems. They do try to size people up quickly to not waste time on those they don't think can cut it or who they do not want to work with.

I do not know if the "three injections" are my idea or if I heard this along the way. I think it is original, but if not, I apologize to the originator, who is anonymously credited for it herein.

9.2   *Venture capital math*

After the people, the second most important aspect of gaining a good understanding of the business model of a VC firm is the fund itself. You may hear about the "size of the fund" at a VC firm you visit. The fund size will tell you what stage they invest in and what their check size might be. Sometimes they will have two active funds. Because a fund may run out of capital prior to the end of its life, larger venture capital firms usually have several overlapping funds at the same time; doing so lets larger firms keep specialists in all stages of the development of their portfolio companies almost constantly engaged.

In a specific fund, the LPs have a fixed, legally binding commitment to the fund that is initially unfunded and subsequently "called down" by the venture capital firm over time as the fund makes its investments. There are substantial penalties for an LP who fails to participate in such a *capital call.*

Let's do the math to begin to understand what makes VCs tick. My focus here is on how they spend their time, because "time is money."

Let's assume the following:

- $250 million fund
- Four partners
- Five years to make initial investments

Other entrepreneurs and I observe that partners for rounds A-B-C can do 1 to 2 investments per year or 5 to 10 in the five-year investment window for a single fund. For four partners, that means 20 to 40 investments in five years. For Series A, a $5 million investment is typically the upper limit of what one VC will do, which means the number of investments such a firm can do is around 25. For every investment, they will see 20 opportunities (just an observation that entrepreneurs, including me, have made). For 25 investments, that is 500 opportunities, or a little more than 8 per month. That means each partner needs to spend time with two new opportunities per month for the duration of the fund, 95% of which they will reject. They will have many existing companies in their portfolio from previous funds, and for each of those, they need to interact with the CEO, attend board meetings, make business connections for the company, and provide other assistance, and they need to constantly interact with their own investors (the LPs) to keep them informed and happy. (This is not considering years in which the firm is raising a new fund, in which case partners need to spend considerable time doing their own fundraising.)

Now let's try this with a big fund. Assume:

- $1 billion fund
- Eight partners
- Five years to make initial investments

Fund size doesn't change how much time each partner can spend on a new investment; they still can only do one or two investments per year. Because they have double the number of partners, that is 40 to 80 investments in five years. Let's use the number 50 for investments. Doing 50 investments from half of the $1 billion fund size means $10 million per deal. This is too large for Series A, so this firm has to move up to Series B or Series C deals. Using the same 20 opportunities seen for each investment made means they must see 1,000 opportunities over the life of this fund. That's 200 per year, or almost 7 per month, and that ends up being the same 2 per month per partner. This is the same as the smaller-size fund with half the number of partners—which makes sense because the process and the analysis are roughly the same regardless of the investment size.

An interesting observation about this $1 billion scenario is that they are really putting $20 million into each startup over the life of the fund ($10 million up front and a $10 million earmarked for follow-on investment), and like all VCs, they need to see 10× return on their money to attract the kinds of LPs they want. But not all of their companies can achieve 10×, or will even survive, so on average they need to do at least 5× that (assuming, if they are really good, only one in five of their companies goes bust) or 50× the money they invest. But 50× the $20 million they invest in each deal is a unicorn.

> **DEFINITION**   A *unicorn* is a company worth over $1 billion.

So, if you are a company they do not immediately see as being worth $1 billion by the time it has an exit (and remember, as I said earlier, that timeframe must be within the limits they have on their funds, typically 10 years), you will get a very quick no.

This is why you need to understand their model well before you go asking for money. When you are looking for seed-stage capital of around $1 million to $2 million, be sure you are not putting Series A investors on your list; and similarly, when you need to raise a Series A of around $5 million, drop the seed and Series B investors from your list. Carefully studying what stage investments they make and the size of their funds is critical to you being efficient in your financing efforts.

Now, having said that, it is a good strategy for you to begin to get to know the firms that invest in the next stage beyond where you are today and, even more importantly, have them get to know your company. They will usually be willing to spend some time learning about earlier-stage companies because prospecting is something they constantly do to "fill their funnel" with interesting prospects. Chances are, you are at most one to two years away from whatever that next round is, so getting to know you and your company is not them getting too far ahead of themselves.

9.3   How the money flows within a VC firm

The staff at a VC firm gets paid out of two major streams of income. First is *carried interest*. Strong LP interest in top-tier venture firms has led to a general trend toward terms more favorable to the venture partnership, and certain groups are able to command carried interest of 25% to 30% on their funds.

Second is the management fee. This is what sustains the business with steady cash flow, as opposed to the big payout of carried interest when an exit occurs in a portfolio company. This is an annual payment the LPs make to the fund's managers to pay for the private equity firm's investment operations. In a typical venture capital fund, the general partners receive an annual management fee equal to up to 2% (sometimes as high as 3%) of the committed capital. Large funds are $1 billion these days, and moderate funds are $300 million, with management fees of $20 million and $600,000 annually, respectively. In the latter case, the number of partners is likely four to six; they pay their staff first, so they do not get rich on these fees, but the fees are guaranteed.

9.4   *Life span of venture capital funds*

Most venture capital funds have a fixed life of 7 to 10 years, and firms begin to manage multiple funds simultaneously as they grow. This last point is not just a detail that you can breeze past—it will be essential to you. If they do not manage multiple funds, and they are just getting started on their only fund, which has a life of seven or more years, you can't use this VC, because I doubt you can wait seven years to raise a round of financing. That's because their next fund depends on them having some good exits in the previous fund, both so they have more cash to work with and because they need to prove to their investors that they know what they are doing and have invested their money well. By managing multiple funds (which can only happen if the VC firm has started to grow), they can have some portfolio companies that are exiting and some that are just getting started, perhaps raising their Series A round. These funds need an ending (i.e., at the 7-to-10-year point) because of the LPs who are the source of the money in these funds. LPs are also in the business of making money on their money, and they either want to get a return or they want to write off an investment that has gone bad and take the tax benefit of such a loss. It is important to note that for VC firms to get any return on their investment, they must see an exit via an IPO, a sale to another company, or a sale to a private equity firm. This makes them get very itchy as a fund's end of life looms. And this itchiness is what bit me when I was a first-time CEO at NovaSoft: I was trying to turn it around but had very little time in which to do so because the LPs wanted to call it quits and write off their investment (see anecdote 3, "A venture-backed turnaround: a dangerous place to be").

Let's break down the 7 to 10 years. First is the initial three to five years during which the firm is doing new investments. That is followed by a four- to five-year period managing the portfolio companies they have already invested in and in which they may need to do follow-on investments to those companies moving forward.

It can take anywhere from a month or so to several years for VCs to raise money from LPs for their fund. At the time when all the money has been raised, the fund is said to be closed, and the seven- to ten-year lifetime begins. Some funds have partial closes when one-half (or some other portion) of the fund has been raised. The main thing you need to know about when one fund closes and the next one opens is that if you get to the firm when they are finished with the previous fund, they may not yet be ready to invest out of the next fund. And further, when they are raising a new fund, every partner in that firm will be completely consumed with their fundraising process, and you will not be a priority for them until that is complete.

9.5   *The moral of this anecdote*

If you don't understand the VC business model, you can't understand what makes VCs tick. You must always keep in mind what motivates them and how they apportion their time. This will help you seek the right-size fund for your investment stage. Only with a good understanding of their business model will your next moves be nicely aligned with the VC you are working with. And best of all, you will be better able to predict how they will react to your pitch or, once they are an investor, how they will react to the latest news about your company's performance, especially when it comes to your and their ideas of what a good exit looks like.

10

Seed:
The first priced round

- Have you met all the requirements for seed financing so you don't waste time needlessly?
- Can you decipher pre-money and post-money valuations?
- Wouldn't you prefer the lower stress of a seed financing instead of jumping right into the high-stakes Series A world?
- Once you land your seed, what must you keep your eyes firmly on? The Series A prize!

Seed is the first organized, formal, priced round of equity financing for a startup company. It precedes Series A. (Some legal firms call seed Series Seed.) Series Seed comes after a very young startup is formed and may or may not yet have received any sort of financing. Seed used to be the domain of angel investors, but the recent times I have raised seed, it has included VCs as well as angels. In fact, Dover's seed had VC, angel, and strategic investors.

Think of seed like kindergarten versus the big time of grades and tests and stress; seed is great practice for doing all the things you will have to do for later rounds but with easier grading. We will look at what types of firms invest in seeds so you know where to go when you are ready. Speaking of ready, we will look at the requirements you need to meet before you are ready to close a seed round. This is a good time to explain the meanings of pre- and post-money valuations—terms you will hear a lot from investors from now on.

There will be times when you exhaust the money you raised in your initial seed round but are still not qualified to raise a Series A; this is a situation where you may want to extend the original seed. For this discussion, I will use my cybersecurity startup, Dover Microsystems, as an example.

10.1 Where the seed stage of financing fits

To set the context, what financings might precede seed? The founding team may have lived off savings or family and may not have done any previous financing. Some do a small friends-and-family type of debt financing, as described in detail in anecdote 5, "Friends and family, angels, venture capital, or strategic?" And/or there may have been a small amount of funding from individual angels. Most likely, these small cash injections are debt that will later be converted into ownership shares when the company's value is determined. This is because small investors may not have the knowledge or resources to accurately assess a company's worth. It is easier for them to provide debt financing and then let a professional investor, who has the necessary expertise and resources, come in later to establish a price for the next funding round; they convert their loans into ownership shares at that time.

> **NOTE** *Debt financing* is not a loan—it is an equity instrument because its intent is to be converted into shares in your company, not to have you pay it back. The legal documents for the financing do have a provision to be paid, but that is only if something goes wildly wrong and the conversion to equity cannot happen.

While raising your seed, it is important to keep your future Series A firmly in mind. In fact, I've learned to always, always, always keep the next round of financing firmly in mind, whatever it is. A wise investor in one of my first startups admonished me when I was doing high-fives and cartwheels because I had just closed a round of financing and was expressing relief that it was over and done. "Oh," he said, "and since when was your job as CEO not always raising money?" Even if you are not actively reaching out and talking to investors for that next round, you'd better be clear-eyed about the requirements you have to meet for the next round. Thus, while raising the seed, you need to be driving your company to accomplish all the requirements for Series A.

The requirements Series A investors will place on you, in simplest terms, will be to prove product-market fit (PMF) (see anecdote 15, "Product-market fit: Making sure the dogs will eat your dog food"), which, to most investors, includes having three or more paying customers. Knowing these requirements will help you understand what your burn rate will be to support the size of team you need for the length of time it will take to prove PMF.

10.2   *Typical seed investors*

Typical seed-stage investors fall into one of three categories: organized angel groups, small venture capital funds, and a few large VCs getting into highly desirable startups on their first round. By organized angel group, I mean the rare group that, instead of operating as an informal collection of individuals who need the group only so they have a time and place to hear monthly pitches from prospective investments, has a fund that members can invest in and that is used to make investments under the direction of the membership. They also usually have an employee who is designated as the fund manager or managing director and who is responsible for the fund and the disbursements of its assets to approved startups. Small venture capitalists frequently like to invest early because their smaller funds can have a bigger impact early than if they invested in much larger, later rounds where they are a small fraction of the total amount raised. But there are also a few very large VCs that create special seed funds to invest early in highly promising startups so they can influence them and turn them into very successful companies that they continue to invest in at later stages.

Dover's first seed round ("first" because a year later we needed to expand that seed with more investors and more cash) started with an established angel group called HUB Angels. HUB Angels is one of the groups where individual members invest in a fund, and the fund invests in the startup. Not only is it much cleaner for the startup to have one name (that of the fund) in the cap table, but a professional fund manager represents the fund. This model of investing out of a fund sounds a lot like a VC, but it is still just a group of individuals investing in the fund, as opposed to the huge retirement funds and university endowments that tend to make up the LPs in a VC fund.

> **DEFINITION**   *A capitalization table* or *cap table* is a table that details who has ownership in a company. It lists all the securities or number of shares of a company, including stock, convertible notes, warrants, and equity ownership (option) grants.

Surprisingly, because seed is a priced round and pricing a round is not something most angel groups want to take on, HUB Angels even declared willingness to be the lead investor in our seed round. It did add a caveat that if a VC came in and wanted to lead, HUB Angels would prefer to step aside. Through referrals, I found such a VC called Hyperplane, which specializes in "hard tech." It was only interested in early stages, such as seed and an occasional Series A. In addition, I spent time cultivating a relationship with a partner at a strategic investor called Qualcomm Ventures, and in a highly unusual move, that strategic investor ultimately invested in our seed as well. It is rare for strategics to invest in seed rounds, but in this case it was very interested in what our technology could mean for the parent company. With Hyperplane leading, HUB Angels right behind, and Qualcomm Ventures adding impressive cachet, I was in incredible shape for my first real financing round.

The lead investor sets the price for the round, attracts other investors, leads the due-diligence process, and typically gets a board seat. Hyperplane did all of that, except it didn't need to attract more investors because I had already filled up the round. The other two investors got board observer roles. To understand board observers, see anecdote 27, "Board observers: Observe only, please."

10.3 Requirements for raising a seed round

What are the requirements for raising a seed? To state the obvious, you need to have a real company. It must be formally registered, with a few exceptions, as a C corporation with the secretary of state either of the state it resides in or of Delaware. There are a lot of benefits to that state being Delaware. Many C corps, including every company I've registered, chose Delaware because it does not impose income tax on corporations registered in the state, shareholders who do not reside in Delaware do not pay tax on shares in the state, and Delaware has developed a court system specifically designed for and efficient at corporate work. You also need to have a well-formed idea of what your product or service is or, even better, a prototype you can demonstrate. Some seed investors will require you to have real customers. That's typically a Series A, not seed, requirement—and you can safely avoid seed investors that require this because it is far from the norm.

Unlike the relatively informal types of financing that precede seed, seed is structured and formal, with lawyers involved in drafting many documents (which cost me $35,000 each time I did a financing round, seed or later). This first seed will be your first *priced* financing round.

Types of shares during a seed round
- *Priced shares*—Shares offered to investors at a fixed price per share during a financing round.
- *Seed preferred shares*—A new class of shares created specifically for investors of the seed round. Investors receive these shares in exchange for their cash investment.
- *Preferred shares*—A class of stock that holds some preferential rights not available to a preceding class of shares.
- *Common shares*—The class of shares that founders, management, and employees receive. It is the only class of shares that exists before the seed round.

The seed round became very personal for my Dover founding team and me. We were by far the largest holders of common. In fact, at one point, I owned *all* the shares in the company. First I brought on the cofounders and diluted my ownership—of course, that was in return for having a team that could create something of value, so it was worth it. Then, for a while, common (now the founders) plus a few employees owned it all. But when seed came along, we created a lot of new shares to sell to Hyperplane, HUB Angels, and Qualcomm Ventures. Suddenly common owned a smaller and smaller amount of the overall company (i.e., dilution). But again, without the essential funds from the Series Seed, we didn't have a company. The choice was to own a lot of nothing or accept that raising money meant we did have a company, but we owned a little less of it.

10.4   *Pre-money and post-money valuations*

Once the new shares are created, this offered price sets a monetary value for your company, called *valuation.* This is the company's *pre-money valuation.*

> **DEFINITION**   *Pre-money valuation* is the value someone new from the outside places on your company prior to an anticipated new capital raise.

This valuation is called *pre-* because it is not counting the money that is about to be put in. Investors are giving you cash and—for an instant before you begin to spend it—that cash is sitting on your balance sheet, which adds more value to your company, so the valuation after this investment is called the *post-money valuation.*

> **DEFINITION**   *Post-money valuation* is the value of your company immediately after a new investment. It is equal to the pre-money plus the amount of cash invested in the round.

If everything goes well, the stock price should never go below the post-money valuation. Entrepreneurs and their investors like to think of this as a floor value, which should be the lowest value your company should ever attain. (However, if you make no progress with acquiring customers, the product turns out not to work, the CEO quits, or something equally devastating happens, the company valuation will decline, and this won't be the floor at all.)

Table 10.1 is helpful in seeing how pre-money and post-money valuations work. The first column looks at seed. Investors, in particular the lead investor, will do some calculations about your company and declare a valuation. This is a pretty subjective thing when you have very little product or market progress to show yet. They will use calculations about your team size, any intellectual property (IP) you may have developed, comparison to similar companies if possible, and the stage you are at with your product/service.

Seed First priced round			Series A			values in millions (except PPS)
			Starting valuation	=	$2.50	← same as Seed post
Pre-money valuation	=	$1.50	Investor's valuation	=	$3.00	← credit for achievements
Investment amount for 40% stake	=	$1.00	Investment amount for 40% stake	=	$2.00	← 40% of $5m post-money
Post-money valuation	=	$2.50	Post-money valuation	=	$5.00	← add pre- and amt invested
Total number of shares	=	10.0	Total number of shares	=	16.67	← add 6.67m shares to total
Preferred Seed shares	=	4.0	Preferred Series A shares	=	6.67	← what investors are buying
Price per share (PPS)	=	$0.25	Price per share	=	$0.30	

Figure 10.1   Pre- and post-money valuations for a sample seed and Series A. Values are in millions, except price per share.

Let's go through an example. If you're already acquiring customers, I would use a reasonable pre-money valuation of $1.5 million. The investors at this stage tend to look to own about 30% to 40% of the company because risk is high. The amount they are comfortable investing, which considers your stage and team size and therefore your burn rate, is $1 million. You add this to the pre-money valuation they declared to come up with a post-money of $2.5 million. At formation, your lawyers created an initial number of shares for the company. In this case, I am assuming there are 6 million shares, all of which are in the common share class. To own 40% of the company, investors need to get 4 million shares of what will be the new total of 10 million shares. The investors receive a different class of stock from common: called *preferred seed*. The special preference they get that common does not is how they are treated on an exit or liquidation. They have a preferential ability to sell their shares before anyone else. This becomes a big deal when an acquisition price is low. All the preferred shareholders are paid first, and if there is not much money left after their payout, everyone else (i.e., founders and employees) may receive small amounts or even nothing. Preferred shareholders may also get a premium on the price offered in the case of a liquidation. It is easy to calculate the price per share by dividing the total number of shares by the post-money valuation, resulting in 25¢ per share.

Remember, your entire goal of raising the seed is to get enough capital that you can satisfy the requirements to raise a substantial Series A. This will hopefully take your startup to an inflection point where revenues start to grow rapidly. Therefore, let's look at what happens later when the Series A is raised. The starting valuation is by default the post-money valuation from the last round. (If you hear the term *flat round*, that means the pre-money of this round is the same as the post-money of the last round, and the price per share will stay the same.) For this example, let's say the investors are giving the company credit for some achievements, and they value the company at $3 million instead of $2.5 million. This will then be the pre-money for this round. Again, the investors want to own in the range of 30% to 40%. (This is where you shop around to many investors to get the best deal you can.) For simplicity, let's assume 40% again. If the pre-money is $3 million and the investors want to own 40%, that means they invest $2 million for a new post-money valuation of $5 million. For investors to own 40% of the shares, 6,666,667 shares will be created and added to the 10 million that existed after the previous round. These shares will be in a new class called *preferred Series A*.

> **DEFINITION** *Preferred Series A shares* are shares created in the Series A financing round that have greater rights and privileges than the preferred seed shares. This includes getting paid first on an acquisition or liquidation. Typically, each successive round tries to jump ahead of previous rounds with its preferences in case an acquisition or liquidation pays a relatively small amount.

Finally, with this many total shares and a valuation of $5 million, the price per share ends up being 30¢ ($5 million/16.67 million shares), compared to 25¢ after seed. The big picture about valuation change between the seed and Series A in the simple example in table 10.1 is this:

- Company valuation doubled, going from $2.5 million to $5 million (excellent!). And . . .
- Common (management and employees) collective ownership of the company went from 60% ownership to 36% ownership, a dilution of 60% (seems to be bad). But . . .
- Value of common shares went from $1.5 million to $1.8 million, a gain of 20% (very good!).

The last two points in this list address a common misconception: many believe dilution of common is categorically bad. Too many employees at my startups have been fixated on dilution, but that is the wrong piece to focus on. You should care most about the value of your shares, because on an exit, that determines what you will make. If going from seed to Series A has enough of a valuation uptick, that more than makes up for dilution.

10.5   *The sequence of steps in a financing round*

I think looking at the usual sequence of steps (simplified slightly here) is really useful as a reminder of what's in front of you as you work on a new financing. This list is pretty much the same for any round: Series Seed, A, B, C. Remember, timing is critical for a financing round because there is a closing date by which all investors have to commit and sign documents, and then they must wire money, usually within a handful of days after closing:

Step 1   A round needs a lead. Usually new named (Seed, A, B, C) rounds get a new investor who leads from the outside, and the insiders follow them. If it is an inside round, there still needs to be a lead.

Step 2   The lead sets the terms of the investment, which include setting a price they will pay for shares of the company. This sets the valuation of the company (offered share price times the number of shares outstanding).

Step 3   The lead's term sheet must be negotiated with the company through the board and signed by the CEO. It gets a little strange if the lead is already on the board, which is likely if it is an inside round.

Step 4   The signed term sheet needs to be shared with existing investors to see who is going to participate and whether they have serious issues with any of the terms. Sometimes the terms do not allow insiders to participate or only lets them participate at a certain level. This socialization of the terms enables management to determine whether the requisite number of votes to approve of this financing on these terms will be forthcoming or if some terms need to be changed to make sure shareholder approval will be achieved.

Step 5   Once the terms are agreed on and the commitments from investors achieve the minimum required (the term sheet will specify minimum and maximum amounts to be raised), the investors codify the terms by signing the term sheet, which is now binding[1] on them. The term sheet must be turned into a set of definitive investment documents by the company's lawyers (this is very expensive legal work; I typically budget $35,000 for major rounds or $15,000 for insider rounds).

Step 6   The final documents are approved and signed by the board, finalized by the lawyers, and ready for investor signatures and execution. The next step is when the most challenging cat herding occurs.

Step 7   The last step is to find each individual who is able to commit their firm and get them to sign the definitive documents and commit when they will wire the money. (Investors who signed the term sheet could, theoretically, change their minds and not sign the corresponding definitive document, but I have never seen this happen. If they did, word would spread that the firm was unreliable, and they would be shunned. It is a small community, and peer pressure works extremely well toward good behavior.) For each firm, even insiders, this can take several calls, and many times you end up speaking to voicemail. All the while, the closing day deadline that everyone must meet is looming.

10.6   *Extensions to the seed round*

You have a lead investor, you have others who filled out the round, you have all your legal documents in place, and everyone has signed the papers and wired their money to your bank. Enjoy that incredible moment of joy! But then get back to work; there is lots to do to achieve a set of requirements that are critical to you being able to build a great new company.

What should you focus on? Here's a good start to your to-do list:

1   Determine who your customer is in the vertical markets you will be focused on. Defining who your customer is will be the most important thing you do.

2   Determine the minimum viable product (MVP) that this customer will purchase and use.

3   Find your product-market fit: get customers and turn your MVP into a *whole product* with high quality, a complete set of features, good documentation, services, and marketing collateral on your website and in white papers.

4   Meet valuation benchmarks by filing patents and signing partners.

---

[1] It is only binding on them until it is not. I have had a so-called binding term sheet signed by two investors who decided, at the moment we were supposed to close the deal, to just walk away and leave me hanging.

    5 Complete any additional milestones: get going on other things investors and you have agreed on.

It may be that your seed only provides enough money for 12 months at your current burn, and that is not enough time to accomplish this entire list. That means you may not be ready for Series A when your money runs out, but you need money to keep going. What do you do? In my experience, if you are doing well on the accomplishments list and working toward everything said during the runup to the seed financing, most investors will not walk away yet. A follow-on round (not the A) is likely. This is called *Seed II* or *Seed Extension* (I'll just call it *Seed II*). This happened for Dover, where we raised a Seed II one year after our Seed I. You don't want to get to a *Seed III* because if your company remains in the seed stage for too long, it can scare off potential Series A investors.

The investors in Seed I prefer a new lead for Seed II to share the risk and perhaps set a new price, but usually the price remains the same (i.e., a *flat round*). Note that if the price per share remains the same but new money is being invested, meaning the number of shares needs to be increased, there is pure dilution with no corresponding valuation uptick.

If you get to the end of Seed II and are still not quite ready to raise the A, a debt round is a good option because investors who are confident you will eventually raise the series A will be interested in investing in convertible notes that convert (at a discount) into the future Series A. Because this investment is debt, not purchasing stock, it is nondilutive, so existing investors also prefer it to dilution.

10.7 When a seed round is not needed (or rewarding)

A seed round is certainly not required to raise an A. That's because you can qualify for a Series A without ever raising a penny. In fact, there was a time not many years ago when you rarely heard of a seed round. My first several startups (MasPar, Webspective, GeoTrust, Service Integrity, Ambric) went straight to Series A, for instance.

There are good reasons to choose to have the first formal priced round be a seed, even if you could convince some VCs to invest in you and call it an A. The most important reason is that if you get ahead of yourself—for example, if you raise an A but don't have a customer and can't prove PMF—and then hit a speedbump, the repercussions are severe. You never want to have a *down round*, which is when the price offered for your equity is lower than it was at the last priced round. A down round can scare off future investors, and it can scare your team, who may get discouraged about the future potential value of their equity and begin to look at other options.

10.8 The moral of this anecdote

Closing a seed is an enormous accomplishment. Not being able to raise a seed is how a lot of startups end. If you did it, congratulations! It is the most critical first step toward raising a Series A, making seed a warmup for future financings. Seed is like kindergarten in that there is not as much pressure, the grading is pretty easy, and the teachers are not nearly as tough as when you get to Series A. Seed teaches you how to find investors, how to sell to them, how to pitch to them, how to shop a term sheet among multiple lead-candidate investors, and how to turn a term sheet into a full financing that results in cash in your bank. All of this is essential for the next big step: the Series A.

If you need a bit more fuel in the tank before you are ready for the Series A and need to raise a Seed II in the meantime, don't think of that as failure. It isn't even close. I have raised a couple of seed rounds on several of my startups that ultimately had very good outcomes. Go ahead and raise a Seed II, and focus like a laser beam on accomplishing what is required for the Series A.

Term sheets:
An institutional investor wants to invest in you

11

- Unlocking a VC investment—what will it take to see a term sheet from them?
- What are all these terms in the term sheet, and how do you make sense of them?
- Difficult and maybe harmful terms—can you spot such deal-breakers in time?

After you have been operating self-funded, or friends-and-family funded, or maybe individual-angel-funded, your next step is an institutional round. You should have the following in place and feel good about them:

- Your team, and how perfectly they are suited to this opportunity
- Your messaging about the problem, how it is not being sufficiently solved, how you solve it, and the size of the opportunity (see anecdote 6, "Angels: Your bridge financing solution")
- Your pitch for institutional investors, which is ready for prime time because you have practiced it with your team, some friendlies who are not part of your team, and anyone else you can get feedback from (see anecdote 7, "The art of pitching to institutional investors")
- Your chosen business model (see anecdote 13, "Your business model: The beating heart of your business")

- Your minimum viable product (MVP), which, with the guidance of one or more lighthouse customers, has been defined, has at least one customer, and is accepted as a sellable product (see anecdote 14, "Getting to a minimum viable product with lighthouse customers")

DEFINITION *Lighthouse customers* are called that because they serve as a "beacon of light" for the rest of your future customer base to follow. This is why getting a critical mass of them is essential to a successful product launch. They may not guarantee the product they approve of will reflect precisely what the early and late majority customers want, but without them, you will never even have any early or late majority customers—you will not have crossed the chasm.[1]

- Proven product–market fit (PMF) demonstrating that you are in a good market with a product that can satisfy that market (see anecdote 15, "Product-market fit: Making sure the dogs will eat your dog food")
- An initial go-to-market strategy (see anecdote 16, "Go-to-market: How to make your business viable and grow")
- Your investor research (try to get access to Crunchbase and use LinkedIn Analytics as described in anecdote 16)

Now you need to do these three things, after which it will be go-time:

- Get a copy of *Venture Capital Deal Terms* by Harm De Vries, Menno Van Loon, and Sjoerd Mol to use as a reference (it was published in 2016, but deal terms have not changed in 20 years).
- Get a lawyer experienced in startup financing. They are going to charge you about $35,000 for a financing round.
- Download the term sheet template found at www.venturecapitaldealterms.com (free, but it requires you to give an email address). This will help you know what to expect when an investor presents you with a term sheet and as well as what questions to ask your attorney as they prepare term sheet variants and the final definitive investment documents derived from it.

11.1 Your first institutional investor term sheet

Recently I had a startup of 12 people, 6 of them founders, with a working prototype product and a multibillion-dollar lighthouse customer that had paid us handsomely for engineering work. For each round of financing, especially the very first one for a new startup, getting that initial term sheet is an almost-magical experience. Someone who is an experienced, professional investor likes you, likes your team, agrees with your premise about an unsolved problem in the market, agrees that the market is big, thinks your product is good, and thinks it solves a big problem in the market. I certainly felt this feeling of relief and exhilaration for the seed financing for my most

---

[1] Jay Fuchs, "4 Ways Lighthouse Customers Can Predict a Product's Future," HubSpot Blog, September 04, 2020, updated June 15, 2021, https://blog.hubspot.com/service/lighthouse-customer.

recent startup, but it was also true for every startup before this one. That feeling never gets old, and I never take for granted that I will even get a term sheet.

For this discussion, I will use a term sheet from the seed financing for imaginary NewCo. It is a simple, clean financing—it is hard to get simpler than this in an institutional financing, and there are no "harsh" terms the founders would have had a hard time accepting. Our company counsel wrote this term sheet to show the lead investor what we wanted. This is a good thing to do and can lead to better terms than if you let the investors dictate initial terms. That investor accepted most, but not all, of these terms when creating the eventual signed term sheet.

11.1.1 A clean, standard seed financing term sheet

Our lawyer is very experienced at constructing term sheets—the term sheet given in tables 11.1–11.10 is the real deal. Read it, and you can learn about standard terms and what they mean. Below each term, in *italic text*, I offer a brief explanation of the term, especially with respect to its effect on the founders. The following appears at the top of the term sheet:

> *This nonbinding term sheet (the "Term Sheet") summarizes the principal terms of the Seed Series Preferred Stock Financing of NewCo, Inc., a Delaware corporation (the "Company").*
>
> *This Term Sheet is for discussion purposes only and does not constitute either an offer to sell or an offer to purchase securities. This Term Sheet shall be governed in all respects by the laws of the Commonwealth of Massachusetts.*

Table 11.1   Offering terms, part 1

Investors	Accredited investors selected and approved by the Company; minimum investment of $25,000 per investor (each, an "Investor," and together, the "Investors"). *The investors will be explicitly named in the final term sheet.*
Targeted Amount	$1,000,000 of new cash plus conversion of all outstanding simple agreements for future equity ("SAFEs") in an aggregate amount equal to $696,000. The new cash shall be funded, and the SAFEs shall be converted at closing to occur no later than November 15, 2024 (the "Closing"). *The amount desired and expected to be raised. If any notes, such as SAFEs, are being converted, that needs to be stated here because they are becoming part of the new equity financing.*
Security	Seed Series Convertible Preferred Stock (the "Seed Series Preferred"). *The type of stock being purchased is defined. In this case, its official designation is Seed Series Preferred.*
Price per Share	$1.40 per share (based on the capitalization of the Company set forth below) (the "Original Purchase Price"). *This is the per-share price calculated from the proposed valuation divided by the new total number of shares: i.e., existing plus newly issued.*

Table 11.2   Offering terms, part 2

Pre-Money Valuation	The Original Purchase Price is based upon a fully diluted pre-money valuation of $7,000,000. *This does the math for investors. It shows how the investors are valuing the company. "Fully diluted" in this term means "counting all stock options, warrants, and purchased shares."*
Use of Proceeds	General working capital and other general corporate purposes of the Company. *This is not as obvious as it may seem. This term makes sure the funds are not used to, for example, service debt or functions other than approved in the business's documented plans. But in this case, "general working capital" is not very restrictive.*
Capitalization	The Company's capital structure on a fully diluted basis before and after the closing is set forth on Schedule A attached hereto. *Also called Capital Structure. In this term sheet, this is a reference to the capitalization table (often shortened to cap table) for the startup in question, which looks like the one shown later in table 11.1. (CSE means common stock equivalent.)*

Table 11.3   Charter, part 1

Dividends	No dividends payable on Common Stock or any other class of preferred stock of the Company without payment of similar dividends to the Seed Series Preferred on an "as converted" basis. *No better terms can exist for prior classes of stock, so no dividends shall be paid to common stock investors unless seed gets it too.*
Liquidation Preference	In the event of any liquidation, dissolution, or winding up of the Company, the proceeds shall be paid as follows: First, pay one times (1×) the Original Purchase Price; thereafter, all remaining proceeds shall be distributed exclusively to the holders of Common Stock (the Seed Series Preferred shall be nonparticipating). A merger or consolidation (other than one in which stockholders of the Company own a majority by voting power of the outstanding shares of the surviving or acquiring corporation) and a sale, lease, transfer, or other disposition of all or substantially all of the assets of the Company will be treated as a liquidation event (a "Deemed Liquidation Event"), thereby triggering payment of the liquidation preferences described above unless the holders of at least 66⅔% of the Seed Series Preferred elect otherwise. *Upon a liquidation, this specifies how much of the proceeds the preferred shareholders collect before any other holders are paid. If there are several classes of preferred, this term will specify the order in which they are paid. This term as written is very favorable to founders (who hold common) and probably would be rewritten in the final approved term sheet by the lead investor to favor them such that they get the 1× purchase price first.*
Voting Rights	The Seed Series Preferred shall vote together with the Common Stock on an as-converted basis, and not as a separate class, except (i) as provided under "Protective Provisions" below or (ii) as required by law. The Company's Certificate of Incorporation will provide that the number of authorized shares of Common Stock may be increased or decreased with the approval of a majority of the Seed Series Preferred and Common Stock, voting together as a single class, and without a separate class vote by the Common Stock. *The arrangement typically is not "one share, one vote" because special conversion terms (see table 11.4) turn preferred shares into a larger number of shares when they are converted into common. The voting for preferred is done with common on the as-converted basis. These are votes on major issues that are not handled just by the board of directors, such as approving new financings or acquisitions.*

Table 11.4   Charter, part 2

Protective Provisions	So long as 10% of the originally issued shares of Seed Series Preferred are outstanding, the Company will not, without the written consent of the holders of at least 66⅔% of the Company's Seed Series Preferred, either directly or by amendment, merger, consolidation, or otherwise: I liquidate, dissolve, or wind up the affairs of the Company or effect any Deemed Liquidation Event; II amend, alter, or repeal any provision of the Certificate of Incorporation or Bylaws in a manner adverse to the Seed Series Preferred; III create or authorize the creation of or issue any other security convertible into or exercisable for any equity security, having rights, preferences, or privileges senior to or on parity with the Seed Series Preferred or increase the authorized number of shares of Seed Series Preferred; or IV purchase or redeem or pay any dividend on any capital stock prior to the Seed Series Preferred, other than (X) stock repurchased from former employees or consultants in connection with the cessation of their employment/services at cost and (Y) stock repurchased pursuant to contractual rights of first refusal approved by the Company's Board of Directors. *Also called Consent Rights. This guarantees rights for certain situations not covered under Voting Rights, such as liquidation or merger, creation of new equity, or paying dividends on other classes of stock.*
Optional Conversion	The Seed Series Preferred initially converts 1:1 to Common Stock at any time at option of holder, subject to adjustments for stock dividends, splits, combinations, and similar events. *Also called Voluntary Conversion. In this term sheet, holders of seed preferred are allowed to convert 1:1 to common at the holder's option (i.e., whenever they want). In other situations, this can be much more complex than just 1:1 conversion.*

Table 11.5   Charter, part 3

Mandatory Conversion	Each share of Seed Series Preferred will automatically be converted into Common Stock at the then-applicable conversion rate (i) in the event of the closing of a firm commitment underwritten public offering with a price of five (5) times the Original Purchase Price (subject to adjustments for stock dividends, splits, combinations, and similar events) and net proceeds to the Company of not less than $20 million (a "QPO") or (ii) upon the written consent of the holders of at least 66⅔% of the Seed Series Preferred. *Also called Automatic Conversion. This term deals with what happens at an IPO. Multiple classes of stock with different terms are not attractive at an IPO. This term makes sure everything is put in a single class of common automatically for all shareholders in advance of an IPO.*

Table 11.5 Charter, part 3 *(continued)*

Anti-Dilution Provisions	In the event that the Company issues additional securities at a purchase price less than the current Seed Series Preferred conversion price, such conversion price shall be adjusted on a broad-based weighted-average basis, subject to customary exceptions.
	Hopefully the price/valuation of the company will steadily go up. But early-stage valuations are subjective and are established more by negotiations than by metrics, unlike later stages. So, if there is a down round, existing investors will normally be diluted. This term says that the conversion of these shares will use a price based on a "broad-based weighted average," where the weighting is based on the number of shares being held. That formula looks like this:
	$$\frac{P_1 Q_1 + P_2 Q_2}{Q_1 + Q_2}$$
	where
	P_1 = *price in the previous round*
	P_2 = *price in the new round*
	Q_1 = *total shares outstanding prior to the dilutive financing*
	Q_2 = *total shares issued in the new round*

Table 11.6 Investment documents, part 1

Representation & Warranties	Stock Purchase Agreement to include standard representations and warranties by the Company.
	Statements that will be put into the definitive legal documents about company capitalization, key personnel, financial situation, liabilities, ownership, intellectual property, and compliance with all relevant laws.
Conditions to Closing	Standard conditions to Closing, to include satisfactory completion of financial and legal due diligence, qualification of the shares under applicable Blue Sky laws, and the filing of a Restated Certificate of Incorporation establishing the rights and preferences of the Seed Series Preferred.
	This says due diligence will occur and must be satisfactory; that you must be in compliance with Blue Sky laws, which are laws in the state of formation (Delaware, in this case) regulating the offer and sale of securities; and that a filing (with Delaware) of a new certificate of incorporation will be done codifying the rights and preferences of the new seed preferred class of stock.
Information Rights	Any Investor who invests at least $100,000 (a "Major Investor") will be granted access to Company facilities and personnel during normal business hours and with reasonable advance notification. The Company will deliver to each Major Investor (i) annual and quarterly financial statements; (ii) 30 days prior to the end of each fiscal year, a comprehensive operating budget forecasting the Company's revenues, expenses, and cash position on a month-to-month basis for the upcoming fiscal year; and (iii) promptly following the end of each quarter, an up-to-date capitalization table.
	These rights are especially important for investors who are not part of the board as members or observers. This term stipulates that all investors will receive certain specific financial and operational information about the company. This also protects the company from intrusive or overly burdensome small investors because it restricts these rights to larger investors.

Table 11.7   Investment documents, part 2

Pro Rata Rights in Future Rounds	All (x) holders of Seed Series Preferred and (y) holders of Common Stock who hold greater than 10% of the outstanding shares of the capital stock of the Company (determined on a fully diluted basis) shall have a pro rata right, based on their percentage equity ownership in the Company (determined on a fully diluted basis), to participate in subsequent issuances of equity securities of the Company (subject to customary exceptions). In addition, should any stockholder choose not to purchase its full pro rata share, the remaining stockholders shall have the right to purchase the remaining shares on a pro rata basis. *Also called Pre-emptive Rights. This term allows, with some conditions, investors in an earlier round to purchase shares at the same price and terms as are applied to other buyers, up to the number of shares that keeps their fractional ownership in the company constant.*
Right of First Refusal/Right of Co-Sale	Company first and (x) all holders of Seed Series Preferred and (y) holders of Common Stock who hold greater than 10% of the outstanding shares of capital stock of the Company (determined on a fully diluted basis), second shall have a right of first refusal with respect to any shares of capital stock of the Company proposed to be sold or otherwise transferred (except for estate planning purposes) by any stockholder holding greater than 1% of the outstanding capital stock of the Company (determined on an a fully diluted basis), with a right of oversubscription for stockholders who elect to purchase shares unsubscribed by the other stockholders. Before any such stockholder may sell or otherwise transfer capital stock, such stockholder will give the other stockholders an opportunity to participate in such sale or transfer on a basis proportionate to the number of securities held by the selling stockholder and those held by the stockholders who elect to participate in the sale of shares. *This is a right of a shareholder to meet the terms of a third party's offer if another shareholder intends to sell their shares to this third party. The purpose is to keep the company's shares in friendly hands while the company is still private. The co-sale right (or tag-along) is a shareholder's right to include their shares in any sale of shares by another shareholder under the same terms and conditions.*

Table 11.8   Investment documents, part 3

Drag-Along Rights	All holders of Seed Series Preferred Stock and holders of Common Stock who own or have the right to vote 1% or more of the outstanding shares of capital stock of the Company (determined on a fully diluted basis) shall be required to vote in favor of any (x) merger or sale transaction and/or (y) post-closing equity or convertible debt financing that is approved by (i) the Board of Directors of the Company and (ii) the holders of at least 66⅔% of the outstanding shares of the Company's outstanding shares of capital stock (voting together as a single class on an as-converted basis). Such holders of Common Stock and Seed Series Preferred shall, subject to the foregoing, also be required to use commercially reasonable efforts to affect the consummation of such merger or sale transaction and/or equity or convertible debt financing, including without limitation entering into all customary agreements and other documents as may be necessary or required to effect such merger or sale transaction and/or equity or convertible debt financing. *This enables all seed and significant holders of common to force all other investors to sell when the right conditions are met for a sale of the company. In this case, those conditions are approval by the board of directors and by two-thirds of the outstanding shares of stock.*

Table 11.8 Investment documents, part 3 *(continued)*

Lock-Up	Investors shall agree in connection with the QPO, if requested by the managing under-writer, not to sell or transfer any shares of Common Stock of the Company (excluding shares acquired in or following the QPO) for a period of up to 180 days following the QPO (provided all directors and officers of the Company and 1% stockholders agree to the same lock-up). Such lock-up agreement shall provide that any discretionary waiver or termination of the restrictions of such agreements by the Company or representa-tives of the underwriters shall apply to Investors, pro rata, based on the number of shares held.
	This term makes sure the IPO can be tightly controlled by the underwriter, such that investors holding shares that were not included in the IPO can't sell those shares for an extended time (in this case, 180 days).

Table 11.9 Other matters, part 1

Definitive Agreement	Except with respect to matters included under the caption "Counsel and Expenses" and "Confidentiality," this Term Sheet is not intended to be legally binding. The material terms and conditions of this Term Sheet will be set forth in a definitive Stock Purchase Agreement and other related agreements and documents.
	The term sheet is not a legally binding agreement. It is a document meant to be concise, clear, and easy to understand (by nonlawyers). This calls out that a stock purchase agree-ment (also called a subscription agreement) and related legal documents will definitively define the financing in legal, contractual language.
Counsel & Expenses	The Company's legal counsel will draft the Stock Purchase Agreement and other invest-ment documents reflecting the terms set forth in this Term Sheet. The Company and each Investor shall bear their own legal and other expenses with respect to the financ-ing contemplated by this Term Sheet.
	This states that the company's counsel will write the definitive legal documents, and the company will pay them. It says that each investor will pay their own legal expenses. This is a nice try—every financing I have done calls for the company to also pay the investor's expenses, perhaps with a cap, if you are lucky. The $35,000 estimate I use includes investor expenses, but those can be hard to control, so budget a bit more to be on the safe side.

Table 11.10 Other matters, part 2

Expiration	This Term Sheet expires on November 15, 2024, if not accepted by the Company by 5:00 p.m. (EST) on that date.
	This is meant to force everyone to make decisions quickly. In practice, if the lead wants a different date, you use their date.
Confidentiality	Each Investor acknowledges that all information concerning the Company and this Term Sheet is confidential and nonpublic and agrees that all such information shall be kept in strict confidence by such Investor and neither used by such Investor (other than in connection with the financing contemplated hereby) nor disclosed to any other party for any reason (other than to such Investor's legal, financial, and tax advisors in connection with the negotiation and closing of the financing contemplated by this Term Sheet).
	This entire term sheet and process, and even the fact that a financing is being contem-plated, are confidential because much of this could be harmful to the company, especially if the financing falls through or is heavily modified and the company needs to seek financ-ing elsewhere.

Table 11.11   **Capitalization table (cap table) for the company described in the term sheet**

	Pre-financing		Post-financing	
	CSE shares	**% of total**	**CSE shares**	**% of total**
Series seed stockholders				
New investors		0.00%	714,285	11.35%
SAFE holders		0.00%	579,072	9.20%
Total investors		0.00%	1,293,357	20.55%
Other stockholders				
Common stock	4,200,000	84.00%	4,200,000	66.74%
Options granted/outstanding	505,000	10.10%	505,000	8.02%
Options available to grant	295,000	5.90%	295,000	4.69%
Total other stockholders	5,000,000	100.00%	5,000,000	79.45%
Total	5,000,000	100.00%	6,293,357	100.00%

Once you start talking with several interested investors, it is ideal (an entrepreneur's dream, really) if you get multiple term sheets from investors competing for who will lead. But this does not always happen, especially early, when evidence of the value of your company is not objective and quantitative. If you do get lucky, you can play one investor off another and negotiate for the best terms, including price/valuation.

11.2 *Problematic terms*

You may be faced with some terms I would consider problematic even in the first round you raise. Why do I say "even"? Because the terms used for one round tend to carry forward to successive rounds, including problematic terms. This means after several rounds, there can be a lot of terms that are problematic for you. Tables 11.12–11.14 explains these terms and why I think they are problems that you should try to negotiate away if you can. Having said that, I've usually had to accept them, and so may you; these are by no means deal killers.

> **DEFINITION** A *tranche* is one of a series of payments in an investment to be paid out over a specified period, subject to certain performance metrics being achieved.

> **DEFINITION** A *drag-along* is a right that enables a majority shareholder to force a minority shareholder to join in the sale of a company.

Table 11.12 Problematic terms, part 1

Tranches or milestones	Tranches, a synonym for milestone investments, are a way for investors to hold onto their money: you only get it if you achieve the conditions attached to the next milestone. If you never *precisely achieve the milestone as described*, the investors may never complete their investment. This puts all the control in the investors' hands and leaves very little wiggle room for things you may learn or situations that change. You may have to argue that the milestone, as written, no longer makes sense. On the other hand, I have also been in situations where the investor I wanted would not invest unless I agreed to tranches. At the very least, be very careful with the language used to specify the milestone. *One of the term sheets proposed to me, for a smallish $2.5 million Series A when we were in a challenging situation, got extremely difficult tranche terms:* • Tranche 1: $500,000 on the initial closing date; • Tranche 2: $1 million on completion of the first version of the MVP • Tranche 3: $1 million on obtaining a formal sales engagement from at least one customer deemed to be significant by the Investors I considered this totally unacceptable. I rejected it and believe this would have destroyed my company. It was barely even "spoon-feeding" us cash we desperately needed. And in our case, $500,000 would not get us to the point of the MVP they were envisioning. This is an extreme example of investors hoping the entrepreneur is so desperate that they will accept an egregiously bad deal. In this case, I think they were planning to replace me and take over the company.

Table 11.13 Problematic terms, part 2

Drag-along provision	This term allows 66⅔% of outstanding shares, plus the board, to force seed and common (which includes founders) to vote for a sale of the company, which may not be what founders want at whatever stage the company is in. Although it is true there are many stories of the founding team rejecting offers to sell, thinking the offer was too low, only to never get close to that much later, it is still ideal not to have this term in your financings and to let the board plus management determine when the right time is to sell. Remember, the board has a fiduciary responsibility to the investors, so they are an excellent buffer between investors wanting a quick return and management, who may be looking for a larger outcome. The board members are much better informed (usually) than the average investor about the market and the company's current opportunity. *I have more often had the opposite problem: the board and founders want to sell, but the investors do not. And the investors could block us from selling because a sale requires a majority stockholder approval. Fortunately, in the two situations where I got good exits over $100 million, the board and investors were perfectly aligned on it being the right time and the right offer to sell.*

Table 11.13   Problematic terms, part 2 *(continued)*

Founder's shares	If the allocation is left up to the investors, it is one more example of losing control over something I believe should be taken care of before there are even any investors. *I have never left the allocation of shares for founders up to the first institutional financing, so this term has never been in a seed or later financing of mine. I get this done at formation and highly recommend the same approach for anyone. In my view, the founders and the company can both be well-served by structuring founder's shares as stock grants at a very low price that reverse vest at the same schedule as regular employee options (one-year cliff followed by $1/36$ of the $3/4$ of the total of the remaining stock grant per month for the remaining 36 months). If the founder stays with the company for the full 48 months, they keep all the shares they were granted (and bought); but if they depart early, the company buys back (at the same price the founder paid) the shares they are not entitled to. This does what the Founder's Shares term is trying to do without the punitive aspect of that term.*

Table 11.14   Problematic terms, part 3

Noncompetition	This very complicated and fraught term historically was handled in opposite ways by the opposite coasts of the United States. Most foreign countries tend to side with the East Coast approach, which required this term, whereas Silicon Valley never dealt with this because noncompetes were illegal in California. Now, this term is moot since noncompetes have been made illegal throughout the United States. If a founder dedicates four years to a company and for whatever reason decides to leave, I believe they should not be constrained about what they do; the work they have done for that preceding four years is in their field of expertise, and not being able to do that elsewhere is very punitive for someone who helped build their previous startup. For this reason, I am very happy this issue has finally gone away.
Observers	Observers are frequently mandated by investors who know they can't win a board seat but still want more ability to observe what is going on than the Information Rights afford them. I consider observers a big problem. I cover this issue in the anecdote 27, "Board observers: Observe only please." I once had a board of 13 people, but 8 of them were observers. That's untenable and needs to be avoided. Don't agree to observers being put into the legal investment documents, or it will be almost impossible to fix later.

11.3   *Terms in follow-on rounds*

Your term sheet is not "one and done." With each round of financing, terms can be added and changed. As you progress through the stages of early financing, watch out for the terms listed in table 11.15.

Table 11.15   Follow-on round terms

Cram-down	When new investors buy shares of a company at a lower price than previous rounds, which dilutes the ownership percentage of existing shareholders. In many instances, the investors in follow-on rounds solely focus on getting the best deal for themselves, with little regard for investors in previous rounds. In fact, I have seen follow-on investors literally delight in "cramming" previous investors, which is to say diluting them or making their investment worth very little while making their own deal great. This is especially true when the company is struggling and having a down round. One reason I caution all entrepreneurs not to be too aggressive about how fast and far they try to push their valuation, even if investors go along with that pace, is that if you get ahead of yourself and then there is a stumble—perhaps because sales do not develop quite as fast as you anticipated or because your competition is stronger than expected—the subsequent financing may require you to lower the price of the shares below what it was at the previous financing (the definition of a down round). Many bad things happen when there is a down round. The cramming of previous investors, where the price is much lower than what they paid for their shares, is just one of these things. Another is that it is demoralizing to employees and especially to founders who were counting on the steady rise in share price to reward them for the sacrifice and hard work they have been doing for years. In one of my startups that was struggling with a business model that was not working well, new investors presented a term sheet that proposed taking the seed price of $1.40 per share down to 14¢. This made seed investors throw up their hands and consider giving up on the company and made founders who held common wonder if they should stick around. (This did lead to a restart of the company, but we did not accept those terms, and the seed investors and employees/founders were kept whole.)
Full-ratchet protection	A mechanism whereby previous investors are able to recover their equity diluted by a down round upon achievement of certain targets on an exit. This term is related to anti-dilution, which, importantly, common holders do not have the benefit of. Let's say that full ratchet protection was in force for the Series Seed investment, and when it is time for the Series A, it is a down round, and the price per share is less than the seed. Full ratchet protection focuses on the new price per share and compensates the previous investors for the full difference in share price, regardless of the real impact of the dilutive event. This will significantly dilute the value of the shares held by shareholders who are not protected against dilution (i.e., founders and employees). The shareholders may likely see the full ratchet anti-dilution protection as a severe injustice, and it may have a demoralizing effect on them. For this reason alone, you should try hard to avoid having full ratchet in any financing you do. Instead, try to negotiate a much less onerous form of anti-dilution, known as broad-based weighted-average protection, which we discussed in table 11.5.

Table 11.15   Follow-on round terms *(continued)*

Pay-to-play	Penalizes investors who do not participate on a pro rata basis in a financing round by canceling some or all of their preferential rights. I like to think of this as the anti-freeloader term. I really like it when early investors are dedicated to the company and will invest their percentage share in subsequent rounds. That will be a lot smaller than the amount they initially invested, and most investors specifically reserve funds to do their pro rata on at least one subsequent round. Most investors, especially those who invest early, don't want to be diluted as new money comes in, which is why they like to do their pro rata—it keeps them at the exact same ownership percentage they started with. Investors who only invest once and then sit back and don't invest again are, as I like to say, freeloaders. The pay-to-play term can be a bit harsh, but it is good for common holders like founders because it prevents them from being diluted under investors' anti-dilution clauses. This also makes the pay-to-play a valuable tool in the term sheet negotiations.

11.4   *The moral of this anecdote*

When it comes time to develop a term sheet and negotiate with investors, I hope you will find this anecdote invaluable. Remember, the term sheet is not a legal document, but it is still full of legal-type language and all the associated arcane constructs and subtleties. In this anecdote, we looked at a real term sheet for a company's first financing and explained the *why* and the *so what* of each term.

There are a handful of terms to really watch out for and try to avoid or tamp down:

- Multiple tranches for the investment
- Drag-along provisions
- Dealing with founder's shares
- Board observers

There are also some terms that only come into play in subsequent rounds and some of those can be bad for the company and initial investors.

Due diligence:
An exam you must pass

- What is due diligence? Why is it needed? Who is it for?
- What does a comprehensive due diligence checklist look like? Streamline the process with readiness.
- How can setting up a data room dramatically streamline the due diligence process for you and your investors?

Due diligence is a critical process that occurs prior to any financing or exit. It enables the prospective investors (or buyers) to thoroughly assess you, your team, and your company so they know exactly what they are getting for their money. In this anecdote, you will see what kind of information they will need and how best to give it to them. I outline some actionable steps here that it would be prudent for you to get on top of long before that first investor says they want to start the process.

12.1 What due diligence means

Due diligence is a very old term, going back 500 years. In the literal sense, it means "requisite effort." Due diligence has extended its reach into business contexts, meaning to apply requisite effort before engaging in a financial transaction.

DEFINITION   *Due diligence* means a thorough investigation that a prospective buyer conducts to evaluate a company's complete financial picture, including assets, liabilities, and commercial potential.

Before I entered the entrepreneurial world, and before I had seen the words written down, I (and, I have since learned, many other entrepreneurs) thought, when hearing the phrase "due diligence," that the first word was the verb "do" and that it was a command to go be diligent about something important. Given how important due diligence is and how diligent it requires both the provider and consumer of the requisite information to be, that is not a bad variant of the definition.

I have always considered due diligence to be an *all-hands-on-deck* operation. The CEO usually leads the process, with major involvement from the chief legal officer and the chief financial officer—but literally every function within the company provides content for the process.

PROCESS OVERVIEW   The management team provides information regarding everything important about the company to the prospective investors. This includes information about financing, technology, product, market, business model, team, financials/returns, and important documents.

The process must be carefully managed because the investor has still not invested enough time and expense to feel inclined to deal with negative issues that come up. If there are big issues, the investors are still in a frame of mind to look for a reason *not* to invest, so be careful not to give them one. In other words, the term sheet is great, but although it signifies serious intent, the financing is not yet secure—and if the due diligence process does not satisfy the investors, it won't happen. So, the management team must take this process extremely seriously and make sure it delights the investors.

There are multiple phases of due diligence. You might say that when you first connect with a partner at a VC firm, they are starting their due diligence. They are evaluating you, the problem you are going after, the size of the opportunity, your pitch deck, and your proposed solution. Then they share this with their partners and "sell" it to them. By the time they have had a second meeting, they are pretty far along in their assessment of your deal. If they are excited about it, they will put in a term sheet and specify that it is strictly confidential, trying to hold their position as the lead investor. But even at this point, they have not committed much, and they still have a lot of due diligence to do before they will invest a single penny.

This potential lead, plus any additional investors, will submit their initial due-diligence checklist for you to respond to. All investors, especially the lead, will have a second phase of due diligence, during which they will be very interactive with you and your team. This phase is driven by things they have learned about you and a set of questions that are specific to your company and product—now they are digging in deep, working to make sure every question and concern they can come up with is answered.

12.2 Phase I: The investor's due-diligence checklist

Let's examine a checklist of information you'll need to organize and questions you'll need to answer in preparation for the due-diligence process. The 49-item list in tables 12.1–12.7 is one I constructed based on an amalgam of many lists I've received over the years from about 10 different investors. It has been through a lot of scrutiny and has been used to make investment decisions by these 10 investors hundreds of times.

Being prepared ahead of time to answer this basic set of questions quickly and easily will do wonders to impress investors. Work through this list ahead of engaging with investors, and put all the responses, as well as any other topics they may want to examine, in a *data room* that either you or the investor can access. (We'll go over how to set up a data room later in this anecdote.)

Table 12.1   Due-diligence information to prepare in advance: financing details

	Information	Due diligence questions to answer
1.	Company address	Provide contact details of the main office.
2.	Financing round	What round is this?
3.	Amount raised	How much money are you raising in this round?
4.	Other new investors	Do you have an investor who wants to lead the round or a group of new investors who want to participate in this round?
		How much money will the existing investor be committing to this round?
5.	Amount invested	How much total has been invested prior to the new round?
		How much in grants and loans has the company received?
		How much of those has to be paid back?
6.	Post-money of last round	What was the post-money valuation of the previous financing, and how much was invested?
7.	Expected pre-money	What pre-money valuation are you expecting?
		If you already have term sheets in place, outline their key metrics.
8.	Timing	What is the timeline for this round? When do you expect to close?
9.	Existing investors	Provide a shareholder/capitalization table.
10.	Founding; history	Provide some history on the company: when and why it was founded, how the founders/team came together, major milestones achieved, etc.
11.	Main activities	What is the company doing (broad description of activities)? If available, point also to company/product videos.

Table 12.2   Due diligence information to prepare in advance: technology

	Information	Due diligence questions to answer
12.	Technology details	Describe the product and its functionality.
		What is the technical invention? If available, show a white/technical paper describing the technology.
13.	Target application	What are the main applications of your technology and your product (application areas, industries, use cases)?
14.	Competition	With which other technologies (that solve the same/similar problem) are you competing?
15.	Differentiation	How does your product differ from the competing products (functionality, price, time to deployment, availability, etc.)?
		What kind of advantages does your technology offer compared to competing technologies/technologies used in the competing products?
16.	Uniqueness	What is proprietary about your technology? What is your main intellectual property (IP)? Why couldn't someone quickly replicate it?
17.	Freedom to operate	Does any IP belong to third parties? If so, explain the modality (license agreements, royalty payments, etc.). How do you protect your IP? Do you have any patents? How do you protect your trade secrets? Have you performed a freedom-to-operate analysis? Did you have any IP disputes in the past, or are you having any ongoing IP disputes?

Table 12.3   Due diligence information to prepare in advance: product

	Information	Due diligence questions to answer
18.	What is sold	What is your offering? Describe your product lines and other revenue-generating offerings (services, customization, maintenance, installation, etc.).
19.	Product description	How do you describe your product to your customers?
20.	Product portfolio	Provide an overview of all your products and services.
21.	Value proposition	Provide economic/quantitative data (if data is not available, then calculations) for your product's value proposition. Provide real examples from customers demonstrating the value proposition. What is the return on investment for the customer when using your product? What is the payback time?
22.	Development status	At which stage (idea, prototype, pre-series, commercial, etc.) is each of your products? What is the timeline?
23.	Key milestones	What are the key milestones ahead, in terms of technology and product development?

Table 12.4   Due diligence information to prepare in advance: market

	Information	Due diligence questions to answer
24.	Global market size	What is the size of the theoretical total market in terms of units and in terms of dollar amount? How did you arrive at those numbers (e.g., bottom-up estimations/calculations)?
25.	Addressable market	Given your product's feature set, price, complexity to use, etc., what is the realistic addressable market in terms of units and in terms of dollar amount?
26.	Growth rate	What is the past growth/decline rate of this market? What drivers will drive the future growth/decline of this market?
27.	Key buying factors	What are the main reasons customers are buying your product? Are there any external drivers (regulations, national incentive programs, upcoming laws, etc.)?
		What are the average cycles from initial contact to proof of concept to commercial deployment?
28.	Selling hurdles	What are the main hurdles when trying to sell your product (e.g., unfamiliarity with the technology, high capital expenditures [CAPEX], no single decision-maker, IT security/compliance concerns)?
29.	Competitors	Who are your main competitors? How do your company and offering differ from them? (Are there any other differentiations than the ones listed in the "competitive advantage" section, such as business model, number of partners, target markets, size of company?)

Table 12.5   Due diligence information to prepare in advance: business model

	Information	Due diligence questions to answer
30.	Internal activities	Which activities in the value chain are done in-house (research, material sourcing, product development, manufacturing, assembly, marketing, sales, etc.)?
31.	External activities	Which activities in the value chain are outsourced, and in which way (research, product development, manufacturing, assembly, marketing, sales, etc.)?
32.	Revenue model	What is your revenue model, including pricing structure, depending on market, sales channel, volume, etc.?
33.	Customers	Who are your main customers? How many units have you sold to each of them?
34.	Sales cycles	What are the average sales cycles? Provide an example of the entire sales process from initial contact, full license, and after-sales services.
35.	Distribution channels	Do you have partnerships in place with distributors, system integrators, consulting companies, original equipment manufacturers(OEMs)?
36.	Key dependencies	What key dependencies do you have (e.g., suppliers, exclusivity contracts, noncompete agreements, key partnerships)?

Table 12.6   Due diligence information to prepare in advance: team

	Information	Due diligence questions to answer
37.	Key team members	Who are the founders, management team members, and other leaders of the company?
38.	Board members	Who are the board members, and what are their roles with respect to external activities in support of the company and internal roles in terms of mentorship and advice?
39.	Team size	How big is the entire employee base?
40.	Missing key people	What roles that you deem critical are not yet filled and how do you plan to rectify this? (Investors love to offer help here.)
41.	Advisors	Who are your advisors, and what do they add? What additional ones do you want/need to add, and why?

Table 12.7   Due diligence information to prepare in advance: financials/returns

	Information	Due diligence questions to answer
42.	Revenues	Provide detailed financials for the past two years, budgeted and projected financials for the current year, and projected financials for the next three years. The financials should include detailed revenue streams (recurring, installation revenue, hardware revenue, non-recurring engineering [NRE], grants, etc.) and a detailed cost structure, including gross margins and a list of major fixed costs. Provide the year-to-date (YTD) revenue and, if applicable, the current monthly recurring revenue (MRR). For software/SaaS companies: elaborate on how you calculate the gross margin (i.e., which costs you account for in the cost of goods sold [COGS]).
43.	Pipeline and backlog	Provide as much information as possible supporting the financials of the current and upcoming year, such as weighted sales pipeline and current bookings.
44.	Financial metrics	Provide average customer acquisition costs (CAC), average customer lifetime value (LTV), and customer churn (if possible, for the past two to three years). For SaaS companies: provide MRR churn, net MRR churn, and magic number (a term specific to SaaS products: Revenue this Q – Revenue prior Q) × 4) / Sales & Marketing expense prior Q).
45.	Break-even timing	When do you plan (month and year) to break even?
46.	Capital to break even	How much capital is needed until the cash flow break-even point, and what is the timing of it?
47.	Burn and runway	What is your current burn rate, and when will you run out of cash?
48.	Exit	Who are the most likely buyers of the company, and why? Does the current senior team have IPO experience?
49.	Comparables	What, if any, comparable transactions to that proposed here do members of the team have in their experience base?

12.3 **The data room**

Most investors want to look over all of the company's most important documents, including formation, financings, employees, marketing strategy and collateral, legal agreements, licenses, patents, sales materials and agreements, and more. You will want to create a data room to hold copies of all relevant documents plus the answers from the 49-point checklist and any other questions any investor asks. I suggest following the theory that what one investor asks, another will, too.

> **DEFINITION** A *data room* is space used for storing information such as contracts and corporate documents with the intent to share that information in a secure fashion with potential investors or acquirors during due diligence.

Here are some tips for creating your data room:

- Build the data room using a file-sharing technology like Box, Dropbox, or Google Drive so it is easy for you to share directly with the investor without copying a bunch of files and running the risk of making a mistake and leaving something out.
- Make a copy of your source data room with the name of one investor on it. When you create a link to it for that investor, make sure that link has an expiration date. This way, you won't risk the lifeblood of your company floating out in the ether and losing control of that information. If that investor goes away, remove their entire data room and don't reuse it.
- Make two types of data rooms: one for investors in later stages of evaluation asking for more details about the company, and one for the investor just getting started with due diligence. Name them "full" or "partial." Full adds all employment records for everyone, all financing documents from every investor, and specific things an investor asks for. There may be some documents you don't offer to all investors and only add when an investor asks for them.
- Resynchronize the master data room to one or more of the data rooms extant. As you are asked questions, or as time goes by, these two data rooms can get more and more out of sync.

Table 12.8 shows a data room layout (in my case, using DropBox) that I've used for years.

Table 12.8 Top-level folders (11)

📁 1.	Pitch Deck & Related
📁 2.	Main Corporate Records
📁 3.	Financials & Insurance
📁 4.	Marketing
📁 5.	Sales
📁 6.	Technology Papers

Table 12.8   Top-level folders (11) *(continued)*

📁 7.	Historical Technical Papers
📁 8.	Patents & Trademarks
📁 9.	Employees, Advisors Consultants
📁 10.	Past Financing Rounds
📁 11.	Legal Agreements

Tables 12.9–12.18 drill down on the 11 folders listed in table 12.8.

Table 12.9   Pitch Deck & Related

📁 1.	Pitch Deck & Related
📁 a.	Current Pitch Decks
📁 b.	Previous Financing Documents
📁 c.	Previous Due Diligence [from previous financings]
📁 d.	Supporting Material

Table 12.10   Main Corporate Records

📁 2.	Main Corporate Records
📁 a.	Articles of Incorporation
📁 b.	Board Meeting Records
📁 c.	Bylaws
📁 d.	Cap Table
📁 e.	Certificate of Good Standing (Delaware)
📁 f.	DUNs [your DUNs number assignment from Dun & Bradstreet]
📁 g.	EIN IRS Letter
📁 h.	ESOP Documents [Employee Stock Option Plan]
📁 i.	Founders Restricted Stock Agreements
📁 j.	Investor Rights Agreements
📁 k.	Export Control (Technology)
📁 l.	State Foreign Qualifications
📁 m.	Stockholder Approvals

Table 12.11   Financials

📁 3.	Financials	
📁 a.	409a Valuations	
📁 b.	Budget Planning	
📁 c.	Debt	
📁 d.	Financial Statements	
📁 e.	TAX	
📁 f.	Insurance	

Table 12.12   Marketing

📁 4.	Marketing	
📁 a.	Competitive Assessments	
📁 b.	Go-to-Market	
📁 c.	Market Intelligence	
📁 d.	Videos	
📁 e.	White Papers	

Table 12.13   Sales

📁 5.	Sales	
📁 a.	Sales Forecasts	
📁 b.	Sales Materials	
📁 c.	Sales Agreements	

Table 12.14   Reference Papers

📁 6.	Technology Papers
	Misc
📁 7.	Historical Technical Papers
	Misc

Table 12.15   Patents & Trademarks

📁 8.	Patents & Trademarks
📁 a.	Domains
📁 b.	Patent Portfolio
📁 c.	Trademarks

Table 12.16   Employees, Advisors, Consultants

📁 9.	Employees, Advisors, Consultants
📁 a.	Employees
📁 b.	Board of Directors
📁 c.	Advisors
📁 d.	Consultants

Table 12.17   Past Financings

📁 10.	Employees, Advisors, Consultants
📁 a.	Blue Sky
📁 b.	SAFE Notes
📁 c.	Series Seed
📁 d.	Convertible Notes
📁 e.	Series A

Table 12.18   Legal Agreements

📁 11.	Legal Agreements
📁 a.	Top Five Vendors & Customers
📁 b.	Form of Commercial License
📁 c.	Form of Evaluation Agreement
📁 d.	Form of NDA
📁 e.	License Agreements
📁 f.	Office Lease
📁 g.	Service Providers

12.4 *Phase II: The interactive due-diligence phase*

If the investors are satisfied with your answers to their checklist and they have scrutinized everything in your data room, you are in a good position as they enter the interactive phase of due diligence. If the investors have gotten this far, they have determined that you are worth the significant time and effort their many staff members have expended to analyze the phase I due diligence. This means it is likely they are thinking they'll make this investment. But hiccups are still possible, so you and your team must remain on your game.

This interactive phase typically happens as a series of deeper and deeper dive meetings where the CEO is no longer the focal point. Instead, investors are now getting to know the sales, marketing, and technical teams much better. They typically send ahead a set of questions arising from their study of the materials you provided in phase I or in your data room. You and your team need to carefully work up answers to their questions and prepare a presentation for them. That gives them a chance to ask the experts more questions on each topic. These meetings will indicate to you what direction each investor is heading with respect to an investment. Your team will be able to tell, too.

During this phase, investors check the professional references of the CEO and, potentially, members of their senior team. In one case, we had a prospective Series A investor who believed nothing was more important than the team. He and two members of his team drove up from New Jersey to spend two full days of exhausting sessions with us, going through everything they could think of. Throughout the day as well during the dinner sessions, a steady stream of comments and body language from the partner and his team told us they were really interested. Then the partner went much deeper when he got to reference checks. In my case, he wanted names of people who had managed me, people I had managed, peers, board members, investors, and character references. He ultimately *personally* called 26 references on me, including going back 20 years and speaking to various venture capitalists from both successful and not-successful startups in my distant past. This ultimately led them to put in a term sheet, which was the goal. Success!

12.5 *The moral of this anecdote*

Due diligence is a deep dive by prospective investors into every aspect of your company for the purpose of assessing their risk if they proceed with the proposed investment. You'll want to get well ahead of this phase in your search for an investment to avoid (a) having this be the thing that delays an investment decision that you have control over or (b) having something spook the investor and cause you to lose them. This anecdote provides a thorough 49-point checklist. Spend time gathering the answers for it. Create a data room where all your documents live and that you can give investors direct access to. Do this before your first meetings with investors so you are ready for all their questions well in advance. No doubt about it, due diligence is a major exam for the CEO, the senior management, and the company, but it is one you must pass with flying colors to succeed in raising money from investors.

Part 3

Business strategies, models and plans

Part 3 gets into some very meaty topics that are essential to understand to make your startup succeed and grow. You must get these topics right early on, because if you don't, your startup is likely to be a statistic in the wrong way. The anecdotes in this part are as follows:

13 Your business model: The beating heart of your business
14 Getting to a minimum viable product with lighthouse customers
15 Product–market fit: Making sure the dogs will eat your dog food
16 Go-to-market: How to make your business viable and grow
17 A formal business plan in 10 steps
18 Burn rate and runway—or, where is the edge of that cliff?
19 Achieving cash-flow positive: A startup's Holy Grail
20 Your startup's valuation: Up up up (hopefully)

Your business model is how you make money on your product or service. Who pays you for what, and when? Sometimes the real innovation a startup makes is its business model. More often, the big breakthrough is elsewhere, but it is still essential for you to fully understand and be able to articulate the business model. Most startups are product-based, and once you have done the work to determine what market segment(s) you will go after, building out the minimum viable product that customers in those segments will buy is the next step. Once you do that, you can focus on determining product–market fit (PMF), which is arguably the most important anecdote in this part. Why? Because I assert that no startup has ever been successful without proving PMF.

PMF is critical but not sufficient for the startup to scale and grow. For that, you need to build out a go-to-market strategy that integrates all the functions in your company to find customers efficiently, take advantage of partnerships to find even more customers, close business with those customers rapidly, deliver and service the product to those customers, and, when ready, expand into adjacent markets to truly scale and grow. I include an anecdote on the best way I know to build a formal business plan, which, although it is not normally needed up through Series A rounds, is essential for subsequent rounds and when an exit approaches.

The last three anecdotes in this part discuss operational topics that need to become second nature to the early-stage startup CEO. I learned that you must know the up-to-the-moment accurate cash burn and how many months of runway you have at that burn rate to be fully prepared to act quickly if the runway gets too short and preserving cash becomes essential to survival. That is why I call gaining cash-flow positive the Holy Grail.

Finally, valuation is important, and there are things you can do to improve your valuation. Keeping those things in mind and driving your company to achieve them can raise your valuation and make a significant difference to the size of your exit.

Your business model:
The beating heart
of your business

- What is a business model? How do you determine what yours should be?
- Who is your real customer: consumer or business?
- What are examples of standard business models to provide you guidance in nailing yours down?

The *business model* is the heart of your *business* and of your *business plan*. It's tempting to think, "I have a product, and I just go sell it, right?" Well, *how* are you going to sell it, and how do you get paid? That's the critical question a business model answers. To determine the right business model for your company, you will carefully consider all the possible business models that might make sense and choose the right one for your product and how you want to get it to customers. You must also be able to clearly articulate why it is the right one to achieve the goals you have set out for your company.

> **DEFINITION** *A business model* is how a company sells and delivers its product and generates revenues from customers.

105

A business model explains . . .
- How you will make money
- How your customers will pay you
- How you will deliver your products and services to your customer

The business model is not the same as your business plan. We will focus on how you create a business plan in anecdote 17, "A formal business plan in 10 steps," where the business model takes up at most 1/20 of a business plan. As I explain in that anecdote, full written business plans are not commonly done for early-stage (pre–Series B) startups anymore because entrepreneurs and investors seem to have agreed that the pitch deck will serve as the business plan instead. But *every* business must have a business model.

There is not necessarily only one right answer as to what your business model should be, and the business model is among the many things you can change as your company grows. But if you pick a business model that does not work at all, it is challenging to recover. It is critical that you go through an iterative process to develop the best possible model that you, and those advising you, can think of. Following are several business model options for you to consider, along with some of my experience with them.

13.1 Business-to-consumer

To begin, ask yourself what type of customer you are selling to. Is your customer a consumer? Then your model is business-to-consumer (B2C). For example, Apple is primarily a B2C hardware company (which also sells software and services in support of its hardware), and Norton is a B2C software company.

13.2 Business-to-business and its variants

Is your customer another business? Then your model is business-to-business (B2B). Next you must ask, is that business the end user, or does it include your product in what it sells to yet another business (B2B2B) or consumer (B2B2C)? Either form of this last model is frequently called an original equipment manufacturer (OEM). Several of my startups were a form of B2B, as highlighted in table 13.1.

Table 13.1 B2B variant business model companies I founded

Company	B2B type	Description
MasPar	B2B hardware	MasPar was a supercomputer company that sold to businesses that bought our machines as "major capital equipment hardware" in terms of how the machines showed up on its books.

Table 13.1 B2B variant business model companies I founded *(continued)*

Company	B2B type	Description
Aguru	B2B hardware or B2B2B services	Aguru Images made a giant half-geodesic dome with 400 computer-controlled cameras and lights mounted all around the inside. A movie actor would sit in the middle, and thousands of images of tiny portions of their face were taken from many different angles in many different lighting conditions in 14 seconds. This made it possible for the very first time to create computer-generated images of the actor's face that viewers could not tell were computer-generated. These devices were sold to large movie studios in a B2B model or to service bureaus that then sold their image-creation capability to movie studios in a B2B2B model.
Ambric	B2B OEM	Ambric was another hardware startup. It designed and built a semiconductor chip that contained 300 processors and replaced a dozen or more boards full of expensive chips. The Ambric chip could encode and "shrink" the signals transmitting high-resolution video images on their way to consumers, signals critical to *streaming*. To make streaming of high-resolution images practical, bandwitch utilization had to drop from 25 megabits per second to 7 megabits per second with no loss of fidelity. Ambric's chips could do this shrinkage for a fraction of the cost and space that the dozen old boards required. This was B2B OEM because Ambric sold its chip to a company that added something to it and then sold it to Apple and the makers of broadcast equipment and set-top boxes or modems in people's houses.

13.3 *Software-as-a-service (SaaS)*

Another very popular business model in the technology sector is software-as-a-service (SaaS). This is software that's delivered to users via the internet. There is a distinction between the user being a business versus being a consumer, but the similarities are stronger than the differences, so we will lump them together to avoid adding complexity. When you interact via a browser with your bank, Amazon, Google, Facebook, or literally millions of other sites, you are using a SaaS application. There are many benefits to this approach to application development. It is a great business model, and investors love it. Obviously, companies have become huge using this model.

13.3.1 *GeoTrust*

GeoTrust was a very early SaaS provider in a somewhat unusual way. We sold the security technology that turns on the lock symbol in your browser to indicate that data to and from the site you are interacting with is encrypted and therefore it's safe to transmit personal or financial information. Without this technology, no online shopping would occur because people would quickly learn that their credit card was being transmitted out in the open for bad guys to grab. The name of this security technology is *Secure Sockets Layer* (SSL). SSL was not technology you could sell to consumers; it had to be sold to a company that wanted to offer secure transactions. And the best time to sell it to them was when it was acquiring the domain for its website.

GeoTrust's technology

In the late 1990s, when there was a need for one web server to directly interact with another web server, this was done using screen scraping. The developers programming the server would access the target web page, examine its HTML, and codify the HTML elements on the target page into their application. So if there was an element to capture a person's first and last names into two fields, the developers built that into their program; using the interface on their web page, they could capture someone's name, and later their server could access the target server and have it insert the first and last name into the corresponding elements on the target site's page. As the term implies, these developers were scraping elements of interest off the target page and programming their server to interact with them as if it was a human sitting at a browser. As you can immediately see, if the owners of the target site changed anything on that web page, it could break this very fragile application.

It turns out that this capability was needed a lot in the days before one company could access the data of another (which happens constantly now). If you were at an airline site and the airline wanted to offer you a rental car for your trip, it needed to access the rental car site on your behalf as if it were you. If it let you click a link to the rental site, you left its site, which was then and still is a strict no-no. The site you start on wants to keep you there so it can interact with you; it knows that if you leave, you probably will not be back.

GeoTrust's entire sales and growth strategy was to sign up as many resellers of Geo-Trust's digital certificates as it could. All these resellers were business-facing sites that sold domain names, email and website services, backups, databases, and many other services and tools. At first GeoTrust worked with each reseller so the reseller's servers would know the interface at GeoTrust for registering and purchasing a digital certificate. That approach was brittle and not scalable. Plus GeoTrust would only achieve its growth goals by signing up 600 resellers, and the engineering team would never have been able to keep up.

A recent standard had emerged called Web Services, and it was designed to solve this exact problem. It made it easy for a site like GeoTrust to publish a machine-readable application programming interface (API) for all of its B2B interfaces to any sites that wanted to do business with the company. A small amount of training was all that was needed for the developers at a new reseller to program their servers to utilize GeoTrust Web Services. Now a site can change its look and feel and not break the Web Services and all the sites depending on them.

As soon as this capability was fully operational, GeoTrust started growing as fast as the salespeople could sign up resellers. Its market share grew by 1% per month for 25 months, and then it was acquired.

End users like SaaS because it is convenient—they don't need to install a new application; they just use their browser. Big SaaS vendors like Salesforce like it because they can almost constantly update and improve their products without users even knowing it is happening. Also, because the application is paid for based on how many users (designated as seats) are using it at an organization, revenues are smooth and predictable. And big corporations that buy SaaS seats love it because they are spending operational expenditure (OPEX) dollars instead of capital equipment expenditure (CAPEX) dollars to purchase it. This means they don't have to put large expenses on their balance sheet, and if times get tough, they can cancel subscriptions (i.e., decrease the number of seats they are paying for) and reduce their operational expenses instantly. Investors love SaaS because a small company can get a product to market extremely fast and can prove product-market fit (PMF) quickly while testing various aspects of that fit to rapidly improve the product and increase their revenue stream. But most of all, investors love it because it is annually recurring revenue (ARR) that repeats and grows year after year.

13.4   *B2B services*

One way to build a company where you retain most, if not all, ownership is to provide a valuable service to companies (B2B services), which can also pay well. Then what frequently happens is that you build out software tools to make your service delivery more and more effective and efficient. In this way, you are turning your business gradually into a product business model (B2B software). Selling a product (hardware or software) has much higher margins than a services business. Efficient services companies generate on the order of 35% gross margins (and frequently lower), whereas product companies achieve 80% or even higher, sometimes reaching as high as 95%. If you can pull this off, it is a fantastic way to go, because the services revenue pays your expenses. This means you don't need to raise any, or at least not as much, venture capital, which keeps your and your employees' equity position from getting as diluted.

A dominant company that started out delivering pure services and then added B2B enterprise software was the huge German software company SAP, whose category is enterprise resource planning (ERP). Most large companies use SAP or one of its smaller competitors. Even after SAP created large amounts of software to manage a company's resources, it still charged a substantial amount for its after-sale B2B services. It is common for Fortune 500–size companies to spend $100 million on a full ERP install of SAP's software system.

13.4.1   *Open Environment and Borland*

I witnessed this services-to-product transformation once in a company called Open Environment Corporation (OEC), which my company, Borland, bought. OEC built software that utilized a technology called Distributed Computing Environment (DCE). The technology was powerful but hard to use, so OEC was the rare company that had collected a cadre of people who knew a lot about it and could deliver services to companies needing *distributed systems* that worked across multiple servers in different locations. To be successful, OEC had to make the service it provided to its customers more and more efficient (and less costly), so it relentlessly looked for steps its field delivery team performed that were common and could be automated into a set of software tools. The customer still almost always wanted some services, but they were no longer all custom code written in the field. Now the services were "glue" code to interface the product components to special systems the customer was using. This was such genius that Borland, then the third-largest software company in the world, bought OEC for an excellent price.

The genius move was that because OEC started with a service model and then saw that software tools could make its services more efficient, eventually it was able to turn that into a full-fledged product. OEC was stone-cold certain it had PMF because it had worked with its customers and could see what worked and what didn't and what customers would pay for and what they wouldn't. More on PMF and how vital it is for a startup in anecdote 15, "Product–market fit: Making sure the dogs will eat your dog food."

13.5   *Internet advertising*

Probably the most lucrative internet-based business model of all (for companies in the United States) is advertising. In 2022, according to Oberlo, ads represented about 85% of Google's $224 billion in annual revenues[1] and almost 100% of Facebook's $136 billion in annual revenues.[2] Many others also use an advertising business model, but not nearly to the same magnitude as the big two. To make money charging others to display ads through your web platform requires that the platform attract a very large number of unique viewers. Because Google and Facebook take most of the oxygen out of an ad-based business model, be very cautious about proposing this business model, or your company my suffocate.

Table 13.2 summarizes the categories of business models discussed in this anecdote. It includes a couple of examples of well-known companies that generate a significant portion of their revenue using each model.

Table 13.2   **Basic business models covered in this anecdote with example companies**

Short name	Description	Examples
B2C	Business to consumer	Apple Microsoft
B2B	Business to business	Microsoft Cisco
B2B2B	Business to business to business	NXP chip ($\rightarrow$ GE device $\rightarrow$ electric grid)
B2B2C	Business to business to consumer	Qualcomm ($\rightarrow$ Apple $\rightarrow$ consumer)
SaaS	Software as a service licensed by named users (Salesforce) or as an application with built-in fees (Fidelity)	Salesforce Fidelity
Advertising	Advertising (eyeballs)	Google Facebook

---

[1] "Google Ad Revenue (2013–2023)," Oberlo, last modified November 2023, www.oberlo.com/statistics/google-ad-revenue.

[2] "Facebook Ad Revenue (2017–2026)," Oberlo, last modified November 2023, www.oberlo.com/statistics/facebook-ad-revenue.

13.6   *How your business model affects hiring*

The choice of business model has a profound effect on who you hire. For this reason, it is paramount that you nail down the business model before you staff your teams.

B2C requires extreme attention to simple, clean, consistent user interfaces, so engineers who specialize in UI/UX (user interface, user experience) will be essential. Documentation, either shipped with the product or available online, needs to be simple, clear, and translated into many languages. Quality expectations are about as high in this category as in any—users who run into bugs will stop using the product and not come back.

B2B hardware needs electrical engineers, hardware designers, and hardware-verification engineers just for the hardware component. In addition, there is always software that interacts with and controls the hardware, so a team of software engineers must be paired with the hardware team. The combination is a large, expensive engineering group.

B2B services need generalists who can go to the customer site and adapt and configure the vendor's systems into the customer's systems. Because these technical people are on-site at the customer, they need to be very good with people, or harm could be done to the relationship with that customer.

SaaS is a combination of backend systems that usually run in a cloud coupled to a frontend that is an application built to run in a browser. The backend component requires expertise in servers of all sorts including web servers, database servers, and specialized servers unique to this application. If the expectation is that the system, if successful in the market, will have to scale to millions of users, the team working on the backend must be well-versed in how to engineer highly scalable systems. The browser-based frontend team are mostly software UI people experienced in web technologies. Although quality is always important, SaaS vendors have the ability to quickly fix issues with their systems and release them without customers having to take any action to get the new version.

Advertising technologies have a software component that controls what ads are delivered when and to whom. They also have software that automates the sale of advertising to buyers and the reporting of results to them. These are separate and distinct software teams that may ideally report to different functions within the company.

13.7   *The moral of this anecdote*

The business model you choose for your company is one of the most important factors controlling whether you will succeed or fail. It is how you get the company to be profitable. Choosing the right one is not easy, but it is critical that you do it first thing—before you fully staff, before you fully develop your product, and before you land your first customer. This is because the business model affects all those elements in major ways. If you create a detailed business plan, your business model is at the heart of it. And if you do not create a business plan, you still need to have a business model, a strong understanding of it, and conviction that it is the right one. Although it is possible to change business models midstream, doing so can be painful and potentially damaging to your young company.

Getting to a minimum viable product with lighthouse customers

- Can you use your LinkedIn connections to identify lighthouse customers?
- Does your product solve their problems, and what is the MVP that does that?
- What are the product gaps to address from customer interviews before you enter the market?

You are working hard to get into the market and begin bringing in revenue. But you need to nail down a few things before you do that so you can be confident that you have something that solves the big problem you wanted to solve as the premise for starting your new company. The first big step in getting the right product into the right market the right way is to make sure the product is something people in your chosen market will pay for. But you don't want to build too much product, because that takes more time; and you might not be building "necessary" features, which is a complete waste of time and delays your getting into the market. This anecdote is about how you zero in on what is called a minimum viable product (MVP) for which real customers will pay real money.

We will talk about finding early-adopter customers called lighthouse customers by getting out and talking to the market. We are going to see how you can use resources you already have, such as LinkedIn, in a new way. Once you find a lighthouse customer, you work with them to define just the right set of features that solve their problem and that they consider valuable enough to pay you for.

14.1 *Minimum viable product*

Startups should follow this progression:

1 Identify a market with a big problem.
2 Find a lighthouse customer that helps you define an MVP.
3 Prove product–market fit (PMF).
4 Develop a full go-to-market (GTM) strategy.

In this anecdote, we focus on step 2. An essential part of PMF and then GTM is having an MVP. Your MVP has just enough of the features you eventually envision in your "final" product to satisfy early adopters. If you have been lucky and you have a lighthouse customer, you will use their needs to drive your MVP. If not, you will use your vision and knowledge of your target customers to establish what you think the minimum set of features is. You take that initial MVP out to show customers and start to iterate on what the real MVP needs to be. That iteration process involves gathering feedback and requirements from your early adopters, building in those capabilities, and going back to show the result to those customers. After you have enough feedback from this early-adopter group, you can declare victory on having an MVP. Teams always seem surprised by how different their final MVP is from their initial vision.

The term minimum viable product was coined by Frank Robinson, cofounder and president of SyncDev, who focused on having product development and customer development executing in parallel. MVP was then further popularized by Eric Ries, founder of The Lean Startup methodology.

> DEFINITION *The minimum viable product* is the version of a new product that requires the least amount of development yet is something real customers will use, give useful feedback on, and pay for.

The effort put into the MVP is best done using agile development, where the product is developed in an iterative fashion that adds capabilities incrementally and keeps the team tightly focused on only putting in features that will garner the most customer feedback. This is important because you don't want the team developing features customers end up not caring about—that is extremely wasteful, and startups don't have time or resources to waste. Because by definition the team does not yet have the intimate customer knowledge to build precisely what their customers need to solve their problems, using this process allows startups to create an MVP with the confidence that as their customer development process proceeds and they gather more and more input about what the product needs to grow into, they will be able to apply the agile development process and morph the MVP into a fuller, more complete, and high-value product that they can sell broadly. Startup teams have proven this method to be successful for 30 years.

14.1.1 *MVP vs. prototype*

An MVP is different from a working prototype, which is a version that a development team builds to prove to themselves that the various technologies they are creating, combined with technologies they bring in from outside (purchased or open source), work. In such a prototype, a development team rarely tries to incorporate a smoothly working user interface. I like to call these "demos only a mother can love." I've seen a demo print out thousands of lines of gobbledygook text and end with "DONE" and the watching team members explode in raucous high-fives and celebration. Such a thing does not ever see the light of day outside the lab.

A candidate MVP is clearly not such a thing. It is based on the prototype but is designed to have the exact minimal set of features early-adopter customers require, which can be added to the candidate MVP in an iterative design process until those early adopters agree that this is an MVP that will deliver real value and generate sales to initial customers.

14.1.2 *Different MVP definitions*

I should note that there are minor differences of opinion about the precise definition startups should use for *MVP*. Some define it as the product's "first version," others think of it as a "stripped-down version," and some call it "a full-scale, but simple, version." A definition that has worked for me in several startups is "a stripped-down, but fully functional version of the product," with lots of room to add significantly to it to excite and delight future customers when our startup is further along.

At Dover, the giant semiconductor company NXP was our lighthouse customer, and it had a pretty demanding set of requirements even for a "minimal" product suitable to be incorporated on the next version of one of its chips (which would be shipped in the hundreds of millions). Our product provided what is called *oversight* for the processor (also called the *CPU*) NXP put on its chip, which could tell whether a specific instruction the processor executed was okay or was the result of a cyberattack. Our product identified a cyberattack using a set of rules that was installed on the chip when it was turned on. We decided, with NXP's input, that there would be a small set of only three rules, support would be only for simple processors, and protection would only be provided for one simple operating system; that would define our MVP. We knew from conversations we were having with lots of other semiconductor companies that some wanted support for multiple processors at a time, some wanted additional sets of rules beyond our base set of three, and some wanted protection for lots more complex operating systems; all that fell onto our roadmap of future capabilities we would develop *after* we started to see sales of our MVP. Additionally, this was all for a single vertical market we were targeting. Once we developed a beachhead in that market, we would have the knowledge to improve the product such that we could go after adjacent markets with different features we would add to the MVP we started with.

MVP examples from the field

Here are a few examples from my startups of cases when we worked with a lighthouse customer to define an MVP and were able to collect revenue for it. We then worked on product–market fit for this MVP.

WebSpective (1996)

Fidelity was WebSpective's lighthouse customer. It understood the need for website load balancing and wanted to help shape the product. What Fidelity and WebSpective defined was as simple as possible, with a server acting as the monitor at fidelity.com. The server's job was to redirect incoming requests to a hidden server that was the most lightly loaded with other web traffic. This is what Fidelity initially paid money for, as did other large companies. Later the product was expanded as WebSpective learned more from its initial customers.

GeoTrust (1999)

GoDaddy was GeoTrust's lighthouse "reseller". GoDaddy and GeoTrust defined an MVP as a single digital certificate created via a 10-minute automated authentication process. The interaction with GoDaddy as a reseller of GeoTrust's certificate meant that when a customer bought a domain from GoDaddy, they were offered a digital certificate from GeoTrust. GoDaddy required that it keep control of that customer on its site, so GeoTrust's servers operated through GoDaddy's servers. The customer got the certificate from GeoTrust without ever leaving GoDaddy's site. Later this was significantly expanded using Web Services technology, enabling GeoTrust to enlarge its market footprint to 600 certificate resellers.

14.2 *The critical importance of lighthouse customers*

A lighthouse customer is an early adopter that embraces a product soon after (or even slightly before) launch. According to marketing software tool provider HubSpot,[1] lighthouse customers typically compose 13.5% of the first 15% (that's 2%) of customers to adopt a new idea or technology. They are proverbial early adopters in the nomenclature that Geoffrey Moore, author of the seminal book *Crossing the Chasm*, uses to describe the technology-adoption curve shown in figure 14.1. Moore describes the various stages of adoption of a new technology or product as innovators, early adopters (or lighthouse customers), early majority, late majority, and laggards. Where they are in time and how many of them there are is represented by the bell curve shown in the figure.

The lighthouse customer helps you establish your MVP, without which you will not be able to move forward with investors or with your go-to-market strategy. In Moore's world, you will not cross the chasm and will never get to the early majority, which is essential for your product and your company to take off—and, frankly, for its survival.

---

[1] Jay Fuchs, "4 Ways Lighthouse Customers Can Predict a Product's Future," HubSpot Blog, September 4, 2020, updated June 15, 2021, https://blog.hubspot.com/service/lighthouse-customer.

Here are some of the ways the lighthouse customer can help you achieve MVP:

- They tell you whether the feature set you have chosen is missing anything critical (i.e., if you defined MVP correctly).
- They expose flaws in usability.
- They may provide early revenue (the product may be free for the first few).
- They provide your first base of significant influencers who help spread the word for you and attract more customers.
- They show, once there is a critical mass, that your product has caught on and has a solid head of steam as you get ready to launch.

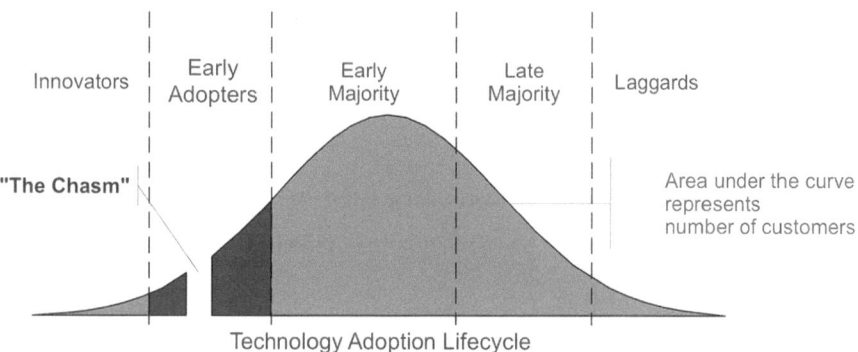

Figure 14.1   The bell curve of new technology adoption and the chasm that is so hard to cross. Licensed under the Creative Commons Attribution 3.0 Unported license.

14.3   Talking to the market

A product concept is sufficient to start fishing in various markets with a variety of stakeholder roles. Through these interactions with stakeholders, you can begin learning how you will be perceived, what language you should use to describe yourself, and what markets resonate better with your message than others. Ultimately, talking to a minimum of 15 people (ideally more, up to as many as 40) will provide you with the information you need to come back well-armed for the GTM strategy development process. During this interviewing process, you may have the opportunity to turn one to three of these stakeholders into a lighthouse customer.

How do you find 15, much less 40, high-quality interviews? Begin with people you already know who are relevant to your vision. Most people starting a company have been in and around the general market area where this new company will play. Or someone on the team has these connections. That was true for all my startups. But those connections may not get you to 15. You can augment them with LinkedIn, using the search capability that LinkedIn calls LinkedIn Analytics.

How to exploit the hidden LinkedIn Analytics user interface

Before you begin, make sure you expand your first-degree, and therefore second-degree, connections as much as you can by adding anyone related to your venture to your network. It's not useful to try to go beyond second degree, as it is too hard to get effective introductions that far out. You need good, warm introductions to your second-degrees, which come from your first-degrees. Your first degree connections are people who know you, understand you, respect you, and are the most likely to assist you in opening closed doors. Because these are people who hold you in high regard, you can now use your reputation to facilitate introductions to the key contacts they know (your second-degree connections).

These contacts are part of the LinkedIn social networking community, and they have indicated a willingness to network (unlike cold-calling or following up on a letter to an executive surrounded by an army of gatekeepers). You will now be using your reputation and have the greatest chance for a positive outcome.

The following screenshots demonstrate how to open the hidden LinkedIn Analytics user interface and explore the possibilities. Note that LinkedIn may change its user interface periodically, but these basic elements have been stable in LinkedIn for many years.

1   Run a people search by clicking in the LinkedIn search box and clicking Enter to get the search options:

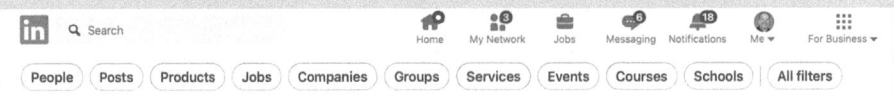

2   Click People. Then click the button to the right that says All Filters.

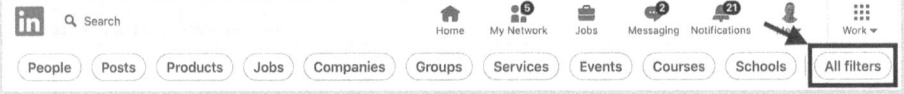

3   Filter by first- and second-degree connections, and click the blue Show Results button. You will see a list of all of your first- and second-degree connections.

4   Click All Filters again, and scroll down to the Industries section. You will see a listing of the top five industries where your first- and second-degree LinkedIn connections work. This is where you should begin to take advantage of your connections, because your business connections have generated those industry results. By checking and unchecking each industry, you can see the number of possible referrals for each one. If you want to check for industries that are not in the top five, you can do so by clicking Add an Industry and then typing in the name of the industry. As you make industry selections (think verticals), the list of the top five companies in the industry also changes. You may wish to start with those companies because they are the leaders in a vertical.

When you get a connection, tell them you just need 30 minutes. The truth is, you need more like 2 hours, but you don't want to scare them off. Besides, they may turn out to be wrong for you, or they may not really be interested in helping you. The reason they may be willing to do this in the first place—other than the case that they know you well and will always agree to help you—is that your vision struck a nerve. And just maybe they want to be a lighthouse customer and have a chance to influence your product roadmap. If so, you won't just get a 2-hour follow-up meeting; it could be more like an all-day meeting. At Dover, NXP's technical team and ours spent 4 hours together, followed by a full day of technical and business site visits, at which point NXP announced that it wanted to be our lighthouse customer. Ultimately, it paid $1 million and invested in us as well. They worked closely with us—yes, influencing the product every step of the way—for 5 years, and the technical teams met every Friday.

After making sure your new connection understands what you have, why you think it is needed, and why you think it is unique, you need to interview them with a list of questions to suss out as much as you can about the market, competition, ecosystems, and other details they will want to tell you.

Here's the minimal set of questions I like to use in these interviews (I'll use NXP's responses as Dover's lighthouse customer for the example answers):

Dover: Do you know this is a real problem in the market?

NXP: Clearly cybersecurity is affecting all our customers.

Dover: Do you have the problem we solve?

NXP: Our customers do, so we do.

Dover: Do you think, based on what I have told you about our product, that we solve this problem?

NXP: There is nothing like your product, and no one else comes close with theirs.

Dover: What is our minimum viable product (MVP), in your opinion?

NXP: Just stopping the most common type of attack, called buffer overflow, will be a huge step up and a differentiator.

Dover: Who do you think is our competition?

NXP: Mostly it is going to be Arm.

Dover: Is the competition a close call, or are we radically better?

NXP: We would say radically better, but the noise in the market [overwhelming marketing communication] makes the message from Arm stand out and confuse most customers [into thinking their solution is all they need].

Dover: What markets are the best for us to go after?

NXP: Probably industrial, like automation and robotics, but then automotive after that.

Dover: What is the business model(s) that work best in this world?

NXP: We are used to paying a fee up front and then a per-chip royalty, which is called IP Licensing, and that is standard in our industry.

Dover: Is our solution complete such that we will be able to close sales, or is it missing something critical?

NXP: We have the missing components ourselves, so we are going to be a real solution when combined. Other customers might not have what we have, and you will need it.

Dover: What existing systems does our product have to work with to be accepted by prospective customers?

NXP: Really, it is all about working with various Arm processors, because they are the "800-pound gorilla" and dominate.

Dover: Who is the buyer? Who influences them and needs to support a purchase decision?

NXP: The head of a business unit, but they need the head of hardware, the head of software, the head of marketing, and a senior architect to buy off on the decision.

This is not an exhaustive list, and there may be more specific questions you need to include. But answers to this set, especially from a few potential lighthouse customers, will be invaluable for entry into their market and achieving PMF.

Back from these interviews, focus on product first and map out what the gaps in the product are, according to the aggregate of all interviews. Ask:

- How will you get that technical work done (homegrown, purchased, or partner with someone)?
- How long will that work take?
- How much will that cost?

This last question may drive a financing round before you are ready to enter the market. But it is critical to know this now, before you try to enter the market, get shot down, and then must withdraw, rework the product, and reenter the market.

Dover Microsystem's technology

Dover's CoreGuard is a hybrid hardware/software oversight solution. Oversight is a term from the Department of Defense's (DoD) 1983 so-called Orange Book that described its desired way to secure the Pentagon's most critical systems: those tasked with command and control. The Orange Book defines an oversight system as independent from the execution system, watching every instruction the execution system processes and determining whether it is the correct instruction. If not, it is likely part of an attack. CoreGuard's hardware is unassailable—unlike software, no one can manipulate hardware that is etched in silicon—and it provides oversight by having access to each instruction in the companion execution system. Micropolicies are security, safety, and privacy rules defining what types of oversight are to be done based on the types of attacks that must be prevented from succeeding. Micropolicies are small and are focused on a specific type of software flaw that can be exploited and turned into a cyberattack. Micropolicies are also fungible so that they can be updated over time. They drive the hardware and inform it about what decisions are to be made for each type of instruction being executed. The third and final component of CoreGuard is metadata, which is application-specific data that informs micropolicies about the software being executed.

For each instruction being executed by the execution system (also known simply as a processor), CoreGuard hardware gains access to that instruction via an instruction trace port coming out of the processor and decodes it. It then looks for the relevant micropolicies for this type of instruction and provides appropriate metadata to that micropolicy. The ultimate job of the hardware is to ascertain, in real time, whether the instruction is correct and should be allowed or if the processor needs to be stopped and notified that it is being attacked.

Three policies are considered essential and are always present: a heap micropolicy for buffer overflow, a stack micropolicy for stack smashing and return-oriented programming attacks, and a read–write–execute micropolicy that will not allow unauthorized writes to memory, thereby blocking code-injection attacks. Metadata comes in two forms: static and dynamic. Static metadata is generated in a build-time by the software compiler (either of the two standard C/C++ programming language compilers called GCC and LLVM) for the program (where functions start and exit, where global variables reside, the layout of the stack for each function, etc.). A micropolicy linker uses this information to generate metadata that is loaded as the application loads. Dynamic metadata comes from functions Dover provides that need to generate metadata at runtime, such as buffer information generated by a standard memory allocation library routine called malloc.

14.4   *The moral of this anecdote*

An MVP is the simplest product you can provide to early adopter (aka lighthouse) customers that they can use sufficiently well to provide feedback about it and that they assert is valuable enough to purchase. An MVP requires intense focus and whole-company obsession and may require team and product changes along the way. Getting it right is a prerequisite to proving PMF. As anecdote 15 ("Product–market fit: Making sure the dogs will eat your dog food") makes clear, there is never a startup that succeeds without it.

Product–market fit: Making sure the dogs will eat your dog food

- What is the law of startup success, and what is the most important factor for success? Answer: market!
- How should you think about determining your product–market fit?
- No startup is ever successful without PMF. Do you have a companywide obsession to achieve it?

Proving PMF is what defines the success of a startup. There are things in a startup you can work on and improve, and there are things you can't. The most common thing a startup can't fix later is PMF. Get this wrong, and it is difficult to back up and go at it again fast enough before your cash runway gets too short (see anecdote 18, "Burn rate and runway—or, where is the edge of that cliff?"). Stating this more positively, if you get PMF right and your customers (aka "the dogs") like your product (aka "your dog food") so much that they will buy it (aka "eat it"), your chance of success is very high.

On this topic, I will share quotes from two very good sources:

- A blog post from Marc Andreessen, the cofounder of Netscape (the first widely used web browser) and Andreessen Horowitz (one of the most successful Silicon Valley venture capital firms)[1]
- Andy Rachleff, the founder of Benchmark Capital and a professor at Stanford Business School, who coined the term product–market fit and created Rachleff's Law of Startup Success, which I outline later[2]

15.1 Pillars of startup success

PMF is tightly coupled with anecdote 14, "Getting to minimum viable product with lighthouse customers," and anecdote 16, "Go-to-market: How to make your business viable and grow." In the GTM process, a critical step is proving PMF. This anecdote focuses on that, so when you get to GTM, the PMF step is done, and you can then fill out the rest of the GTM process.

I like to motivate this PMF discussion by examining the three foundational pillars of a startup: team, product, and market. I will go through each of them to consider which of these pillars has the strongest correlation to startup success. It is also important to recognize the flip side: of team, product, and market, which is most dangerous if weak? To use the metaphor from this anecdote's title, which would most contribute to the dogs *not* eating your dog food?

15.1.1 Team

Most people, including most entrepreneurs and many VCs, will say without hesitation that team is the most important factor in the success of a startup. Certainly, as you go through the list of people who make up the team, that seems self-evident. The CEO must be experienced, have vision, understand the problem and the startup's solution, know how to raise money, attract good people, and be a good manager, among many other important attributes. The CTO needs to be technically rock solid if it is a tech company, as do the founders. During every due diligence I have witnessed, the thing the investors spend the most time on is always the team. The reason team seems obviously to be the most important factor in the very early days of the startup is that it's what you and the early investors know. You may not even have a product yet or have had time to fully explore the market.

No doubt about it, team is of vital importance. In many areas, the expertise you need is hard to find, and once you find it, you don't want to let it go. Really, the key question about team, as Marc Andreessen said in his "Product/Market Fit" blog post, is "You look

---

[1] Marc Andreessen and Andreessen Horowitz, "Product/Market Fit," *Business Management for Electrical Engineers and Computer Scientists* (blog), Stanford University, June 25, 2007, https://web.stanford.edu/class/ee204/ProductMarketFit.html.

[2] An interview with Andy that highlights his views on how you know if you have PMF is available at https://greatness.floodgate.com/episodes/andy-rachleff-on-how-to-know-if-youve-got-product-market-fit-XxGvX8DH/transcript.

at a startup and ask, will this team be able to optimally execute against their opportunity?" In that same blog, however he points out that prior to a Series B, experience has been proven to be overrated. He said, "[T]he history of the tech industry is full of highly successful startups that were staffed primarily by people who had never 'done it before.'"

All of this makes it just feel right to say that team is the most important component of startup success. But it's not.

Certainly no one wants to take the position that people are not important. Of the three pillars, team is what you have the most control over. You are hiring them, and you can fire them. Of course, it is the team that creates the product. Hopefully a great team gets you at least a decent product and ideally a great one. Let's look at product now.

15.1.2 Product

If you ask engineers which of the three pillars is the most important, you will uniformly hear product. Great products are what created Silicon Valley and Boston's startup community, they will argue. From San Francisco to San Jose, and along Boston's Route 128, you will see plenty of evidence of huge companies that are built on highly successful products.

Let's face it: the technology business is a product business. We have come to identify tech startups with the invention of innovative products that millions and millions of people buy and use. In "Product/Market Fit," Andreessen said, "Apple and Google are the best companies in the industry today because they build the best products. Without the product there is no company. Just try having a great team and no product, or a great market and no product."

Lots of great teams have not created great products. Microsoft is a huge, successful company that didn't necessarily have the best product. But Microsoft had a *sufficient* product aimed at huge markets at just the right time and grew those products to dominate almost every market it entered. Another example is Adobe Flash Player, which was so buggy and insecure that Steve Jobs refused to allow Flash on any Apple products. Winning products are extremely hard to create. It is not just a matter of excellent engineering. The best products have the right features presented in an easy-to-use fashion that is high-quality with few bugs. Again, Apple and Google are cases in point. They consistently create the best products in whatever industry they are selling to. And they make it look easy. But it isn't. A product is only great if it is applied to a great market. I strongly agree with Andreessen when he says, "*[M]arket* is the most important factor in a startup's success or failure."

15.1.3 Market

The *New Oxford American Dictionary* defines a market as "an area or arena in which commercial dealings are conducted." Arena is the part of that definition we want to focus on. New Oxford American says an arena is "a place or scene of activity."

This is why we can say, for example, that financial services, oil and gas, and consumer electronics are markets: each is a scene of activity where commercial dealings are conducted. The stock market is a market because public companies have stock (ownership) in their companies that they want to offer for sale, and institutions, funds, and individuals want to buy stocks to own portions of various companies they think will get more valuable over time so they can sell those shares and make a profit. In these and thousands of other markets, some people have something to sell, and some people want to buy those things.

How did so many technology companies, from Adobe to Google to Apple to Oracle, get so big? They did not all have the best products. It was market that made them grow so big and dominate their industry. In this assessment, I completely agree with, in addition to Andreessen, the other thought leaders of startup success and PMF, Andy Rachleff of Benchmark Capital and Don Valentine of Sequoia Capital, as well as organizations like HubSpot, Mailchimp, Intuit, and others: huge success comes from having a stupendous market!

Team and product are things you control, and you can change them if that is essential—you can add or subtract people from your team, and you can add or subtract things from your product. But you don't control the market, so you must find (or create—that's really hard) it.

Andreessen explained, "In a great market—a market with lots of real potential customers—the market pulls product out of the startup." It's sort of like how bacon in any form seems to just pull a dog in and get them to eat what's being offered.

For me, this is what happened with WebSpective, which launched its website load-balancing product in 1997 just as the world was realizing that this new Web thing was going to be a way to interact with customers directly and dynamically, and the market was going to perhaps be the biggest market ever conceived. It is also what happened with Google. When Google arrived on the scene in 1998 with its incredibly fast PageRank search algorithm, AltaVista from Digital Equipment Corporation (DEC) was the de facto internet search leader. It seemed like overnight, Google was in, and AltaVista was out. Google was so much better that the market shifted instantly to the better product.

> **REMEMBER**   As Andreessen put it in his "Product/Market Fit" blog post, "The market needs to be fulfilled and the market *will* be fulfilled, by the first viable product that comes along."

Andreessen should know—he wrote the very first browser, called Mosaic. Microsoft quickly came out with its Internet Explorer browser, and because it was bundled with the operating system, it immediately became dominant. But Andreessen then founded Netscape and showed how a browser is supposed to work. Once Netscape did that, no one wanted to go back, and Netscape raced past Microsoft to become and stay number one in the market for several years. The market *will be fulfilled.*

When the market is great, the product doesn't also need to be great; it just needs to basically work (AltaVista grew quickly when it launched and was alone). Also, the market doesn't care how good the team is. All that matters is that the team can produce the viable product that meets the market needs. When the market is that good, it is relatively easy to upgrade your team as you go. (The great market also literally pulls great people into your startup who want to join your team.) I am describing a dream come true where customers are knocking down your door to buy your product. You just must be ready to respond to that rapidly growing demand (an enviable problem to have).

However, flipping this around, if you are aimed at a weak or nonexistent market, you can have the best product backed by a dream team, and it will not work—your startup is going to fail. The first incarnation of Dover was in this situation, but, hanging on by its fingernails, it got a second chance.

In the late 1990s, even though Apple, Netscape, Lotus, Stacker, and Borland were no longer startups and were established in their markets, Microsoft used some techniques that violated US antitrust laws to take those companies' markets away from them.[3] In the case of Netscape, Microsoft put features in the Windows operating system that only Microsoft Internet Explorer could access, so it worked much better than Netscape Navigator and Navigator sales went through the floor. In the case of Stacker, whose very popular product did disk compression, Microsoft built that capability into the operating system, removing the need to ever buy Stacker's product. Suddenly, without a market, Netscape and Stacker disappeared, and Borland and Lotus followed behind them a few years later.

Lots of startups—most, actually—that have *a solution in search of a problem* can spend years in a frustrating search for customers who don't exist for their marvelous product built by their marvelous team. They started with a vision and built a great product, but none of that matters when there is no market. Unfortunately, many tech founders have a solution in search of a market. This anecdote is hereby dedicated to them.

Andy Rachleff teaches marketing at Stanford, where he is considered *the* professor of PMF. He created Rachleff's Law of Startup Success, which he used in his Stanford class and is reproduced in Marc Andreessen's blog.

Rachleff's Law of Startup Success

The #1 company-killer is lack of market:

- When a great team meets a lousy market, the market wins.
- When a lousy team meets a great market, the market wins.
- When a great team meets a great market, something special happens.

Andreessen wrote about this law and said in his "Product/Market Fit" blog post, "You can obviously screw up a great market—and that has been done, and not infrequently—but assuming the team is baseline competent and the product is fundamentally acceptable, a great market will tend to equal success and a poor market will tend to equal failure. Market matters most."

---

[3] *United States v. Microsoft Corp.*, 87 F. Supp. 2d 30 (D.D.C. 2000).

And with that discussion of startup success and a clear understanding that the market is what matters most by far, we are ready to discuss PMF.

15.2 Defining PMF

Here is the broadly accepted definition of PMF, found on the VC firm Andreessen Horowitz's a16z[4] blog:

> Product–market *fit is being in a good market with a product that can satisfy that market.*[5]

The definition says "a good market," and that is, most importantly, one that is growing. For a startup, it is hopefully one that is growing rapidly. And perhaps it's a changing market that is creating new opportunities a startup can take advantage of more easily than a large company can. Sometimes what is going on—which startups are expert at taking advantage of—is that a market is being disrupted.

In some cases, the startup is going after a market that is not yet mature or one that might not even exist yet. Although it is possible to create a new market from scratch, it is exceedingly rare. With the iPod, Apple created the market of portable music libraries and then turned around and created the smartphone market.

Another helpful example of a PMF that disrupted its market is Airbnb. Before Airbnb, people could find a bed and breakfast using various travel sites, but travelers typically booked through the bed and breakfast directly. Airbnb totally disrupted that market, changing how B&B owners rented their rooms to guests, and that created an impressively large market for Airbnb to have a dominant market share in almost instantly. It sold services to the B&B owners as a customer-friendly way for them to create and deliver their property listings to potential renters in an attractive, browser-based SaaS application that few B&B owners could have achieved on their own. Airbnb also delivered customers to those owners, giving them real value (financial transactions handled by Airbnb) they were willing to pay for (fees to Airbnb on successful transactions), which, according to Statista, generated enormous 2022 revenues of $8.4 billion.[6] Matching available bed-and-breakfast rooms to prospective renters is *the good market* for which Airbnb has a SaaS product, which satisfies that market—Airbnb has PMF.

WebSpective, a startup I cofounded in 1997, was also disruptive in the market it entered: the 2-year-old Web. As people began to realize the Web was going to turn into applications where financial transactions would occur, a new market emerged called *website load balancing*. Our tool pulled an array of web servers into service to keep a website from crashing when there was an influx of visitors. Website load balancing was *the good market*, and WebSpective had a product that satisfied that market—WebSpective had PMF.

---

[4] A *numeronym* is a word, usually an abbreviation, composed partially or wholly of numerals. The a16z blog is named using a numeronym of Andressen Horowitz, which is the letter a followed by 16 letters and ending with z.

[5] Tren Griffin, "12 Things About Product-Market Fit," *a16z* (blog), Andreessen Horowitz, February 18, 2017, https://a16z.com/12-things-about-product-market-fit/.

[6] "Revenue of Airbnb worldwide from 2017 to 2022," *Statista*, March 2, 2023, www.statista.com/statistics/1193134/airbnb-revenue-worldwide.

Notice that in these examples I did not talk about how good or bad its product was, just what it was. I also never mentioned how good the CEO or any other member of the team was. This is because market is *the* most important factor in PMF; and more importantly, as discussed earlier, it's ultimately the most important single factor in startup success.

PMF lessons from the field

MasPar (1988)

MasPar had both a strong CEO and a strong CTO. The company created a massively parallel supercomputer product that quickly attracted a strong marquee customer following, including the NSA. But its value proposition was its performance advantage against the conventional computers that quickly caught up with it. Essentially, its market (and initial PMF) disappeared, and MasPar faded into nothingness.

WebSpective (1996)

WebSpective had a weak CEO but a talented technical team with a useful product and an enormous (all of the Web) market. WebSpective had a blockbuster—53× revenues—exit. (It had great dog food that a heck of a lot of dogs wanted to eat!)

GeoTrust (1999)

GeoTrust had an okay team and an okay product but a PMF that was incredibly effective at achieving rapid growth in a huge market based on the growth of the Web. It was purchased in a "defensive" acquisition by a competitor that was bleeding market share to GeoTrust. The result was that GeoTrust had a nice 5× revenue exit. (Good dog food!)

Service Integrity (2002)

Service Integrity had a great team, a struggling CEO, and an okay product, but the market was a complete dud. Service Integrity hit the wall with no skid marks. The competitors also realized there was no market, but they scrambled faster and harder, and they all got bought as a feature in a much bigger company's much bigger product. No one did great, but none of the others just liquidated.

Aguru Images (2006)

Aguru Images had a great team led by a visionary CEO/CTO who created a world-class product to create computer-generated images of actors' faces. However, the market was miniscule—too small to determine PMF. Aguru was sold for pennies on the dollar.

Dover Microsystems (2017)

Dover had a great team who produced a technically very impressive product. The commercial market was very bad to nonexistent, but the DoD market was strong. Dover almost died—I had to do a 180-degree pivot, lay off the entire team, and hire a new CEO from the DoD world to survive. Dover 2.0, a company servicing only the DoD market, where PMF was excellent, now continues its journey to whatever the final outcome may be.

15.3 *The obsession necessary to obtain PMF*

Getting product fit right takes persistence and a whole lot of luck. As many in the startup world have observed, companies (that is, teams) often stumble into PMF. That is not to say you should just pray and wait and you, too, will eventually stumble into it. No, teams are trying and trying, and then they eventually get it right. They don't follow a straight line to the perfect outcome right out of the gate, and they rarely just form the company and have PMF pop out of their heads without interacting with any customers. Luck is a big factor in finding fit. That might surprise you, as you think "Well, how do I control luck?" I believe luck comes because of hard, focused work. You find it when you keep at it over and over, learning as you go, until you get multiple prospects giving affirmation that your constantly evolving MVP fits many (enough) of your prospective customers' needs.

Okay, it's more than just hard, focused work; it's a flat-out obsession. It's that important. You need to do whatever is required to get to PMF, including changing people who are not cutting it, altering the product, and maybe even rewriting it completely. Perhaps you need to switch to a different vertical market or change your business model. Sometimes the right answer is to say no to a customer when what they are asking for just doesn't make sense for the stage you are at or when you can't find any other customers asking for the same solution. On the other hand, you may have to say yes to a customer, even though they are asking for something unique to them, because they are so important and all the other things they need are universally needed in their vertical, which makes saying yes the right thing to do. This obsessive quest for PMF is so important that you must do whatever is necessary to achieve it, ignoring everything else you wish you could do but that will have to wait.

You will never meet a successful startup that has not reached PMF. Once it has achieved PMF, it may not yet have done a bunch of operational tasks that startups eventually have to do, like develop a partner strategy, have a solid marketing plan, create solid hiring and compensation plans, have a smart sales model, put a customer pipeline process in place, lay out financial controls, establish standard IP policies, and so forth. But do these things after proving PMF. In my experience, companies that have all this stuff buttoned up perfectly but still have not achieved PMF will soon hit the wall and fail.

> **The Lean Product Playbook steps to achieve PMF[7]**
> 1 Determine who your target customer is in your target vertical market.
> 2 Identify underserved needs of these customers (the problem).
> 3 Define your value proposition.
> 4 Specify the minimum viable product (MVP) set of features.

---

[7] Dan Olsen, *The Lean Product Playbook: How to Innovate with Minimum Viable* Products and *Rapid Customer Feedback* (John Wiley & Sons, 2015).

(continued)
5   Build a prototype of the MVP.
6   Test the MVP with the target customers from step 1.
7   If you do not get strong affirmation, iterate back to step 4 (as many times as necessary).
8   MVP is done. Start selling!

15.4   *The moral of this anecdote*

Startup success fundamentally requires team, product, and market. Most assume team is the number one, and a great team is important. But market is the most important factor by far and must be figured out by getting PMF right. PMF is about being in a good market with a product that can satisfy that market. Remember, team and product are fungible, but market is not. There is not, and never has been, a successful startup that did not achieve PMF. You must get there so you can be one of those who succeed!

Go-to-market:
How to make your business viable and grow

- Have you got minimum viable product and product–market fit nailed? Time for go-to-market.
- Did you get 40 customer interviews across all your prospective vertical markets? It's worth the effort.
- How do you go from initial revenues to market engagement and profitability? With a solid GTM strategy.

This topic is closely tied to anecdotes 14, "Getting to minimum viable product with lighthouse customers" and 15, "Product–market fit: Making sure the dogs will eat your dog food." Here we will be building our *go-to-market* (GTM) strategy on top of *minimum viable product* (MVP) and *product–market fit* (PMF). In my first two startups, where I was going from academia into the technology startup world, I was not cognizant of what GTM really meant or of how to develop a strategy for it. But this did not hurt me because at my first startup I was down in the trenches of product development, and my second one was during the dot-com bubble so, without a GTM at all, we managed to sell it for $106 million on only $2 million in revenues. I literally thought all there was to GTM was getting out into the market, intuiting who the customers were who needed our product, knocking on their doors, and selling to them.

This meant I had a real knowledge gap when it was up to me to drive the next company and make it into a real business. I had to learn how to develop a disciplined process to get customers and grow revenues.

If there is a problem with the product once you engage with the market, you can fix it—assuming it's not completely the wrong product. If there is a problem with the team, you can fix that, too, with the right hires and surgical layoffs. You may think that if your GTM turns out to be wrong, you can adjust it once you engage with the market, but I've lost companies because we were just plain wrong about the correct GTM. My companies with unsuccessful (or no) GTM that failed or had to sustain massive, life-saving pivots include GeoTrust, Service Integrity, and Dover.

Given that you have an MVP and a proven PMF, that means you have a product that will sell into a market that wants and needs it. What you need now is a GTM strategy that incorporates every person in every department of your company doing what they need to do to maximize your reach to prospective buyers and partners who will help you grow and steadily get more and more revenues. What I want you to get out of this anecdote is an understanding of the process of building a strategy for your GTM such that you will find a lot of the right buyers in the right market and start to achieve steady growth. GTM is about getting to profitability and thus to success.

16.1 GTM is one of the most important early activities of a startup

What are the three most important things a startup needs to get right, right away? You may be tempted to say cash, cash, cash. You are not wrong that "cash is king" in the startup world. You are also not wrong to say that most startups fail because they run out of it. But why is cash king, and why do so many startups run out of it? Again, it's perhaps obvious, but it's because the company spends more cash than it brings in. That is just not sustainable. GTM is so critical to an early-stage company because even a year's worth of cash—that might have come via a small equity investment or the founding team—does not give you much time to figure out how to stop taking expensive money (from investors) and switch to the best kind of money (from customers). And that requires a well-crafted, whole-company GTM strategy.

> **DEFINITION** *Go-to-market* is the plan of an organization, utilizing its sales force and distributors, to deliver its unique value proposition to customers and achieve competitive advantage. It helps identify a target audience, outline marketing and sales strategies, and align key stakeholders. It requires that PMF already be proven.

16.2 My introduction to GTM

My first exposure to a formal GTM formulation was at Service Integrity. We had two investors, both named Richard. Luckily, one used the nickname Dick. The other, who went by Richard, was reuniting the WebSpective founding team for this new startup after he found out from a mutual friend that I was between things and might be available. Richard was relatively new to investing after a long stint as CEO of a startup that had a successful exit. He joined forces with three high-school buddies, all of whom had built and run successful companies. They believed deep operational experience (usually as CEO) was essential for anyone doing venture investing, and they decided to have that be their new VC firm's differentiation. Because they were so new on the Boston investing scene, Richard needed to bring Dick into the deal. Dick was a partner at a very established, somewhat conservative firm with offices that looked like a bank. Richard wanted to partner with someone more established on his first few deals as he built his credibility and reputation in the small Boston entrepreneurial community.

Upon first meeting me, Dick made it clear that he would only accept me as CEO for the first 18 months. After that, he expected us to bring in a CEO with a lot more sales and marketing experience. I can't help but wonder if, unbeknownst to me, I had some sort of tattoo on my forehead that said, "This guy is no sales guy"; how else did people keep getting this impression? About a year into building Service Integrity's product and testing it on various vertical market segments, Dick said I needed to hire Peter Brumme, who was an expert on developing a GTM—a process, Dick warned me, that would take three months and a lot of money, as well as total commitment from me and my whole senior team. That seemed weird to me because I still thought GTM was just marketing to, and then selling in, the market we *guessed* was going to work for us. But what I and many inexperienced entrepreneurs do way too much of is opportunistic selling to anyone they happen to get some interest from. That's unpredictable, expensive, not scalable, and therefore not sustainable.

Having an investor force this on me made me wonder whether Peter would help or simply provide another reason for the investors to be overly involved in running the company. Peter assured me that he worked directly for the company and not for the investors, a critical part of his advisory model that the investors also understood. Despite the strained introduction, Peter very quickly won me over, and we developed a strong partnership that has lasted through two decades and two stints of developing a GTM for two of my startups: Service Integrity and Dover Microsystems. Peter had developed a well-oiled GTM "training process" through his work for dozens of startups, including a couple of his own. It was immortalized in a 100-slide PowerPoint deck by this point. Unlike most business consultants I know of, Peter invested significant time (about 96 hours in person plus another 48 hours working at his home office) in each engagement—a commitment he was fairly compensated for (direct cash compensation plus some equity). But Peter's compensation was only part of the expense of developing an effective GTM. Service Integrity's entire senior team also spent valuable time on this effort, to the tune of several tens of thousands of dollars. It was well worth the expense because none of us realized how essential this consultation was to teach us how to build a GTM, and none of us had a clue how complex it would be.

At our first meeting, Peter informed me that we would be meeting for two half days per week for three months to develop our personalized GTM strategy. As CEO, I had to be at all meetings, as did the head of sales, the head of marketing, and often the head of product. Others, such as legal counsel, business development, and even the CFO, would be pulled in as deemed appropriate. Many of these half-day sessions also generated homework assignments that took an additional half day per week for at least the head of marketing, plus some engagement with our head of sales and me. Most of these homework assignments had to do with engaging with key stakeholders in potential vertical markets to soak up as much as we could (and as much as those individuals had time for) about markets, business models, and competition.

A good GTM requires a good architecture. It's sort of like not wanting to write too much code "from the hip" without a software architecture. The goal of a good software architecture is to be a framework and set of guiderails or rules so new features can be added without throwing the whole thing away and starting over—something that frequently happens when coding from the hip. A GTM architecture encompasses elements of vision, strategy, and the tactics you use to turn prospects into customers, called a customer development process (CDP). These three major elements fit together and interact as a *GTM machine*, as shown in figure 16.1. Consider this a 50,000-foot view of GTM.

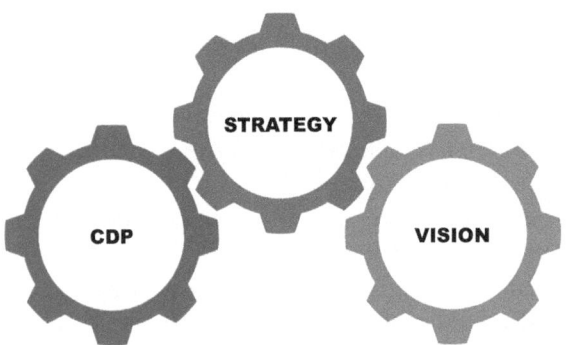

Figure 16.1   The GTM machine showing the three major GTM components

16.3   *Articulating your vision*

Let's walk through a simplified process of developing a GTM machine. The first and easiest of the GTM machine components to define is the vision statement. It's easiest because vision typically is the most fully formed concept in the mind of a founder and their team from the start. However, all too often at technology companies, including several of mine, this vision takes the form of "we have incredible technology that no one else has figured out, and it must be good for something, so someone must want to buy it." We all know that many a tech startup leads with product and then tries to find customers for that product. This GTM formulation process is precisely designed to avoid that trap.

Your vision statement should answer these simple questions:

- Why did you start this company / why did you join this team?
- What is the product or service?
- What problem does it solve?
- Why do you think it is unique such that you can beat any existing competition?

If you begin with the first three questions in the Heilmeier Catechism (see the following sidebar), you will have a good start to answering these questions. Knowing the Heilmeier Catechism will stand you in good stead as you work through the GTM process and when you go to raise money from investors because these are the questions the Defense Advanced Projects Agency (DARPA) requires each of its program managers to answer before it will invest tens of millions in a new program.

The Heilmeier Catechism questions

George H. Heilmeier, a former DARPA director (1975–1977), needed a way to get everyone at the agency on the same page when it came to deciding which of many competing proposals they would approve and fund. To do that, he crafted a set of questions that became known as the Heilmeier Catechism; they have been used ever since by the Technology Council at DARPA that evaluates all program proposals. These are precisely the same questions the leaders of a technology startup need to have answers for when entering the market as well as when seeking investment dollars. It is incredibly valuable to follow this list and recheck it frequently as you move through the evolution of your company:

- What are you trying to do? Articulate your objectives using absolutely no jargon.
- How is it done today, and what are the limits of current practice?
- What is new in your approach, and why do you think it will be successful?
- Who cares? If you are successful, what difference will it make?
- What are the risks?
- How much will it cost?
- How long will it take?
- What are the midterm and final "exams" to check for success?

Early on—or in many cases even before I founded the company—I developed the vision for a new startup. Here are a few of these vision statements aimed at each company's prospective customer:

- *GeoTrust (1999)*—"Since your websites are used in transactions with consumers or other businesses, you need to encrypt all data, and to do that, you need digital certificates on each server. Existing vendors of these certificates use a largely manual process to authenticate a customer's identity that takes four days, but our automated process only takes 10 minutes and is less than half the cost, which saves you money and time for this essential part of your online presence."
- *Aguru Images (2006)*—"Human eyes are incredibly sensitive to minute details in human faces and are not fooled by skin texturing via computer-generated imagery (CGI). This is why, in your movies where no actors or stunt people can do what the character in the film is doing, your directors must pull the camera position way back and use very distant shots so viewers can't see faces at all. With our geodesic dome employing 400 cameras, a single sitting for each actor filmed for 14 seconds will remove this restriction forever. Now close-ups of CGI-created

actors doing impossibly dangerous stunts will completely fool the audience, opening amazing possibilities for writers and directors to pursue in their films."

- *Dover Microsystems (2017)*—"The cybersecurity problem is so severe that no current systems are stopping more than 16% of all attacks. Our technology stops 95% and can be applied to almost every vertical market you service that uses any computers connected to the internet. Being early to market with this unprecedented level of cybersecurity defense will provide you a competitive advantage and will get you ahead of the coming regulations and fines levied on those whose systems allow breaches to occur."

16.4   The GTM strategy

Once you are certain you have a product that fits into several verticals you learned about during your customer interviews, it is time to delve into which of the verticals could benefit most from your product.

16.4.1   Target verticals

Start with between 12 and 20 verticals, and define detailed evaluation criteria you'll need to develop to compare one vertical to another. These criteria are specific to your company and are based on your goals. Each element in the list of criteria needs ranges for what is good, unacceptable, and in between. Now a big research project ensues; an efficient way to get this done is using interns from a business school, if you can find them. You need to fill in a huge matrix with the verticals across the top and your chosen criteria down the left side. Your goal is to identify two verticals that meet the most important criteria with strong scores.

The grandfather of marketing high-technology startups, Geoffrey Moore, in his bowling pin strategy, states emphatically that you should choose one and only one vertical. I almost completely agree with him, but I say two is the right number, not one. It is too easy to be wrong about the one, and when you find out it's not working, you must start over, but you have invested a lot of time and money. Moore's argument for not attacking more than one market at a time comes from seeing so many people think their product is horizontal and applies to almost every vertical. The list of industries (or verticals) LinkedIn uses is hundreds of markets long, and if you went after all of them, the marketing costs alone would break you. This is Moore's rationale for having just one bowling pin. I posit that if you work two simultaneously, it is not like trying to have a GTM with a horizontal approach. And if one of your two is wrong, chances are the other works better, and you are in the market making progress with it, not starting over.

At Dover, we distilled the starting group of 15 verticals down to 5 for our final "traffic light" diagram, where we color the blocks different colors based on the evaluation ranges defined earlier to indicate whether the evaluation resulted in good, neutral, or bad. The idea is that you can look at the diagram from a distance and see the best vertical(s) jumping out at you—the one(s) with the most good and the least bad. The final decision comes from a little more analysis: subjective judgment is also applied to these different criteria because some are overwhelmingly important in one direction or the other.

Table 16.1 shows the final traffic light matrix Dover used to determine the initial verticals to focus on. I decided to re-create it faithfully and not remove specifics used in security or semiconductor evaluations. That means you may not understand these terms, and that is okay. This kind of chart is always very market- and product-specific and so is rife with arcane details. This is just to provide a sense of the kinds of criteria being considered and how the different shades start to jump out and point to the right choices (which were Communications Infrastructure and Industrial IoT).

Table 16.1   Using the Dover evaluation matrix to narrow the final number of chosen verticals to two

Device makers	Automotive	Communications Infrastructure	Industrial IoT	Consumer IoT	Storage
Segment	Infotainment, GPS, & ADAS	Routers, Hubs, & Modems	Industrial	Connected Home	SSD & HDD
# target accounts	100	500+	2000+	500+	<100
# ASIC starts	980	6120	251	455	457
# ASIC sales	70M	1.1B	1.85B	991M	880M
# device unit sales	169M	750M	4.16B	1.2B	600M
SAM	$393M	$350M	$420M	$400M	$91M
Cost per attack	$1.1B	$886,560 (DNS)	$13M	N/A	N/A
Budget metrics	■ R&D budget: $1B ■ Margins: 5%–15% ■ ASP: $49	■ R&D budget: <$500M ■ Margins: 20% ■ ASP: $50	■ R&D budget: >$500M ■ Margins: 19% ■ ASP: $64	■ R&D budget: $50M ■ Margins: < 25% ■ ASP: $42	■ R&D budget: $150M ■ Margins: >50% ■ ASP: $67–$102
Timing	Slow (2–3 years)	Fast (<1 year)	Medium (1–3 years)	Medium (1–2 years)	Fast (<1 year)
Upgrade cycle	Medium (6.7 years)	Short (3–4 years)	Long (8–10 years)	Medium/Long (5–12 years)	Long (10 years)
Current value	Medium	Medium	Medium	Medium	High
Future value	High	High	High	Medium	Medium
Compelling need	Safety	Network security	Operational security and safety	Privacy	Data security and privacy
Top 3 pain points	■ Safety ■ Liability ■ Regulations	■ Service interruptions ■ User privacy ■ Liability	■ Process disruption ■ More points of attack (edge) ■ Safety and trade secrets	■ Broad privacy breaches ■ Reputational risk ■ Liability	■ Privacy of data in motion ■ Commoditization ■ Differentiation needs

Table 16.1   Using the Dover evaluation matrix to narrow the final number of chosen verticals to two *(continued)*

Device makers	Automotive	Communications Infrastructure	Industrial IoT	Consumer IoT	Storage
Buyer profile	▪ Mostly technical	▪ Mostly technical	▪ Mostly technical	▪ Less technical	▪ Medium technical
Competition	Entrenched: few Other: varied, HW & SW	Entrenched: several Other: onus on InfoSec	Entrenched: large firms Other: large firms, HW & SW	All over the map, lots of SW	▪ Encryption (Rambus) ▪ Little else
CoreGuard obstacles	Regulation/standard compliance	Agile development cycles, lukewarm on security	TAM/SAM shrinks w/o low power product available	Consumer apathy and unwillingness to pay	Market only interested in encryption
GTM: technology fit	▪ Complex SW stacks ▪ Consumer OS/interface ▪ High performance ▪ Power/area OK	▪ Complex SW stacks ▪ High performance ▪ Power/area OK ▪ Varied cores	▪ Work with basic OS ▪ Platform compatibility ▪ Quick SW updates ▪ SW integrations/ expansions ▪ Bluetooth/Wifi connectivity	▪ Work with basic OS ▪ Port to more complex OS ▪ Quick SW updates ▪ SW integrations/ expansions ▪ Bluetooth/Wifi connectivity	▪ Flow translation from host ▪ Encryption essential ▪ High performance ▪ Low gate count
GTM: market fit	▪ More security attacks ▪ Bigger risks ▪ Trends (autonomous)	▪ More network attacks ▪ More user risk ▪ Increasing security costs	▪ Process disruption costly ▪ Sophisticated attackers ▪ Distributed attack points	▪ Highly visible risks ▪ Privacy is "hot issue" ▪ Distributed attack points	▪ HW-centric market ▪ Data security critical
GTM: audience fit	▪ Technically savvy ▪ Project managers ▪ PMs ▪ Engineers	▪ Technically savvy-ish ▪ Project/product mgrs ▪ Engineers ▪ Architects	▪ Technically savvy ▪ PMs ▪ Security managers	▪ Less technically savvy ▪ PMs ▪ Security managers	▪ Technically savvy ▪ PMs, CTOs ▪ Security managers ▪ HW architects
GTM: leverage	▪ Upstream ▪ Rental car firms ▪ Ride-sharing firms ▪ Trucking industry ▪ On-demand (e.g. bikes)	▪ Major vendors ▪ Large implementers ▪ Enterprise SW use can drive selection decisions	▪ Existing platforms > Arm, IBM ▪ Managed cyber > BMC, ServiceNow ▪ Other stack players > Rambus, Gemalto	▪ Existing platforms > Amazon, Google ▪ Other stack players > Rambus, Gemalto	▪ SiFive ▪ Western Digital
Top 3 pros	▪ Manageable universe ▪ Safety is need-to-have ▪ Technical audience	▪ Fast time-to-market ▪ Demanding users ▪ Increasing security costs	▪ Expanding market ▪ Security lapses = real pain ▪ Low regulatory overhead	▪ Expanding market ▪ Privacy concerns growing ▪ High-profile market players	▪ Fast time-to-market ▪ Differentiation needs ▪ High margins

Table 16.1   Using the Dover evaluation matrix to narrow the final number of chosen verticals to two *(continued)*

Device makers	Automotive	Communications Infrastructure	Industrial IoT	Consumer IoT	Storage
Top 3 cons	▪ Slow time-to-market ▪ Low margins ▪ Regulatory environment	▪ Slow to address security ▪ Security is after-thought ▪ Infrastructure "inertia"	▪ Lack of standardization ▪ Outdated, specialized HW	▪ Less technical buyers ▪ Pricing pressure (low ASP) ▪ Market used to crowded SW	▪ X86 trending up ▪ Thin market for security ▪ Limited leverage

☐ Bad   ▨ Neutral   ▩ Good

16.4.2 Roadmap

The next big step is to build out the ecosystem map for your company. Who are the competitors and partners, and what future verticals might you move into? What are the standard parameters that vendors are measured against? This analysis is best done on a large physical whiteboard, a digital whiteboard, or mind maps; surprisingly, a wall using sticky notes works well, too, because you need to keep moving parts around. When completed, this needs to be codified and turned into a chart for preservation and presentation.

We worked very hard to distill these different categories (partners, channels, markets) into a roadmap diagram. Figure 16.2 is the Dover roadmap diagram from our

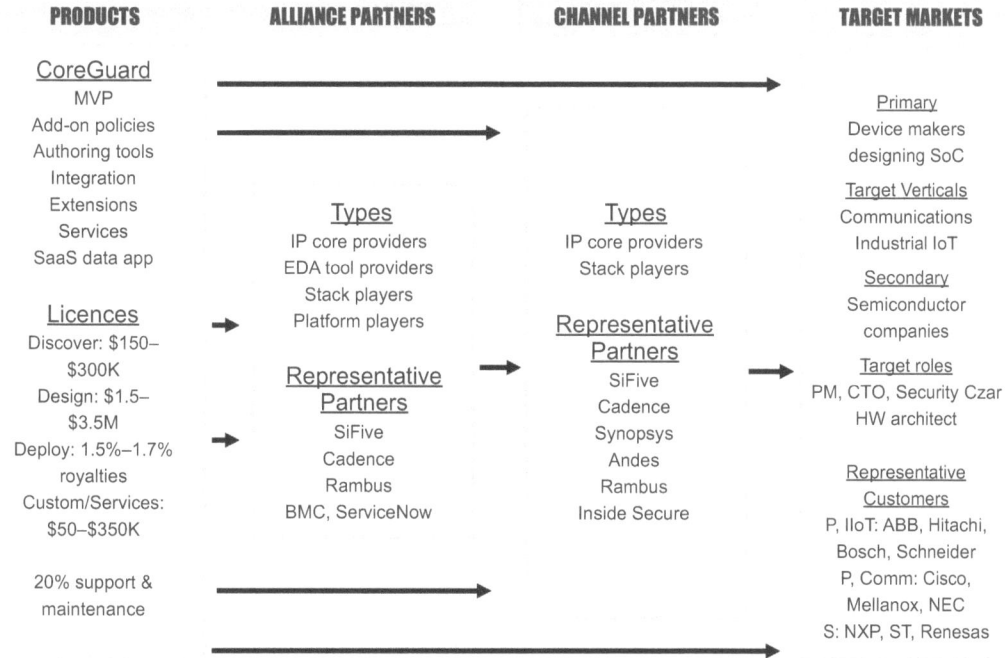

Figure 16.2   Roadmap diagram from Dover's GTM

initial GTM work, which shows how the dependencies begin to be nice and clear when put into this form. From left to right, the first column is about the product and how it is sold. Alliance partners are people who help promote your product to their customers, but they do not take on any role in selling it directly, whereas channel partners resell and take a percentage of each sale. Someone can be an alliance partner and a channel partner: they may start at arm's length as an alliance partner and then want to take a more active role as they see the company progress and a great opportunity emerge. Finally, the target markets are listed with a designation of primary versus secondary, which indicates priority and preference.

16.5 *Making sure your GTM works*

Some elements need to be in place before you can even ask the question "How do I know this GTM is going to work?":

- You need a value proposition that you have validated in discussions with people in your chosen verticals. (Do they have the problem you are attacking, and do they see the solution the same way you do?)
- You need to have a business model that is likewise verified. (How do these enterprises like to buy products like yours? Refer to anecdote 13, "Your business model: The beating heart of your business."
- Your product needs to be ready to engage with customers, meaning it must be an MVP based on what you have learned about your vertical markets in these weeks of outreach. Refer to anecdote 14, "Getting to minimum viable product with lighthouse customers."
- You must have a good understanding of the competitive landscape as well as your competitive posture in your vertical markets.
- A good GTM requires a good architecture, just like good software depends on the solid foundation of a good architecture. This will ensure that your GTM meshes well with your overall vision as well as the tactics you use to engage with prospects and turn them into customers.
- A good GTM must be integrated across all functional areas: R&D, sales, marketing, business development, and customer support. It is a whole-company strategy. Everyone plays a vital role and must work together smoothly with a crystal-clear, shared view of what the GTM is. This way, you avoid redundancies and inconsistencies in how you approach the market, making limited resources as effective as possible.
- The lack of GTM integration across all functions in a startup is perhaps one of the biggest stumbling blocks I've seen, even in smaller companies. Different functional areas get siloed, and soon the limited presence a small company has in the marketplace starts to dissipate due to lack of consistency. That costs time and money you don't have.
- Effective GTMs must be systemic both inside and outside the company. This is critical because by definition, a startup has no leverage in the marketplace. You

are unknown; you don't have strong partnerships yet. And especially if your model is direct selling, all the heavy lifting must be done by your team, who will be resource-constrained.

- Effective GTMs must be hypervigilant about execution because markets are unforgiving, resources are limited, and time is not the startup's friend as competitors change their offerings and target markets evolve and shift.
- Successful GTMs need to be tested. In software development, we like to say, "If you didn't test it, it won't work," even when the feature in question is trivial to implement. The same is true for GTMs. The idea is to do controlled experiments that test market adjacencies, new product functionality, different channel partner types, unique alliance structures, and so on.

By far the most important GTM formation step at this point is to spend time talking to prospective customers in your chosen verticals and, if you are lucky, to identify a lighthouse customer that is so interested in your product that it will get involved early and help shape the product to fit its, and hopefully the market's, needs. Along the way, you need to verify or modify the business model you believe is right for your product and determine the service-addressable market (SAM) size for your chosen verticals to make sure for yourself—and for your ability to attract investors—that you have something that is a big opportunity ready to take off.

Serviceable-addressable market

In the past, entrepreneurs frequently quoted total addressable market (TAM) to express the opportunity size they were chasing. This is the number you get when you read about the size of the automotive market, for example. It includes everything from tires to navigation systems. It bears very little relation to how big the opportunity is for you. Some people would literally say, "Okay, the TAM is $2 billion, and our goal is to get 1% of that in two years." That's a nice round $20 million in revenue, and to get that in year two of your startup's existence is worthy of writing home about. But what was the basis for predicting you would get 1% of that market? Likely it was a pure stab in the dark. That approach never fools venture capitalists these days, and they will consider you not credible if you try it.

Instead, what works is to calculate the SAM. SAM answers this question: "If everyone in this vertical market who *could* buy my product did, what would the total revenue to me be?" You take the number of companies in each of your chosen verticals and assume that each one (that makes sense) buys your product. Add up that many sales, and that is your SAM. When Dover added up the SAMs from all 15 vertical markets we considered, we came up with $8.5 billion as our total SAM, which investors and employees considered a plenty big opportunity to go after.

The rest of GTM is setting up systems and processes to execute the strategy you have established and testing how it is working as you go with a once-a-year tune-up to keep the strategy on track.

With this, you have a strong set of tools to use to prepare for entering the market, and your whole company is ready to deliver your products and services to the right vertical markets in which you can begin to grow. Of course, no matter how good your planning is, you should get out there, test the messaging and hypotheses you developed during this planning, and evaluate how you are doing, whether sales are happening, and whether your revenue is growing; if not, time to modify some of what you developed for your GTM and then go out there again.

Some of my GTM lessons
GeoTrust

GeoTrust, which started out delivering B2B online trust to facilitate trusted transactions between businesses, had to go through two significant GTM recraftings. One was to switch from being a provider of online trust certification for businesses to being a website certifier that prevented someone from hijacking a website to trick the unsuspecting partner into confidential transactions with the wrong party. Neither of those GTMs worked. We ultimately ended up with a GTM of partnering with third-party resellers of digital certificates used in B2C secure online commerce.

GeoTrust's goal was to get bought. Its entire business strategy was to sign up 600 resellers because the process we used to create these certificates took only 10 minutes versus the standard four days required by our competitors. Consequently, our cost was the lowest, and customers loved the speed advantage. Further, with a rapidly growing cadre of resellers, we were gaining one point of market share per month against the entrenched market leader, Verisign. We joked about how many points of market share gain it would take before Verisign would feel so threatened that it would buy us. The consensus was 25 points, and that turned out to be accurate. As soon as we took away 25 points of its market share, Verisign bought us for 5× our revenues, or $125 million.

Service Integrity

Service Integrity was delivering real-time business process intelligence that enabled businesses to see what was happening in real time with its B2B transactions. This allowed them to predict business trends and adjust critical business parameters to improve their financial results. For instance, if a company saw that suddenly there was a huge uptick in orders for a certain product, it could quickly increase its inventories so it could meet the demand and not lose customers. But even after an extensive GTM study group, we found that one vertical market after another did not agree that our proposition was compelling enough. The fact is, like many startups, this was a technology in search of a market, and it never found the right GTM before it ran out of cash and liquidated.

Dover Microsystems

Dover Microsystems is a hardware-plus-software cybersecurity provider. Using public data chronicling every cyberattack since 2005, we proved that we stopped 95% of all known cyberattacks. Using the same data, our closest competitor stopped 16%. Dover's GTM for entry into the commercial market was to sell to giant chip manufacturers globally. These are companies like NXP, Qualcomm, and Renesas that would build our product into their chips. Then they would sell those chips to companies making devices, and the device-makers would sell their products to end-user companies in hundreds of markets, including electric grids, industrial automation, medical, and automotive. The value proposition was that those end users would now be highly protected from cyberattacks.

Here, our GTM miscalculations were the willingness of the commercial market to pay for this level of cybersecurity protection, the difficulty for a small startup to license hardware to huge semiconductor companies, and the interest in this tech to companies two steps removed from the entity being attacked. We did not have enough proof of market success to attract venture capital, and we had only one small Air Force contract. We were on a path to run out of cash—certain death.

I had to lay off the entire company and pivot to a new "DoD-first" GTM, acknowledging that although the commercial market wasn't sure it needed our high level of protection, the Department of Defense never saw security it did not want to add. In its first year on the new GTM, Dover had 3× the revenues of the previous GTM in five.

16.6   *The moral of this anecdote*

As we all know, most startups fail, and the conventional wisdom is that this happens because they run out of cash. But why do they run out of cash? I believe it's because they got their GTM wrong and spent a lot of money thrashing and not executing a well-thought-out GTM strategy. The three most important things you must get right, right away, in a startup are product, team, and market, and market means GTM. Entrepreneurs understand product and team much better; it is GTM that trips many of them up. This is partly because the GTM strategy involves every function within the company. Many entrepreneurs either misunderstand what GTM really means or, to their peril, don't value using a rigorous process to develop the GTM strategy.

A formal business plan in 10 steps

- What's the compass that guides you through stages of company development? A formal business plan.
- How should you leverage your great go-to-market strategy? By baking it into your business plan.
- What is the key to a great strategy business planning process? Asking the right questions and an absolute focus on customers.

Business plans are not expected (and, quite frankly, are considered a waste of time) for early-stage (seed and Series A) startups because everything changes so fast that it's hard to keep a business plan current, and three-year plans are pretty much wild guesses at the early stages. But even if you are early stage and not required to create a written business plan, the strategy process I describe here is still important:

- We will talk about how to develop a long-term strategic plan—a business plan is just the written document that comes out of that. Going through this process makes you and your entire team a lot tighter, better aligned, and more certain your approach is the right one. It is simply best practice and very good discipline to go through this process even if you are not creating a written business plan. Period.

144

- You may need to create a written business plan for later-stage investments (Series B and later); having done this early makes it all the easier later.
- The same is true if you are in line for being acquired or are heading to an IPO. In both cases, the acquirer or the public market needs to be able to fully understand your strategy, which they will look to find in your written business plan.

This three-year strategic planning process is a superset of the go-to-market (GTM) work we discussed in anecdote 16, "Go-to-market: How to make your business viable and grow." In fact, as you will see soon, steps 3, 4, and 5 in this strategy-planning process are what the GTM strategy focuses on. If you skipped that anecdote and came straight here, then when you get to steps 3–5 you may want to shift to the triumvirate MVP, PMF, and GTM anecdotes because they have more detail and insights about how to accomplish the customer interviews necessary for these steps.

Compared to the GTM process, this business-planning process goes much further, especially in its consideration of every function in your company, and it has a three- to five-year time horizon. But again, I do not recommend this for an early-stage company prior to a Series B unless an IPO or potential for being acquired appears sooner.

17.1 Origins of this process

I went through this exact process while at Borland, the third-largest software company in the world at the time (only behind Microsoft and Lotus), as we were trying to transform the company to deal with major shifts in our market—a situation that always requires a hard rethink of one's strategy. The Borland senior management team was caught flat-footed and was behind Microsoft in supporting the client-server business computing model. So, in 1995, to help develop a strategy to rapidly take Borland into this new world, we hired the small team of Dave Chen, his partner Karla Friede, and one other staff researcher, all former McKinsey consultants, to drive the business planning process that I outline in this anecdote and that Dave kindly gave me permission to use here.

17.2 Introduction to strategic planning

Strategic planning, done correctly, focuses first and foremost on the customer, because the goal is to get the company on a path to growth, and growth comes from customers and their money. But it also digs deeply into the company itself and creates actionable plans for each functional area.

Strategic planning can be distilled down to *four purposes*:

1 To focus a microscope on the needs of the customer
2 To translate the strategy and company objectives into specific, actionable plans for each functional area
3 To create team alignment within the company
4 To share learnings from one functional area to another across the entire company

This process is so important to the company that a cross-functional senior team must be actively involved in all aspects, which can be summed up in *four main areas of team involvement*:

1 Data collection and synthesis
2 Leading and delivering key components of the plan
3 Developing conclusions and decisions
4 Communicating the project's results to the rest of the company

And *four phases of the strategic planning process* drive how the process works logically in time:

1 Data collection
2 Opportunity selection
3 Implementation and implications
4 Three-year strategic plan creation

The following four sections briefly outline each of these four phases. Then we will dive into more detail on how the 10-step strategic planning process uses these four phases.

17.2.1 Data collection

There are three steps to the data-collection phase:

1 Developing a market segmentation model along with an assessment of the target market's needs
2 Understanding your competitors' and your planned response to each one
3 Assessing your strengths and weaknesses in each targeted segment, and planning to overcome these weaknesses

Start by gathering basic research and data from industry analysts such as Gartner. Then look carefully at a variety of markets and develop a model to slice those markets into segments that are a reasonable size for you to enter and become dominant in within just a couple of years. By adding direct input from prospective customers in these segments to the analyst data, you should be able to get a very clear understanding of each segment's needs that you and your product will be able to address. As a founder or senior executive of a small company, you probably already have a good understanding of your ecosystem, but put extra focus on all competitors and your response to them, both product and messaging. In a dispassionate fashion, articulate your product's and team's strengths and weaknesses in each targeted segment.

17.2.2 Opportunity selection

Opportunity selection involves identifying and prioritizing target markets. Identifying candidate markets comes from a combination of gut instinct, your founders' past knowledge of markets that fit the product, and some basic research from firms like Gartner and IDC. Prioritizing these candidate markets results in considering market size and other aspects of attractiveness, which we will discuss later. Then factor in how your products can and should be positioned vis-à-vis the competition and how strong that positioning will be. For each potential segment you are considering, evaluate a set of critical success factors that apply to that segment to measure how your product does relative to products being used in that segment. Next, for each segment under consideration, apply a set of critical success factors to that segment to measure how your product stacks up against others that are used in this segment. The final step will be to consider the requirements to build a whole product acceptable in this segment, as doing this can be quite different and more of a heavy lift in one segment versus another.

17.2.3 Implementation and implications

That point about whole product has major implications for your development team. This part of the selection process involves taking the requirements you discern from the segment and mapping that into the product implementation work needed to meet those requirements as a whole product. Whole product is a topic that startups frequently ignore.

> **DEFINITION** *Whole product* is your core product augmented by everything the customer needs to have a compelling reason to buy. Usually this includes what products or systems it needs to interoperate with, as well as service and support for the core product. *Whole product modeling* is an exhaustive analysis of what it takes to ensure the fulfillment of the target customer's compelling reason to buy.

I say this without equivocation: any company that competently executes a whole-product strategy significantly improves its probability of success.

Other implementation factors to consider are the critical milestones you need to achieve versus your ability to meet the timing windows. Similarly, consider the critical technologies you must incorporate or your product needs to be compatible and successful. And then, from the viewpoint of partnering, consider who the critical partners are and what impact there would be on your present or future channel to choose these partners (or, for that matter, to choose this segment). Finally, consider any implications for your organization and team that may be detrimental if you choose this segment.

17.2.4 Creating a three-year strategic plan

The fourth and final phase is the creation of a three-year strategic plan. This involves taking all the factors you used to choose segments and expanding them in terms of timeframe. This means you need to turn the target markets, the whole-product definition, the competitive positioning, and the technology plan into a 36-month product development plan. Then you will build out the full three-year plans for channels, partners, business mode, revenues, and high-level financials.

The 10-step strategy and business planning process is illustrated in figure 17.1. A step 11 is shown, but it is not part of the business plan; it is the actions the plan prescribes for the first year of following the plan. The plan, when presented, is not the same as the order in which the plan process is followed. The numbering of the steps shown in the figure is the order in which the steps are followed during the development of the plan; the layout of the steps in the figure shows the order in which they are written into the formal business plan document.

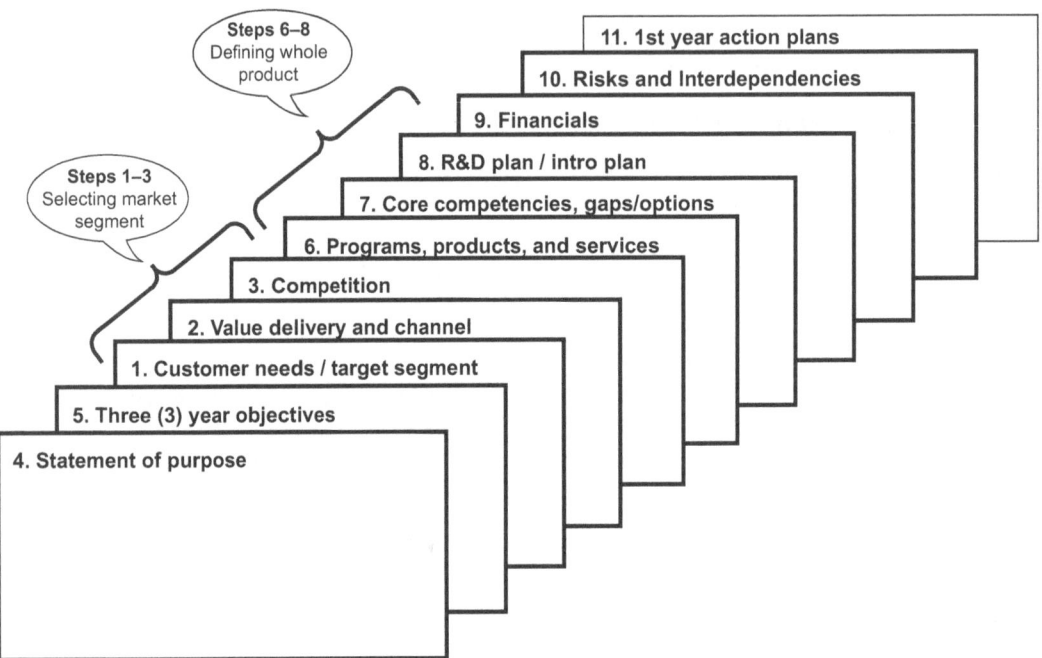

Figure 17.1   Pictorial representation of the 10 steps in the creation of a business strategy/plan. (Step 11 is not part of the plan; it is the actions the plan dictates for the first year of operations.) Note that the order in which the steps are taken during plan development is not the same as the order in which they are presented in a document. The numbering shown here is in the order in which the steps are taken in the plan development process.

FIRST: TARGET MARKET SEGMENTS

You begin with steps 1, 2, and 3, where the goal is to understand your customers' needs and select a target segment. This means considering your potential channels, key customers, market research data, analysts' views, field visits, and anything else relevant to your general industry to gather data and understanding.

DEFINITION   *Market segmentation* is the practice of dividing your target market into approachable groups. Market segmentation creates subsets of a market based on demographics, needs, priorities, common interests, and other psychographic or behavioral criteria used to better understand the target audience.

DEFINITION *Channels* are how a company sells products through another company. Depending on the relationship between these companies, the other company is referred to by different names: partner, distributor, affiliate, etc.

This market segmentation part of the process seeks answers to the following questions:

- How/where is value created for that customer?
- How do you serve that customer better than your competition?
- What are the major trends and key discontinuities that create opportunities for you?

Eighty percent of the planning cycle is spent here on market segmentation. But most teams tend to jump straight to steps 6 and 7.

SECOND: BUSINESS PURPOSE
Next come steps 4 and 5: defining your business's purpose and objectives.

THIRD: WHOLE PRODUCT
Now you tackle steps 6, 7, and 8: defining and introducing "programs, products, and services," or whole product, to solve that target segment's needs (defined in steps 1–3) creatively and uniquely to take advantage of your core competencies.

FOURTH: FINANCIAL RETURNS
Fourth is step 9: investments and returns. Can you make acceptable financial returns in this market and in the value delivery chain you defined in steps 4, 6, and 7?

FIFTH: RISKS AND INTERDEPENDENCIES
Fifth are steps 10 and 11, cataloging risks and interdependencies and, outside of the business plan itself, mapping out the first-year action plans to implement this business plan.

FINAL: VALIDATE
Later, once you have engaged with the market (which always changes some of your assumptions), be sure to send that feedback back to steps 1 and 2 so your business's purpose and objectives will track these changes.

In summary, the sequence of plan creation is as follows:

Target market segments (1-2-3) →
Business purpose (4-5) →
Whole product (6-7-8) →
Financial returns (9) →
Risks and interdependencies (10-11) →
Validate (market segments onward) ↑

The 10 steps ground rules

To be successful, this 10-step strategy must be built on a solid foundation of ground rules, as follows:

- *It must be fact-based.* Anecdotes and opinions can be the basis for ideas; however, ideas are tested through customer research, experiments, and data. These are all hard things that take time. Part of the team must be dedicated to finding suitable prospective customers and then having the calls with those prospects who agree to meet with you—this is by far the most important data you will acquire.
- *It must be customer-needs-based.* This means getting a detailed understanding of the customers' problems, usage, needs, and requirements as well as the segmentation and selection of specific target customer segments.
- *It must be team-developed.* Cross-functional teams create the project plan, inputs, and results. This means you will need active involvement of channel resources and their customers, as well. This is crucial to cement buy-in and commitment to the result.
- *It must be an evolving process.* The plan is not static and must be executed and evolved yearly. This process will generally take two to three cycles to realize the full benefits.
- *It must involve innovative and creative solutions for customer needs.* This forces you to understand customers' problems and develop creative ways to meet that need by employing all the elements of the value delivery chain.
- *It should use a standard format to facilitate communication.* Figure out what format (Word, PowerPoint, Google Docs, etc.) works best for you. Then consistently use that format, and make sure the results are always widely communicated and understood.

17.3   *The steps in working order*

This section outlines the key issues in each of the steps. Crucially, I have organized this in *working order*, not the presentation order as the steps would be laid out for a business plan or an investment pitch (as shown in figure 17.1 earlier).

We start with steps 1–3, which are heavy on data gathering and analysis. Step 1 is customer needs, step 2 is value delivery and channel, and step 3 is competition. The most critical portion of the plan and the planning resides in these three steps. Why? Because no matter what you do in business, you must thoroughly understand your customer. Doing these well means you will have a solid understanding of the user's real needs and how to deliver these values to the user. You will understand how to define and select a defensible niche where you can create a sustainable advantage over your competitor(s). The result of steps 1–3 is the selection of a target market segment and the definition of how to uniquely create value for that customer set who self-identify as being part of that segment. A clearly defined and well-understood market segment is the key to efficiency for your startup. Such a segment has many similar customers that your marketing can reach and that you can find via shows they attend and things they read. Work you do for one customer translates to all customers in a well-defined segment.

Steps 1–3 are the starting point for the plan. And most, perhaps 80%, of the planning time will be spent here. Steps 1–3 should be approached simultaneously, potentially with parallel teams but even with a small team. They will need to time-slice these three steps into their work schedules because information learned in one of these steps informs what is being done in the other steps. The key to steps 1–3 is a segmentation model. A segmentation model is not how you bucket the customer; it is how they define themselves, their needs, how they use, and how they buy. It is the basis for determining your PMF.

17.3.1   Step 1: Customer-needs target segments

For step 1, focus on a key set of questions you need to answer:

- Do you understand what problems users are trying to solve today and over the next three years? This is not the same as asking "What products do they need?"
- Can you divide these users into segments that share common needs and usage patterns or buying criteria and/or are served by the same channel?
- How different are the needs in each of these segments? Can you build differentiation in these segments? Does the customer value this differentiation?
- Which target segments offer the most attractiveness? Consider the size of the market, growth, ability to make a profit, ability to create barriers to entry or differentiation, threat of substitute products or technologies, saturation, existing levels of competition, degree of user power, and the ability for you to be in a number-one or -two market position in the three-year planning horizon.
- Are there substitute technologies or solutions that are new ways of solving the customer's problems that can impact your business?
- Consider major technical trends. Are they evolutionary or revolutionary? Do they change the economics of suppliers and users?

The outcome from step 1 is a data-driven customer segmentation chart that describes customers, markets, and partners and includes the size and growth rate of this segment plus any major discontinuities and technology trends that are affecting the segment (and might create an opportunity for you). I find a simple spreadsheet is the most effective way to collect, update, and present this data, with the segments laid out across the top horizontally and the attributes you are measuring for each segment down the left vertically.

17.3.2   Step 2: Value delivery and channel

For step 2, these are the key questions you need to answer:

- How and where in the value delivery system is the most value created for the user? Do you understand the points, metrics, and levers of customer satisfaction?

Be sure to consider this from a whole-product, whole-solution standpoint, not just delivering what you might think of as the core product, whether it is hardware, software, services, or all three.

- Do you understand the purchase and distribution (service needs) requirements of the users/customers?
- Have you selected the appropriate channel model for you and your current situation? Be sure to consider cost, required expertise level, service level, geographic requirements, and impacts, and whether this partner is selling direct or indirect or is an original equipment manufacturer (OEM).
- How much value, and what value, is created in the channel? Is it valued by the customer?
- What are the requirements for success in using these channels? Are these a fit with the customer set?
- Do you understand the competition's channel strategy? Consider your comparative strengths and weaknesses.
- Have you defined how to best create awareness and reach in this target segment?

The outcomes from step 2 are a channel value chart (by target segment) and channel fit with the segments you are analyzing, along with requirements for success.

17.3.3 *Step 3: Competition*

For step 3, these are the key questions you need to answer:

- What is each competitor's strategy in each target segment? What entry and exit barriers have they built? Can you overcome these barriers?
- Have you compared each competitor's strengths and weaknesses against the key customer satisfaction points or key buying factors in each target segment?
- Have you defined how your solution will create a sustainable advantage against the competition? What points on the value delivery system will you use to create that advantage?
- What user perceptions, if any, will have to change for you to be successful?

The outcome of step 3 is helpful data that you'll put into the following charts:

- A chart of competitors' strengths and weaknesses by segment
- A chart comparing key competitors along with key buying factors
- A SWOT (strengths, weaknesses, opportunity, threat) chart to identify competitive actions, reactions, and opportunities to synthesize key opportunities from steps 1–3.

Once steps 1–3 have produced proposed target market segments, identified each segment's key needs, and determined how to best deliver value to this segment, it is time to begin executing step 4, the creation of the value proposition, which ultimately is the key to the business's statement of purpose.

17.3.4   *Step 4: Statement of purpose*

For step 4, the team can now develop a "working" version of the value proposition for each segment being considered. The key questions are as follows:

- What users are in this segment?
- How will you create and deliver value to them?
- How will you create a long-term advantage for yourself (and what are the sources of that advantage)?

Value proposition template

For [*description of users*] in [*segment name*], we deliver [*your solution*] that solves [*their problem*], unlike competitors who only provide [*competitor's solution*], giving us a long-term advantage based on [*sources of your advantage*].

Next, test the fit of the value proposition for each segment with the long-term corporate strategy and objectives. The results of this step can be added to the chart of all the segments for ease of communication.

17.3.5   *Step 5: Three-year objective*

For step 5, you are taking the results of step 4 and extending them out for three years. This may mean you start with your number-one segment and, after a certain milestone is reached (market share, perhaps), add the next segment. Alternatively, there may be a financial objective that, if met, indicates the next step you should take. The team deliverables to support a three-year outlook are as follows:

- Translate step 4 into tangible deliverables.
- What are appropriate market and financial objectives and ways to measure them?
- What are key nonfinancial goals that are reasonable key success factors for your business?

17.3.6   *Step 6: Programs, product, and services*

For step 6, the key questions you need to answer are as follows:

- Do your solutions, consisting of programs, products, and services, meet the prospective user's, channel's, and partner's needs uniquely and completely?
- Will the user and buyer believe you have the best solution?
- Have you tested and validated that assertion?
- Here it is critical to steer clear of the oh-so-common bugaboo of so many technology startups: confusing a cool technology for a whole product. For example, when the iPod came out, it was certainly considered cool, but Apple knew that was not enough; the company built the iTunes store to accompany the device so people could buy music to load onto their iPods. The *whole product* was the

device plus the iTunes service that users continuously interacted with. Many tech startups would have presented the iPod alone, and without the accompanying service, it probably would have failed.

The outcome from step 6 is a competitive whole-product strategy in the form of a specification of all the components that make up the whole product and how they come together and are delivered. This needs to be based on a realistic hard look at your ability to meet these needs and deliver the specified solutions. This whole-product strategy needs to be examined in the context of the entire ecosystem of partners and competitors. It must be tested and validated with quantitative and qualitative testing. This will be an ongoing process linked to target-segment selection from steps 1–3. Why? Because your solutions are targeted at serving specific segment needs and will not be the same from segment to segment.

17.3.7   *Step 7: Core competencies, gaps, and options*

For step 7, the first task is to assess your current strengths and capabilities in key processes. Then, after a target segment is selected in steps 1–3 and this segment's needs and key success factors are understood, determine any new required critical capabilities (step 6) and identify the gaps between these and your current capabilities. For each new required capability that you do not currently meet, identify a plan to leverage, build, develop, or buy it.

Here is an example list of core competency areas you may want to consider:

- Current sales channel structure and sales model
- Services solution strategy
- Systems integration or consulting
- Post–sales customer support
- Partnering programs
- Customer/field training programs

The team deliverables from step 7 are the identification of your current core competencies and a chart showing the new required capabilities versus your current ones for each segment. This chart needs to clearly identify the gaps and propose options to fill those gaps quickly and efficiently. The chart must also identify opportunities to use and extend your current capabilities to satisfy and delight your chosen segment's needs.

17.3.8   *Step 8: R&D plan*

Step 8 has one very big question to answer: how and when will you deliver on the products and services outlined in step 6, including the development of technology, marketing, and channel, as well as resource (people) planning? The technology plan must include a plan for developing or acquiring the technology and an engineering development schedule, a quality plan, and a support plan.

Your marketing and channel plan must address core planning topics, including these:

- Marketing positioning and strategy
- Alignment of channel and support
- Orders forecast
- Value proposition communication
- Marketing launch
- Demand generation
- Key partners (who, how, when)

Your resources plan is about your organization and about your team and how to match them to the plans being formulated as this process progresses. Are any organizational changes needed to deliver the value proposition to the segment(s)? Are there unmet requirements in the team, and if so, what key skills and new capabilities are called for? How does the current team transition into the new team? The output of step 8 is a document containing the three plans for technology, marketing and channel, and resources.

17.3.9   *Stop: Do a sanity check*

This is the point in the 10 steps to stop and not get so caught up in the process that you lose the view of the forest for the trees. Ask yourself: Do the plans laid out in step 8 address and deliver the product, services, and attributes outlined in steps 6 and 7? And do the plans address the needs of the targeted segments identified in steps 1–3?

To answer those questions, consider:

- Do the action plans support the value proposition?
- Do the action plans hit the business targets for cost, quality, and time to market?
- Is the channel plan consistent with the step 8 plans?
- Can you communicate the value clearly and credibly?
- Have you considered the use of partners in every stage of the value delivery, including R&D, marketing, sales, and support?
- Do you have the capability to deliver on the R&D plan (step 8)?
- Will the plan allow you to win first or second position in the market in a relatively short time (perhaps two years)?

17.3.10   *Step 9: Financial analysis*

Having made it past the sanity check, it is time for step 9, the financial component of the process. That can be summed up by asking this question: with the plans laid out in step 8, can you meet your financial objectives? To answer this, your finance team will have to develop a spreadsheet template that allows all the data to be input by asking a series of "what if" questions, the answers to which form this step's deliverable. A couple of "what ifs" I suggest are as follows:

- Are the cost, revenue, and profit projections in line with your stage of market growth and corporate structure?
- How attractive are the return on sales and return on investment versus your competition's?

17.3.11 Step 10: Risks and interdependencies

The last step in the 10-step strategy development process is about assessing risks and interdependencies. The key outcomes of this step are contingency plans to deal with those risks and interdependencies, to assess their impacts, and to produce a set of action plans. To achieve this, there are three key questions to consider:

1 Have you considered external risk factors: competition (new and existing), economy (spending levels), and shift in usage or adoption rate of your type of product?
2 Have you considered internal risk factors: schedules, quality, resource availability, and issues with skills match?
3 After identifying internal interdependencies and confirming that deliverables and expectations have been agreed to in all cases, are there ways to minimize the identified interdependencies?

The team deliverables from step 10 come in the form of two documents. One identifies risk areas with associated plans to mitigate and the owners of those plans. The other specifies internal interdependencies, the results of negotiating actions to minimize those interdependencies, and the actions' owners. The purpose is to measure the effectiveness of those owners and the actions they are responsible for.

At this point, having completed your first pass through this process, you can pretty simply turn all the deliverables into a business plan, either in a presentation or as a written document.

17.4   *The moral of this anecdote*

As you are starting anything—a brand-new company, a new division, a new product, an acquisition, or an IPO—or being part of a company that acquired you, you need a solid, well-crafted strategy. This is the best process for creating one that I have ever seen. Part of it is the GTM process, so review companion anecdotes 14 ("Getting to minimum viable product with lighthouse customers"), 15 ("Product–market fit: Making sure the dogs will eat your dog food"), and 16 ("Go-to-market: How to make your business viable and grow") when you reach steps 3–5 because those anecdotes go into more detail about how the most critical step of this process works. When you have gone through this process, you are ready to head out into the market for your first year of acting on the plans and strategies you came up with. In addition, or alternatively, you can write a long business plan document and/or a set of slides you can use to raise money from investors in advance of an acquisition or for an investment banker in preparation for an IPO.

Burn rate and runway—or, where is the edge of that cliff?

- What is going to keep you up at night the most? Your monthly cash burn.
- What is the most important number you should track every day? How many months of cash are left.
- What happens when the runway ends? It's game over. The company will wind up operations.

Most startups fail—about 8 or 9 out of 10. The majority of failures are because they run out of cash. There are a lot of reasons your startup might run out of cash, so watching the cash, how fast it is being spent, and how long what you have left will last are the most important things you, or the CEO, must pay attention to. Let's talk about cash and how to think about it, and what to do about it getting too low—before your company runs off that cliff.

18.1 What are burn rate and runway, and why do they matter?

Burn rate is one of the most important metrics you need to track in your startup because you must not just run out of cash "by accident" for lack of attention to it.

DEFINITION *Burn rate* is the speed at which an unprofitable company consumes its cash.

Oh, you're right; unprofitable is not a nice word to use for the way an early-stage startup thinks about itself—but it's accurate. You are unprofitable on day 1, and your goal is to become profitable before you run out of cash (or can raise more).

If we're talking about a venture-backed startup—in this book, we mostly are—burn rate is the rate at which the company is spending its venture capital: i.e., the money in the bank. Another way to describe it is that burn rate is a measure of negative cash flow. This is a major consideration for tech companies, including life sciences startups, which frequently burn a lot of cash before and until they have revenues—and sometimes that can be a matter of years.

Burn rate is almost always quoted in terms of net cash spent (or "burned") per month. We say, "My burn rate is $100,000," which means the net cash spent per month is $100,000; that's $1,200,000 per year siphoned off from your bank account and gone. Scary, right? This relates to another important term: *runway*.

DEFINITION *Runway* is how long the company has before its cash reserves, or operating capital, is exhausted and it runs out of cash, usually measured in months.

Those four words—"runs out of cash"—are hard for me even to write. That is the ultimate nightmare, and it has almost happened to me several times. In fact, it did happen to one of my companies (after I departed).

Burn rate is a measure of your startup's sustainability. Knowing it helps you make informed decisions about how fast you're spending money and when to plan for your next round of funding. If you are going to track one number that every investor will ask you about, that number is the burn rate; then they will ask you how much cash is in the bank, and they will calculate the cash divided by the burn rate number to get how many months of runway you have.

Runway is the number-one thing that keeps the CEO up at night until the company turns cash-flow positive. There is no opportunity for a do-over. If you run out of cash, you have run the company off the cliff, and it's over. When I said earlier that most startups fail because they run out of cash, I did not mean their bank balance goes to zero and they instantly go out of business. Running off that cliff is rare. That's because the board and investors are usually paying attention, and if they do not think your company is worthy of more time and money, they will tell you to shut it down in an orderly way. I have a full anecdote on that process in anecdote 30, "Heaven forbid if you must wind it up."

Back to runway. It is the number-one thing that freaks out investors and makes them haunt you:

"Your burn rate is getting too high; it might be time for layoffs."

"Your burn rate is too high; you must be paying people too much."

"Your runway is too short; you need to make cuts to lengthen it."

"Your runway is too short; you need to go raise more money."

18.2   *The arithmetic of burn rate and runway*

To understand the relationship between burn rate and runway, let's look at a simple calculation. Let's say you have $4 million in the bank, and your monthly cash burn rate is $250,000. This will give you 16 months of runway, as the following equation shows:

$$\frac{\text{Cash in bank}}{\text{Monthly cash burn}} = \text{Runway}$$

$$\frac{\$4,000,000 \text{ dollars}}{\$250,000 \text{ dollars}/_{\text{month}}} = 16 \text{ months}$$

It is important to understand that burn rate is not the same as expenses. Some use the term gross burn as a synonym for total operating expenses, but I find that confusing. That's just expenses. So, net burn, or just burn, is your revenues subtracted from your total expenses. This number is affected by two things you can do: get more revenue or cut expenses. Cash burn tells you a couple of very important things:

- *How much it costs to finance your operations.* This focuses you on increasing your revenues, if possible, by the amount of your burn: i.e., getting burn to zero.
- *How long you can maintain current spending before you need more cash.* This directs you to start raising a round of financing and tells you when you must close that round. Further, the burn rate, plus the requirement that you have at least 18 months of runway after a financing round, tells you precisely how big the round must be. That 18 months is not arbitrary. It is based on experience that says you need 6 months to raise a new round, and prior to that you need at least a year to operate and accomplish the next major revenue milestone to attract outside investors.

In most tech startups, the number-one component of burn rate is employee expenses, especially engineering. Given the ultra-competitiveness of the market for good talent, especially in areas where you are competing with big, rich technology companies for talent, it is very hard to keep good engineers if you squeeze them on salary and benefits.

Consider carefully whom you hire as a permanent employee versus using contractors. If you use contractors and you get into a pickle and need to cut expenses, you can terminate contractors without affecting your team's morale nearly as much. Use these sorts of variable expenses—as opposed to fixed, long-term expenses—judiciously, and it can be a lot easier to control burn rate.

Engineering costs are a major factor in burn rate at tech startups

Hardware engineers

According to Built In,[1] the average total compensation for a hardware engineer in the United States is, as of this writing, about $150,000 (but in my hiring in Boston, this is $25,000 too low). They need access to very expensive tools like those from Synopsys or Cadence. Synopsys hardware design tools for a small team of three hardware engineers cost $70,000 per year. This means, at a minimum, that a single hardware engineer contributes $14,444 in expense to burn rate. That's just to do their basic job and doesn't include standard expense items like insurance, facilities, travel, and so forth. A small team of three hardware designers, plus two additional who work in support roles for the designers, would cost $68,333 per month (five engineers at $150,000 each plus $70,000 in tools divided by 12). It is starting to add up.

Software engineers

Depending on the number of years of experience and the discipline, hiring a software engineer has gotten very expensive. According to PayScale,[2] entry-level engineers make an average annual salary of about $115,000. Senior software engineers make an average of about $155,000 in total compensation. Those with specialized skills are higher, and in competitive markets like Boston and Silicon Valley, we routinely see salaries of $200,000. A typical startup team of five software engineers with a very experienced technical lead (at $200,000) and the rest at the blended rate of $135,000 would cost $61,667 per month.

You can save considerably by using some offshore resources. But you must be very careful about the "extra costs" associated with doing this. Factors such as communication difficulties, time zones, and cultural differences can shrink or remove the savings you might think you are getting by going offshore.

The rest of the company

Assume that a small software startup has a senior team of CEO, CTO, Finance, Marketing, and Sales and overhead of legal, rent, and some miscellaneous (which all comes to $105,208 per month). Add to that the five-person software team monthly of $61,667, which gives a grand total of $166,875 per month. A seed round that gives this company 18 months of runway must be at least $3 million. That's reasonable, but it will take discipline to stick to that level of expense until revenues start flowing.

18.3   How much runway do you need?

So, what is a good burn rate? The more important question is, how much runway do you need? Investors want the money they put in to provide the company with 18–24 months of runway. Once you get below 12 months, you need to be talking actively with investors about your next round. Those discussions easily take six months, and you do NOT want to get below six months of runway without having a clear line of sight on

---

[1] "Hardware Engineer Salary in US," Built In, https://builtin.com/salaries/dev-engineer/hardware-engineer
[2] "Average Software Engineer Salary," PayScale, www.payscale.com/research/US/Job=Software_Engineer/Salary.

the next round closing soon. Further, once you get below nine months of runway, if you have not achieved some very important milestone, such as landing that big contract or signing up an important partner, your investors will start to expect you to make cuts, and that will mean layoffs. They will hound you about this, I assure you. You also do not want to make cuts in your staff early on, or they will lose heart and start considering other options.

The reason your investors will start to panic if you get below nine months of runway without clear, believable sources of revenue or significant progress on a new round of financing, such as a signed term sheet, is that your runway can make all the difference in whether you can even raise that next round. If you don't have enough cash in the bank when prospective new investors start their due diligence, it can hurt the valuation you are offered: the incoming investor (assuming it is not an insider) will try to squeeze you for better terms because they see you getting closer to running out of cash. And trust me, they will also drag things out so you get closer and closer to that zero bank balance.

All is not lost in this situation. This is what a bridge financing is for. Typically, a bridge financing consists of convertible notes. These are debts, but not the kind of debt that is just principal plus interest paid back over time. Convertible notes are equity instruments that convert into shares in a future round of financing, usually at a discounted price in return for the risk the note purchaser took. Investors like these instruments because a group of individuals can get in on a future round they would not otherwise be able to participate in. The institutional investors leading that later round don't mind these if they are not too big a percentage of the eventual round because they kept the company going until accomplishments were made that attracted the institutional investors to commit.

Some of my runway lessons
NovaSoft

I was thrown into the CEO role (my first time) after the previous CEO spent to a $21 million operating plan but only did $11 million in revenues, making the burn rate way out of proportion for the revenue he actually brought in. In a stern conversation the chairman of the board had with me, he made it clear that burn rate had to come way down to match the real revenues, so I had to lay off half the company on day one. And to fill the hole the CEO had made and give us some runway, I also had to raise a Series F insider round, which had to be sized to give us 18 months of runway at our new lowered burn rate. I also needed to find a new market because the one we were in was shrinking fast. You could say we had had product–market fit (PMF) but lost it because that market was going away, and now we had to find PMF all over again (see anecdote 15, "Product-market fit: making sure the dogs will eat your dog food").

(continued)

GeoTrust

GeoTrust was a company that had to go through several pivots until we found a good path to an exit. With each pivot, I had to carefully analyze our burn rate (and runway) and determine if I had to cut burn, raise more money, or do some of both. My cofounder was based in Portland, and I was in Boston, so we had some operations in both places. During our last pivot, I determined that we had to shut down Portland operations and just have an office in Wellesley, Massachusetts. That was a very hard decision, but it was the right one because it allowed us to shrink in size, cut our burn substantially, and raise a Series C. We never had to raise more capital after that because we found the right market, nailed a PMF as part of our go-to-market strategy, and achieved cash-flow positive on our way to being purchased for 5× revenues.

Dover Microsystems

Because Dover was a hardware-based cybersecurity company, and because designing and building hardware is a much longer process than developing something that is pure software, not only was our burn rate high ($400,000 per month), but we also needed a very long runway to give us time to design, verify, and work closely with our lighthouse customer to get our component in their chip and have them manufacture it and ship it to their customers. For a long time, our investors were very patient, and they supported us in raising a Seed II round the same size as the Seed I; but when the runway from the Seed II was still not enough by half, their patience wore thin, and they came at me hard.

Their instinct was to say "Time for layoffs," but I pushed back because cutting the hardware engineering team would mean we were giving up and shutting down. I kept arguing that we were either a hardware-based cybersecurity company or nothing at all. Ultimately, we came within a hair's breadth of running out of cash; I moved fast and laid off the entire company (except myself), lived off one small Air Force contract, hired an outside hardware engineering team on contract, and rebuilt the company, focused on a completely different market (the government contracting market). Now runway was a different calculation because instead of having to wait until our customer shipped their chip with our component in it, we were on a contract that we invoiced monthly, making it easy to predict burn rate and achieve cash-flow-positive operations.

18.4 *The moral of this anecdote*

Burn rate is the speed at which an unprofitable company consumes its cash. Because we are (usually) talking about venture-backed startups, it's the rate at which the company is spending its venture capital. Burn rate is not the same as expenses. *Gross burn* is the same as expenses. *Net burn*, or just *burn*, is your revenues subtracted from your total expenses. A related term, *runway*, is how long the company has before its cash reserves or operating capital is exhausted and it runs out of cash. Knowing your monthly burn rate and your runway is a helpful way to make informed decisions about how fast you're spending money and when to plan for your next round of funding.

There are two things you can do to change your burn rate and therefore your runway: get more revenues or cut expenses. If you can't cut expenses but you don't have enough runway to get to a major inflection point where you can raise a round of financing, you might consider bridge financing. This is usually convertible notes that convert into equity at a discount of the next round when it occurs.

Bottom line: know your cash burn rate and know how much runway you have at all times. Investors will ask, and you need to be on top of these numbers above all others.

19

Achieving cash-flow positive: A startup's Holy Grail

- What does cash-flow positive mean?
- Why is achieving cash-flow positive like finding the Holy Grail? You like sleep, don't you?
- Hit cash-flow positive? How does this reset investor perspectives about your startup?

Every startup founder and CEO starts their company with their eyes on the prize: steady growth, profitability, and a great exit. There are many challenges to getting there. But along the way, there is a moment that is totally transformational for you, your employees, and your investors: the moment when cash burn becomes cash growing. It's where the runway becomes "infinite." This moment is called cash-flow positive, and it truly is like finding the Holy Grail. You feel like falling to your knees and howling in sheer delight.

19.1 Cash-flow positive vs. profitable

The sleepless nights. The cold sweats. The harassment from your board. The harassment from your investors. It all ends once your burn rate (net cash out the door after revenues and total expenses) goes to zero (cash-flow break-even) or negative (cash-flow positive). Becoming profitable may not happen at the same time as being cash-flow positive. This is because you can be profitable even if cash is not

164

flowing in fast enough to stay ahead of expenses. That might happen if you sold something but have not received the cash for it yet. This can be a problem for a startup that may not have the ability to weather the long payment terms some big companies demand. A startup can be particularly sensitive to what is called *debtors days*.

> **DEFINITION** The *debtors days* ratio measures how quickly cash is being collected from debtors that owe you money. The longer it takes for a company to collect, the greater the number of debtors days and the longer the startup is going without cash it is owed but hasn't yet collected.

Debtor days are why you can be profitable and still run out of cash and go away; hopefully your investors will never let that happen. In that instance, they will do a quick insider's round to cover you if the assurance is there that you have strong accounts receivable that really will be paid. If the receivable is from a big, reputable company, then the company is good for it.

"Cash is king," as most of us have heard many times. It is very true. Profitability is great, but first you must be absolutely certain you have enough cash to pay your bills and, most importantly, your payroll. Speaking of payroll, today's startup employees are very savvy compared to when I started in the late 1980s: they understand if you are already, or certain to achieve soon, cash-flow positive. This will have a dramatic effect on your ability to attract the best, most experienced talent.

19.2 Liberation from the shackles of burn rate

Sometimes investors (especially Silicon Valley investors) want the company to grow faster, which means spending more, which means your burn rate goes up and you fall further away from cash-flow positive. That is fine (maybe) if the investors are committed to putting in more money to fund the faster growth. This is safest if the round will be an insider round, because if a new investor comes in to fund this expansion, they may have different ideas about some fundamentals—one of which might be *you*.

> **TIP** As a quick aside, I have known a couple of investors who *always* replace the CEO when they invest unless the startup is cash-flow positive.

All entrepreneurs strive hard and make many sacrifices to reach cash-flow positive because of how much it changes things for you and your company. I have a saying about board voting that explains why:

Board voting formula

Pre-cash-flow positive = one dollar, one vote

Post-cash-flow positive = one person, one vote

This means that early on, regardless of what the company bylaws say, if the one or two investors on the board whose money sustains your company, vote one way on a critical resolution and the rest of the board, a majority, vote another way, the investor still wins. I have literally heard such an inside investor say, "If you go forward with that resolution, we are out and will not invest in the next round." You can't move forward under that circumstance unless you are 1,000% sure you have all the investors you need for the next round. That's seldom the case, so I would not risk it. Suppose you hit a speed bump and the company situation changes, and now you need a purely inside round. Suddenly you need that investor.

But once you pass cash-flow positive, you have lots of options about your next round, or even if there is going to be a next round. And for sure you don't have to tolerate the extortion of investor threats that make a mockery of board voting. It becomes one person, one vote, as it is supposed to be.

More than just board voting is liberated. Your overall company operations change, as do the strategic options open to you. For the first time ever, you are truly in control. That is why becoming cash-flow positive is the startup's Holy Grail. As we learned from the 1989 film *Indiana Jones and the Last Crusade*, the Grail is a cup that has magic powers. The startup CEO who gets to cash-flow positive has achieved something elusive and of profound significance, as well. They will also find it very restorative. It fires you up to keep pushing to get the company to reach higher and higher heights.

My search for the Holy Grail

GeoTrust

GeoTrust had a difficult beginning, including layoffs and shutting down one of our two offices. Our third business plan and an associated Series C investment ultimately got us to product–market fit (PMF) and a go-to-market (GTM) strategy that started to work, and we began to grow and gain market share. Ultimately, we got to cash-flow positive, which, especially after this company's journey, was a huge celebration and party. We continued growing market share by a full percentage point a month. By the time we got to 25% share, we were acquired for $125 million, or 5× revenues, by the undisputed market leader whose market share we had been "stealing." We had established our brand so well that the acquirer kept it. To this day, you will see the GeoTrust mark on a few websites.

Ambric

Another company in Portland that I got involved with early was called Ambric. It never got close to cash-flow positive, but there is still a story to tell. As a hardware company, it had very high expenses and long sales cycles—it takes a large team a long time to use very expensive tools to design a new semiconductor chip. It did not help that the company went almost two years before it realized a brand-new chip with a unique architecture would need a lot of software running on it before customers could use it, and only Ambric could write that software. Only very late did Ambric ask me to join and build it a software organization from scratch. Now it had two major engineering groups, and that was very expensive. But the company found a solid original equipment manufacturer (OEM) customer that sold a finished product to Apple. On the back of Apple wanting the product, Ambric was able to attract three major investors for its Series C round. The round was approved by all parties, but the limited partners in the firms refused the contractually mandated cash call due to the deep recession of 2008, thereby forcing Ambric to shut down.

Although it is expensive and takes a long time to create a new hardware product, once it is ready and starts to sell, the volumes can grow rapidly, and the company can very quickly convert to cash-flow positive. I am certain Ambric would have, if not for the Great Recession of 2008 pulling the rug out from underneath it.

Aguru Images

Aguru was also a hardware builder, but not of semiconductors. Instead, Aguru developed huge, 14-foot-high geodesic domes with 400 cameras mounted on them to support motion picture special effects. We ran it on a shoestring budget, spending the small initial investment capital until the product was demonstrable. At that point, it landed a large customer that was creating a big-budget movie. But the revenue from just one customer was not sufficient to attain cash-flow positive, and the company sold the originally licensed university IP back to the university where it was developed. It will always be a major uphill battle getting a niche hardware device like Aguru's, which is suitable for a small market (even of the magnitude of Hollywood movies), to be cash-flow positive.

Dover

Dover began life as a hardware IP licensing company. Very early on, we managed to sign up a lighthouse customer that paid $1.5 million just for the rights to incorporate our IP in its chips. For a short while, that made the company cash-flow positive, and yes, the celebrations were legend. The problem is, cash-flow positive can be deceiving when your initial revenues from a single customer are large and you have not yet proven PMF. We thought we had, but no other semiconductor companies were jumping on board. We had a lighthouse customer, not PMF. So, cash-flow positive was short-lived, and the company came within a hair's breadth of running out of cash.

19.3   *The moral of this anecdote*

When you found a new startup and you either run for a while on no salaries, maybe as a group of founders, or raise some capital from friends and family, angels, or VCs, you are not going to be cash-flow positive. It is typical for that to remain the case for a while. But if you confidently establish PMF and begin executing a well-planned GTM strategy, sales and revenues will follow. Unless you have huge expenses (e.g., a life sciences company), cash coming in should start to exceed cash flowing out. There is no better feeling in those early days than when you have achieved this goal. Doing so liberates you in many ways. Board votes are "one person, one vote," not "one dollar, one vote." You will find that investors seek you out instead of you having to seek them out. Plus, the financing terms for a positive-cash-flow company are always much better. Further, your strategic options are better, and you can attract better and better talent. This is why I say achieving cash-flow positive is the entrepreneur's Holy Grail.

Your startup's valuation: Up, up, up (hopefully)

- What is your startup really worth?
- How is understanding valuation significant to your startup's future?
- Is there a steady drumbeat of events that you can accomplish to steadily raise valuation?

The valuation of your startup is a very important concept to you, to your employees, to your existing investors, and to new investors. Until you are raising money or are close to an exit, you don't want to obsess over this—along the way, you have many more critical things to obsess over—but you do want to keep an eye on it. I will show you how it is not a factor you have to accept as is—there are things under your control that can directly improve your valuation.

20.1 Determining a startup's valuation

There are essentially three ways to determine a valuation for your startup. The first is to have an independent appraiser do a *409A valuation*. The second is for professional investors who are considering leading a round in your next financing to use their own process to set the price they are willing to pay for your shares. The third, which happens as an exit approaches, is for investment bankers to perform the valuation. Let's consider the 409A path first.

20.1.1 *Valuation via a 409A*

The shorthand 409A—an objective, independent process for determining a startup's value—comes from the name of the section in the IRS code added in 2005 that deals with deferred compensation. It was created because Enron executives were accelerating the payments under their deferred compensation plans so they could access that money before the company went bankrupt. This was considered corrupt, but it was not officially illegal (those executives went to jail for other issues, including fraud and insider trading).

Stock options are also considered deferred compensation. Before 2005, most startups I know, including mine, set the price employees had to pay to exercise their options (the *strike price*) at a very low value relative to what investors were paying. This was not illegal, corrupt, or nonstandard. But the 409A statute called a halt to setting the option price employees have to pay far below fair market value when, long after the options are granted, the employees decide to exercise those options and convert them into real stock (hence a form of deferred compensation).

Since the creation of 409A, establishing "fair market value" has been critical to prevent startups running afoul of this IRS regulation. The key is to establish fair market value for an illiquid startup—its stock is not bought and sold by outsiders—for which there is no public market (i.e., stock exchange). The 409A statute creates a set of valuation standards for companies called a *safe-harbor valuation*.

> **DEFINITION** *Safe-harbor valuation* means the IRS must accept the valuation as valid unless the IRS can demonstrate that the valuation is "grossly unreasonable."

This is done by paying for an independent appraisal by a reputable source. Various organizations have standard processes to establish the share price, which can then be used to establish a strike price for the awarding of stock options. These processes are designed to be a safe harbor and pass muster with the IRS. Early on, 409A appraisals cost as much as $50,000, which most startups cannot possibly pay. Fortunately, they are now very inexpensive. And if you use Carta—the largest provider of 409A valuations—as most startups do, you get an annual 409A as part of your subscription. I have used the Carta 409A process four times now. It is incredibly easy and fast.

You cannot legally issue stock-option grants without an up-to-date 409A valuation that sets the option strike price. And you are required to get a new one every year at a minimum, or more often if you have *material events*, such as raising a financing round or closing a marquee customer, that any outside observer would conclude impacts your company's valuation. Although this sets the value of the company, new investors considering leading a new round of financing—meaning they will set a price that they offer to pay for the company's stock—do not put a lot of credence in what the 409A price is set at. They have their own metrics and set a price for the new round their own way.

20.1.2 *Valuation via a priced round*

A very different way your share price and company valuation can be determined is by the lead investor at a *priced round* for your next financing.

> **DEFINITION**   A *priced round* is a round of financing led by a new investor, as opposed to an *insider round* where only existing investors participate.

In an ideal situation, more than one new investor is competing for that pole position on your new round, and they are submitting competing term sheets, which means they are probably competing on price—and that pushes up your valuation. The price these prospective investors come up with is based on their own valuation process. It's subjective. However, the thing venture capitalists (and private equity investors in general) are the best at is valuing companies they want to invest in. Some of the factors investors have used to value my various startups over the years include the following:

- *Market*—Success is all about market. If you do indeed have a great market, it will substantially increase your value to investors.
- *Company stage*—Is the company seed, Series A, or later? There will be an expectation of a floor and ceiling valuation depending on the stage.
- *Previous valuations*—The investor doesn't want to offer you a valuation that is too high so that if you do well, your follow-on rounds get a bump in valuation and can still fit into the norm for that next round. But they still need to worry about competition from other investors who might offer more than they do. On the other hand, if things have been going poorly, they will offer you less than your last round (i.e., a *down round*) on the assumption that no one else is going to offer you more.
- *Team*—The strength of the CEO, their experience, how well they know this market, and how well they can sell the company and its concept to investors will affect valuation significantly.
- *Departed team members*—The flip side of a great team is having significant team members depart. Have founders, members of the leadership team, or other key members of technical staff already left? If so, you need to have a good explanation.
- *Board of directors*—Not counting the investors on the board, do you have highly experienced directors from the industry you are operating in? Two big questions new investors will be trying to answer are (a) does this look like a board that provides good governance? And (b) is good advice about your market coming from someone on the board with deep experience in it?
- *Product-market fit (PMF)*—Have you proved that you've found PMF? Startups that fail to prove PMF are not successful.
- *Sales*—Your sales successes, plus what is in your funnel and how well your sales process and sales team is working, indicate how likely you are to achieve your revenue and growth goals.

- *Execution*—How well have your achievements adhered to your plan? This speaks to your and your team's abilities to plan and execute. It also shows the strength of the market and how good your solution is at addressing the compelling market problem you've identified.

- *Patents*—Do you have patent filings or, even better, patents that have been issued? Patents help protect you and show that the United States Patent and Trademark Office (USPTO) has thoroughly examined your patent application and vetted it against prior art. Sometimes the patent portfolio alone can float the valuation up markedly.

- *Product maturity*—Part of the due-diligence process will involve assessing the maturity of your offering, which will be a major factor in pricing. Maturity means your offering has been in the market for a while and you have delivered it to many disparate customers who have been actively using it, versus your product or service having just been completed and perhaps having been used by your lighthouse customer for only a brief period.

- *Comparables*—Just like similar houses down the street allow realtors to help you set the asking price for your house, investors will seek out comparables to assist them in setting a reasonable price for your company.

- *Relationships*—It's good to have meaningful relationships with partners and early customers. These help convince new investors that (a) you are a good management team that knows partnerships are critical to achieving your strategic goals and (b) strong partners and customers strengthen you in ways that help you withstand various challenges.

- *Advisors*—A strong set of advisors can fill the need for market expertise or bolster it. They can convince investors that you are strongly supported by, and sufficiently challenged by, experts.

- *Caliber of investors*—If your investors are top-tier, new investors will value that and will feel you have been well-managed by those investors. This will cause their sense of your value, along with their confidence, to rise. The opposite would occur if you used investors not considered high-caliber; new investors would wonder why you had not been able to attract top-tier investors.

- *Cap table*—How clean is your cap table? New investors do not favor your cap table having a substantial number of individual investors (i.e., angels). They much prefer, and value, a few big, professional, ideally top-tier investors. Have you made lots of strange special arrangements with employees, advisors, founders, and executives? That will hurt you, as well.

- *Competitors*—Investors will take a close look at your competitors and apply some of the same metrics discussed here to them. If your competitors are doing much better than you, investors will make a calculation: Is there something you have planned that will catapult you past those competitors, or are you more likely to fall even further behind?

Valuation events

Here are examples of "events," or accomplishments, that you have control over and can manage and that directly impact your startup's valuation positively. There is not a specific monetary value that anyone can associate with these events. All anyone can tell you is that they are worth something positive and will be considered at the next financing, at an exit, and even in the 409A process:

- *Product release*—Releasing a new product, or even a major revision of a product, is an important and valuable event in the life of a startup.
- *Major customer*—When a major customer (sometimes called a marquee customer) is signed, their leadership and notoriety rub off on you. It raises eyebrows (as in, "They must have something really good, to land that company").
- *Meaningful partner*—Some partners also lend gravitas and are worth crowing about.
- *New financing*—A new financing says to the world that this company has professional investors who do careful due diligence to value it and who believe in it. That is a valuable event.
- *Major new hire*—When a major executive or board member is added, it adds value to the company, especially if that person is well-known and has strong, relevant credentials.
- *Adding key advisors*—Because anyone considering what your startup is worth cares a lot about you having the necessary expertise to be successful, they will look at whether your team, your board, and your advisors come from the markets where you will be operating. So, adding an advisor who is such an expert is very important.
- *Patent awarded*—Patents are intrinsically valuable. They say to the world that you invented something the USPTO has thoroughly evaluated and determined is unique and has claims that are valuable. A collection of them protects you by creating what I like to call a *moat*, like the demon-infested ring of water around a castle.
- *Meaningful press*—Not all press is worthy of being called a valuation event. But some is. If something you have accomplished gets written up in by major press outlet, it can be a very value-adding event.
- *Proof of PMF*—Attaining PMF is probably the single most important early-stage valuation event you can have. It says to the world that you have found a market that highly values your product or service and that likes it and is buying it. That means you are on your way!

20.1.3 *Valuation via an exit*

Exit means either a purchase by another company or investment firm or an IPO during which some of your shares are offered to the public on one of the stock exchanges. The bankers involved with either type of exit are even more experienced at setting the value of a company than VCs. Their due diligence is more involved, and there will be no stone unturned or possible question unasked. But the good news? An exit is going to happen! It's just a matter of the price being set (unless something bad is found during due diligence and the deal falls through).

20.2 Why valuation matters

Your startup's valuation correlates to dilution at the next round. Each round adds some dilution. That's because a round of financing creates new shares out of thin air to sell to the new investors. That creation of new shares makes the existing shares represent a smaller ownership stake in the company (i.e., they are more diluted).

20.2.1 Valuation and dilution explained

Let's say I own 1,000 shares in Acme Corp, which has a total of 1,000,000 shares outstanding. Therefore, I own

$$\frac{1,000}{1,000,000} = 0.1\% \text{ or } \frac{1}{10}\%$$

But what happens if Acme, to raise additional capital, creates another 500,000 shares to sell to new investors, and I don't get any more than what I already own? My ownership stake in Acme is now

$$\frac{1,000}{1,500,000} = 0.067\% \text{ or } \frac{1}{15}\%$$

My stake in the company is diluted by a factor of 1.5. I might be pretty upset that I was hit with so much dilution. But we need to factor in the share price to really appreciate what is going on.

If the share price prior to the new investment was $1, then the valuation of Acme was

$$1,000,000 \text{ shares } \times \frac{\$1}{\text{share}} = \$1,000,000$$

and the value of my stake was

$$1,000 \text{ shares } \times \frac{\$1}{\text{share}} = \$1,000$$

Let's assume the new price offered by the new investor is $2 per share. Then after the new round, Acme's valuation is

$$1,500,000 \text{ shares } \times \frac{\$2}{\text{share}} = \$3,000,000$$

and the value of my stake is

$$1{,}000 \text{ shares } \times \frac{\$2}{\text{share}} = \$2{,}000$$

I got diluted by a factor of 1.5, but the value of my stake increased by a factor of 2. How is that possible? Because the valuation of Acme increased by a factor of 3. So, should I *always* be upset about dilution? No.

My startup teams have, for reasons I have never understood, tended to obsess over the dilution of their stake in the company with each round of financing. It is true that dilution is a very big deal if the company has flat or down rounds because without the price per share rising, a current shareholder's stake becomes less valuable, as well as more diluted, as the share price goes down. But if the company has a down round, it is because what is happening with it is not good in the eyes of investors, and that must be fixed. Having said that, your team needs to learn not to focus on dilution if the future looks bright and your valuation will steadily keep going up. I probably had to explain dilution to my entire startup at my every Wednesday all-hands meeting two or three times each year. For some reason, no matter how many times I explained it, some of the team focused on how their actual stake in the company was declining over time and not on the overall value of their potential payout upon an acquisition or IPO.

Acquisition price is sometimes tied to revenues. A lot of companies are in markets where the expectation for acquisition price is typically 5× to 10× *annually recurring revenues* (ARR). When people learn that Webspective sold for $106 million on only $2 million in revenues, they raise their eyebrows almost to their hairlines because, in their heads, they are doing the math and thinking it means a 52× revenues multiple for acquisition price. But in fact, that was the infamous internet bubble year of 1999, when many normal investing rules were suspended. More typical was the acquisition of GeoTrust: in 2006, seven years after Dave Chen and I founded it, the company sold to Verisign for $125 million on $25 million of revenues. A 5× price is totally typical and expected, albeit still good. Either case deserves an unbelievable day of celebration and high fives because most people have never had anything like that happen to them.

Sometimes acquisition price is tied to your valuation with a factor allowing for it to increase in the short term. A service-oriented business will typically fit into this model. Pricing for an IPO often models valuation with an expectation (hope) that on opening day, the market will drive up the stock higher than the company's valuation—that's the dream IPO, at least.

20.2.2 *Valuation changes: Slow and steady vs. jumps*

Getting back to valuation changes, if you plot on a graph each value as valuation changes over time, what matters most is the direction of the curve. Is it going up (good) or down (bad)? And if it is going up, how rapidly is that happening? The faster your valuation is rising, the better new investors will feel about your prospects; they will extrapolate that line out and give you credit for it as they set the price at which they are willing to invest. This "extrapolate the curve out" happens at acquisition time, too. Whether the investors are VCs, corporates, or bankers in the public markets, they are investing in where you are going as opposed to where you are today. In fact, in August 1999, when Inktomi offered Webspective $106 million, it fully expected the company's value to continue to grow—which, in fact, it did. Within six months of acquisition, the value of Webspective, now fully incorporated inside Inktomi, was measured at over $400 million. Ridiculous beyond explanation, I know, but that was what was happening those days. In March 2000, Inktomi peaked its market capitalization (that's the public market term for *valuation*) at $25 billion when its stock reached $241 per share; yet exactly three years later, its stock had dropped 99.3%, and Yahoo!, its largest customer, bought it for only $241 million, or $1.63 per share.

A nice, consistent step function is much better than a huge jump. That keeps everyone looking toward the future. It also gives you breathing room. If the next step takes a bit longer, the pattern is still there.

A steady rise in valuation motivates, incentivizes, and rewards the team. It also helps with retention because they see the value of their holding going up; if it seems likely to keep going up, they understand why they need to stay to capitalize on that.

I strongly advocate this slow, steady rise in valuation as opposed to big jumps because I believe you need to work hard to avoid a down round. Do that by not getting too greedy or impatient and having the valuation jump suddenly by a huge amount. I know how good it feels to see a big increase in valuation, but such an increase makes it more likely that if there is a subsequent stumble, your valuation will fall, whereas only a modest bump in valuation has some built-in room for a little bad news. If your valuation had been rising and then moves backward, the penalty, in terms of a price drop for the next round, can be deep and painful. Plus, your team can be demoralized by a down round. Both their stake in the company and the value of their holdings decline. Worse yet, the options they have been granted could go *underwater*. That means the strike price could be higher than the price of a share. No one will exercise their options when that is true, so until the price rises again, their options are worthless and lose all their value as an incentive to get employees to stay at the company and keep working hard.

20.3 The moral of this anecdote

Valuation is about how much someone thinks your startup is worth. If that sounds subjective, it is. As a startup, your shares are illiquid and can't be sold on any market. But various groups of interested parties have processes to establish your valuation. This is something you need to pay attention to because it affects things like the price at which you can offer stock options and the price you can expect at the next round of financing or an acquisition. It's safer if your valuation does not jump up extremely quickly: a slow, steady rise means if something does not go perfectly, you won't be subject to a painful down round, which can demoralize your whole team. And although valuation may seem like a concept that is entirely in the hands of an outside group, you can affect it and should work toward doing so. By hitting a variety of valuation events, you can cause the nice, steady rise in your valuation that you will see take effect at your next financing.

Part 4

Your team: Building it, sizing it, aligning it

I am co-opting Gloria Steinem's quote about self-esteem when I say "It's not that team is everything; it's just that there is nothing without it." That makes this part of the book very important to make sure you are attracting and retaining the best possible team. The anecdotes in this part are as follows:

- 21   Hire slowly—and correctly
- 22   Beyond foosball: Crafting a positive culture that retains your team
- 23   Does a startup need both a CEO and a COO?
- 24   Marketing: Too often a startup's afterthought
- 25   The right character for your sales leader—and when to hire them

The first anecdote in this part is about hiring. As I like to say, "Hire slowly, fire quickly." This anecdote is also about how to hire correctly. The next anecdote, on culture, is about attracting and retaining the best people you can for what you are trying to accomplish. A key point is that the CEO must create and maintain the culture and that it needs to start on day one—it can't wait.

I then offer a series of three anecdotes that dive into specific roles (or titles) in the ranks of senior staff that create common challenges for the CEO. These three anecdotes cover, respectively, the chief operations officer (COO), chief marketing officer (CMO), and VP sales or chief revenue officer (CRO).

21

Hire slowly— and correctly

- Using smart resources, can you tap into the talent goldmine?
- What can you safely ask, and what should you avoid, when conducting interviews?
- How should you construct an offer that works for both you and the candidate?

One of my top management philosophies is to *hire slowly, fire quickly*. In this anecdote, we will be talking about hiring. This is a critical function that takes time, and even a startup cannot rush it without paying a very high price. Even though we believe in firing quickly when it's merited, that does not make a bad hire cost less.

RESOURCE If you want to dig into this topic more deeply, a good resource is the book *Hire the Best: Find, Interview, and Select Top Talent* by Laura Butcher and Don Lang. This anecdote covers things I consider essential to know and do in hiring, but the topic deserves a book—and Butcher and Lang created such a book. I knew them when I was first a senior leader at Borland in 1995 and their book was just a pamphlet given out as part of their training course. I studied and dog-eared that pamphlet to death as I incorporated their principles into every one of my eight startups since those days.

Making a bad hire is very costly, both for the individual and for the startup. For the startup, which has few people and even less time to waste, not only does a bad hire hurt productivity because that person is a poor performer, but it also hurts the productivity of everyone around them. It is expensive in terms of time and money. It also hurts morale because everyone is counting on you to add positively to the team, not detract from it. A bad hire means you let the team down and potentially damaged their confidence in you (which you can recoup if you react fast and fire quickly). Everyone makes hiring mistakes—hiring is an art, not a science. It is very hard to figure out in an interview—which does not accurately simulate a real work situation— whether someone is really going to fit and help the team. Nothing can give you a hiring superpower, but the information I provide in this anecdote may help you create a process that increases your odds of making better hires and fewer mistakes.

The process for doing this as well as possible is not rocket science; it is simple and logical. Yet, surprisingly, even those of us who know better sometimes short-circuit the following steps out of a belief in exceptions or due to laziness or forgetfulness. A good hiring process includes

1 Creating a well-thought-out job specification
2 Sourcing candidates using a few different approaches
3 Having an interview team, rules of engagement, and a consistent, careful approach to interviewing
4 Doing detailed reference and background checks
5 Onboarding and supporting the new hires as they integrate into your team, culture, and company

21.1 The job specification

The point of the job specification is to clearly document what you require from the person who ultimately fills the open position. This is important for you because the act of writing it down forces you to be clear about what you want, need, and expect from this new person; it's also important for your interviewing team, for the broader team with which the new hire will work, and for the prospective hire.

A job specification is derived from a job description by adding specific, time-based outcomes expected from the person in this role. Start with a job description that focuses on the responsibilities, skills, and experience necessary in candidates. Following is a sample job specification for a DevOps engineer; it is short, clear, and simple. I have left a few things to be filled in that describe your company, market, and so on.

> **Software DevOps engineer**
> Join a high-performing, close-knit team at a fast-growing technology startup in [*city*]. [*New company*] is commercializing a revolutionary technology. [New company] already has significant commercial traction with customers in the [*name-of-the-market*] market.

We are looking for a software engineer to join our growing team. Candidates should be comfortable working in a fast-paced, [*another-exciting-adjective*] environment.

Responsibilities

- Maintain and build automated testing environments for embedded systems software.
- Develop C and assembler tests to run on both simulators and FPGA-based hardware.
- Narrow test cases and submit defect reports to developers.
- Develop test methodologies and testing frameworks for new technology (software and hardware) developments as needed.
- Perform software integration tasks of proprietary tools into third-party development environments.
- Develop improvements to simulator technology and runtime software stack to support usability, testability, and performance analysis.

Skills

- Strong knowledge of the C language
- Experience with assembler code, both writing and debugging, RISC processors preferred
- Experience with scripting languages, such as Python and Linux shells
- Previous work with continuous integration systems like Buildbot, Bamboo, or Jenkins
- Able to work independently

Experience

- BS degree in computer science or equivalent work experience
- 5 to 7 years of experience developing production-quality software
- Experience working in a fast-paced startup environment would be preferred

Culture & benefits

We are located in a beautifully renovated building in the [*location*] area in [*city, state*], [*some other attractive information*]. We have lots of drinks and snacks, plus access to a free on-site fitness center, biking/walking paths, and [*something more*]. We're a small, tight-knit group that works in a relaxed, friendly, and highly motivated environment.

We offer

- Competitive compensation
- Comprehensive health and dental coverage
- A flexible take-what-you-want vacation policy, plus official holidays
- Flexible office hours and work-from-home options
- Participation in an employee stock option plan

Expected accomplishments (12–18 months)

- A set of tests that provides at least 80% test coverage of the entire system
- A fully automated test environment that can do full nightly regression tests

To turn a job description into this job specification for the hiring process, specific outcomes expected in the next year or two were added. This makes the job information more relevant and actionable. Candidates appreciate this level of specificity, as it enables them to imagine more accurately being in the job and self-evaluate if they can achieve those outcomes. Both the candidate and the interviewing team members can now have detailed discussions about how the candidate—and the team they will be part of—would go about achieving the desired outcomes.

21.2   Sourcing candidates

The concept of *talent brand* is worth incorporating into everything you and your company do. Much like your company brand, which projects what your company stands for, what it does, and the perceptions you want to instill in people's minds about you, your talent brand projects your values and how potential hires could grow, contribute, and improve their skills if they came to work at your company. An effective talent brand is essential to attract the best candidates who will advance your company and improve its standing with investors and its standing relative to your competitors.

> **DEFINITION**   *Talent brand* is the social version of your employer brand—the perception people have about the organization and what they say and share about the enterprise as a place of employment.

Effectively projecting your talent brand means a portion of your website—a careers page, access to which is prominent on the home page—shows that you are hiring and expresses your values and culture as well as the job specifications you are currently hiring for. It means wherever you go, you are talking about hiring and the incredible team you already have. It means you, your senior managers, and especially all hiring managers, have the "we're hiring" link on their LinkedIn profile. It means even when you are not hiring, you are still gathering a pool of candidates your company is interested in so that when you are ready to hire, you can first try to dip into that pool to significantly speed up the process.

Establish an employee referral bonus (make it generous, like $1,000–1,500) because your current team is the ideal first place to source your next hires. It is the cheapest, highest-impact way to find qualified candidates. Plus, candidates come with a strong recommendation from someone who is a producing member of your company. Post your jobs on Facebook and other social media channels that make sense, and ask your employees to share them on their networks and spread the word widely. You never know where you are going to find that incredible hire!

21.2.1   Using sourcing services

Indeed is one of the most prominent job boards, but there are many, and some operate in specialty areas that may be of more use to startups. Indeed is different from most job board sites because, like Kayak, it scrapes other sites for listings and reposts them. And like Kayak, the best way for a job searcher to use Indeed is to do a search there and scan the results but then go directly to the original site. To be comprehensive in getting to many candidates, it is wise to list your openings at Indeed but know what you are getting. The best tech talent is probably not using it.

LinkedIn has grown to 1 billion users, making it an effective way to find people—even people who are not looking for a new job. It has always been especially strong for the tech community, and LinkedIn Recruiter is a paid service that helps them find you. LinkedIn offers Recruiter and Recruiter Lite. Lite only looks at first-, second-, and third-degree connections, whereas Recruiter looks at all of LinkedIn. Pricing is tricky until you specify all your parameters, but HeroHunt.ai estimates that LinkedIn Lite runs $1,680 per year and LinkedIn Recruiter is $10,800 per year.[1] I believe a small company can get what they need with Lite.

The downside of job boards and either LinkedIn Recruiter version is that for you to use them successfully, someone at your company must work hard sitting at a computer. Many startups have no one to do that. A hiring manager who makes sure the startup website is effective at broadcasting that you are hiring, gets employees to dig deeply into their contacts for referrals, and uses LinkedIn Recruiter Lite a couple of hours a day is about as cost-effective and successful as you can get. But if you are doing a lot of hiring, it would be more effective to hire a contract recruiter. They can do a comprehensive search that employs job boards, LinkedIn Recruiter, and myriad other resources that these hiring professionals have at their fingertips. Whenever my team is doing a batch of hires, we take this approach. But if we're filling only one or two positions, the hiring manager goes their own way.

21.2.2 *Using recruiters*

If using paid recruiters is justified, there are contract recruiters, or you can hire a full-time recruiter. Sometimes, if you have hired an HR person, they can recruit as a major part of their job. I did this for my first startup because we had to hire continuously for the first 18 months: HR handled everything from job specifications to recruiting, benefits, employment issues, and even firing. Other times, I have used full- and part-time contract recruiters very effectively. Some of these worked on a time basis, and some were contingency-fee-based, where the fee was paid on successful hiring and sometimes was tied to the new hire's salary.

21.3   *The interview process*

Once the candidate flow starts, the hiring manager is the person who filters the incoming candidates to get to the small set who will go through the interview process. They are also the boss of the interview team. Everything I learned about interviewing I learned at Borland, a 1,500-person public company. The company was enlightened about hiring and built one of the best software development organizations I've ever seen. Based on these first-hand experiences, my most important message about hiring is this: Create a tight process for interviewing and stick to it.

---

[1] Yuma Heymans, "LinkedIn Recruiter pricing 2024: What Does It Cost You," *HeroHunt.ai*, December 18, 2023, https://www.herohunt.ai/blog/linkedin-recruiter-pricing.

21.3.1 *The interview team*

The hiring manager creates the interview team as the job specification is being finalized. The team reviews the job spec just before it is finalized and gives their feedback. This team will follow the process for every candidate considered from start to finish. Each member of the team is given a role. It might be to interview for technical skills or culture fit or communication skills, whatever is critical for this role. Some overlap between team members may be intentional, especially in the most critical areas. It is important that someone on the team covers each element required to be present in the candidate.

I think it is important to empower everyone on the team with a veto regarding whether to move forward with a candidate. They can't (and won't, in my experience) be capricious with that power, and it streamlines the entire process because this makes sure you and your team are not wasting time on a candidate who someone important thinks is a bad fit.

21.3.2 *Types of interviews*

I generally see there as being six distinct types of interviews that should be spread out among the interview team:

- *Screening*—The screening interview is the purview of the hiring manager or the recruiter, if there is one. This step is looking for deal-breakers, salary expectations, and location issues (if important).
- *Assessment*—The one place for questions straight off the candidate's résumé is the assessment interview, which is also done by the hiring manager or recruiter. The normal strategy is to go over the résumé from back to front in chronological order to fill in details that don't fit on the résumé. This is also when any questions about the veracity of the résumé can be checked.
- *Technical skills*—A technical expert or two on the hiring team conducts this interview to assess whether the person has the technical skills needed. No tests should be necessary because these skills can be uncovered with the right kind of questions; later, references can verify them.
- *Communication skills*—Someone on the interview team focuses on the person's communication and interpersonal skills. How well do they work in a team setting? Do they show leadership? Do they write well?
- *Culture fit*—Usually I leave this to the CEO for their interview time. Culture fit gets at a core set of shared values (or not). Questions to consider are: Is this someone who can fit into and add to the existing company culture? Do they value feedback? Can they handle criticism? Do they consider customers important? Do they want to learn, grow, and improve? This is not frivolous. It is vitally important because if they don't fit, they will rub everyone else the wrong way at worst or be unhappy and unproductive at best.
- *Selling*—Either the CEO or the hiring manager usually handles selling the virtues of the company. It usually works best at the end and is most impactful if it

comes directly from the CEO. What is the vision for the company? What is the likely exit, and when? How will the company change the world? Get the candidate very excited as they are about to walk out the door.

21.3.3 Rules of engagement

A set of rules of engagement guides the process once a candidate is identified and is going to be invited in.

INVITING A CANDIDATE TO INTERVIEW

When a candidate is invited in for an interview, the team meets and hears from the hiring manager why this person made it through their filter. Team roles are reviewed, and then the team members are scheduled for their slots. A full day of interviews is at most 8 hours, but preferably 6 hours. A few interviews can be as little as 30 minutes. Most should be 45 to 50 minutes long, with a break of a few minutes between them.

Some types of interviews can be held by two members of your team at a time. This can be very effective because the question one asks may spark a new thought in the other, and while one is speaking, the other can think more clearly about the next question they want to ask. Also, having two interviewers helps when reporting results back to the team, as two people see and hear different things and provide a richer set of feedback.

For especially senior roles, one day of interviews may not be sufficient. In rare cases, a second day can be scheduled.

BEGINNING OF THE INTERVIEW DAY

The hiring manager is the meeter and greeter, welcoming and outlining the day for the candidate.

MIDDAY QUESTIONS OR CONCERNS

If there is a yellow flag, members report it to the hiring manager and work up a strategy for how to get more information about the problem area. Maybe later interviewers focus on this area, or the manager does, or the interviewer raising the flag gets an additional block of time to probe further.

MIDDAY REJECTIONS

Anyone who sees a giant red flag goes to the hiring manager immediately after their interview. Their judgment is not questioned, but the hiring manager probes to see if the problem is as serious as they think. Then if the hiring manager agrees, there is no working around it. Chances are this will not be a fit. In this case, the hiring manager politely stops the process, walks the person to the door, and says goodbye. Do not keep the process going out of an abundance of niceness—it is wrong to waste your team's time if one of them is going to veto an offer anyway.

MIDDAY EXCITEMENT

On the flip side, if people are ecstatic about someone, they need to let the hiring manager know because they may want to move quickly with an offer. Presenting a full offer before a person leaves the building blows the candidate away and is virtually impossible at a large company. In a hyper-competitive environment, this move can make all the difference between getting this person or losing them to a huge, rich company like Apple, Google, or Amazon.

NO SUBJECTIVE EXPRESSIONS

During the day, it is vital that no one expresses their subjective views to anyone other than the hiring manager, to keep the final meeting as objective as humanly possible. Don't even allow the ubiquitous thumbs-up and -down gestures to be used during the day.

THE POST-INTERVIEW DEBRIEF

Here, too, do not allow team members to give any subjective expressions of opinions at the meeting outset. There is time for that later. First, go around in interviewing order and ask each member to express their *objective* feedback on the candidate. This should be based on the candidate's behavioral interview answers (explained in detail momentarily). Following this, ask everyone to express their summary *subjective* judgment, even using the thumbs up/down if they like. This will then drive more detailed explanations of those summary judgments, further enlightening others' views.

NEXT STEPS

This is the point when the hiring manager expresses their intent. They consider the following: Is this the candidate they want? Does this candidate need to come back in because some of the team need more time to evaluate them? Do they want the process to continue through the rest of the qualified candidates?

How not to interview

Except for the assessment interview, which is not done on interview day, do not ask factual questions right off the candidate's résumé. Sure, use the résumé to formulate behavioral questions, but asking where they worked in 2015 is a waste of interview time.

I think tests during an interview are a horrible idea. People who use them think they can discern technical capability. In what way does that accurately reflect the day-to-day of the job? If you must see how they program a particularly challenging thing, give them a take-home test instead of making them go up to the board in front of you and others. The worst abuse of this I experienced was when I was interviewing at Borland before the management team came in that transformed Borland into a company with a high HR IQ. I was being interviewed for a position as manager of a seven-person group that was not a coding role. The senior-most member of the team asked me to go up to his whiteboard and write out a C program that could walk the stack from directly inside a function. I got it right because I am a kind of weird geek, but I was displeased, and once I became his boss, I firmly but gently said never to do that again.

As I discuss in anecdote 22, "Beyond foosball: Crafting a positive culture that retains your team," lots of companies have a set of values they like to talk about and get everyone to embrace. And they like to incorporate them into interviews. I have no problem using them in the culture-fit interview, but to ask every interviewer to include them means other critical topics get short shrift. A big offender in this regard is Microsoft, which is legendary in Silicon Valley for its famous and provocative "Why are manhole covers round?" question. Another big offender is Amazon, where I happened to interview for a very senior role. Jeff Bezos developed a list of 14 leadership traits that he wanted to exemplify Amazon. Every single person who interviewed me over an eight-hour day spent at least a quarter of their time asking me questions about a few of those 14 traits. What was worse was that they took me to a small conference room designed for a meeting of at most four people, where I stayed the entire day. A new person would arrive at the top of each hour, plunk their laptop down on the table between us, hunch over so I could not see them nor them me, and proceed to ask questions. While I answered, they typed their notes into their laptop. No eye contact. No small talk, either. No one subjected to that treatment would want to take a job there. I could not wait to get out of Amazon's building and out of Seattle.

21.3.4 *Behavioral interviewing*

If you are not going to ask factual questions directly from the candidate's résumé, how should you structure interviews to learn what is most important about the individual? The answer is *behavioral interviewing*. Not only is this a much more effective way to really learn about how the person thinks and works, but it also helps keep the questioning away from things that could get the interviewer and their company in trouble.

During behavioral interviewing, you have a friendly conversation, getting the candidate to tell you stories. You do this by asking open-ended questions.

My favorite interview questions for a programmer

"When you worked at Acme Corp, what was the best computer program you ever worked on?" Then later, "What made that your favorite?"

"What was the worst program you ever wrote?" Then later, "What made that the worst?"

"Tell me the story of the worst bug you ever had to track down."

"What is the best time you ever had collaborating closely with a colleague?" Then later, "And what was the worst?"

"What was the hardest thing about delivering the <so-and-so> webinar when you were at Acme Corp?"

"Who was your best boss and why?" Then later, "And the worst?"

This can go on and on, and it's fun because they get engaged and sometimes passionate. Follow-up questions come naturally, and you and they can really build rapport with each other. Further, although this is not precisely a simulation of a workday, it's a lot closer than anything else you can do in an interview because you are being told a story of how they really do their work.

Another important benefit to this approach is that you are asking short questions that have long answers; you are not monopolizing the conversation. You want them to be talking about 85% of the total interview time. Now, when the interview team meets at the end of the day, you have some very objective information about how the candidate performs, what they care about, how they handle stress and disappointment, how they are to manage, how good they are at collaboration, and so forth.

21.4 Closing the deal

Unfortunately, many companies have a policy that the only thing employees can say when called for a reference check about a former employee is to confirm dates of employment. Luckily, some people disregard these rules (more often when they have positive things to say about the individual). It is still important to do reference checks, if possible. I have learned some things in reference checking that reversed my decision to make an offer and saved us from the time, trouble, and expense of a bad hire.

In reference interviews, establish the facts first, such as what their role is and what job the candidate did for them. Then use the same behavioral techniques from the candidate interviews to get at the essence of the person's performance.

21.4.1 The offer

If this is a technical hire, there will likely be competition because the whole tech industry is very competitive for acquiring talent. Competing against Apple, Amazon, Facebook, Google, and lots more of their ilk is no fun. They can certainly pay a lot more than you can. But if you've gotten this far and you are thinking about making an offer, you must have a sense that the candidate is very interested in you. You need to capitalize on that with some confidence that your inherent advantages of nimbleness, small teams, great culture, revolutionary technology, and big potential payoffs, will help you add some sugar. Suggestions for benefits you can include that those big guys can't or won't include these:

- Total coverage of the employee health plan cost
- Unlimited vacation time (that does not accrue to your balance sheet)
- Parental leave benefit of at least 8 weeks (offer 12 if you can)
- Generous stock options

21.4.2 Options

Your ace in the hole is stock options. If the prospective employee is savvy about options and startups, they will know what to ask for. To review, *stock options* are a right the company conveys to employees to purchase stock at a certain price called the strike price at a future date. The parameters that matter here are percentage ownership, vesting schedule, expiration date, strike price, change of control protection, and the date and details of the next round of financing.

PERCENTAGE OWNERSHIP

Telling someone they will get 10,000 stock options means nothing to them. If your company has 1 million outstanding shares, that means the person would own 1%. But if it has 100 million outstanding shares, their grant is for 1/100%. Those who understand this will want to know the percentage ownership they will have. Senior people hired before Series A may get between 1/2% and 1%. Rank and file may get between 1/10% and 1/4%.

VESTING SCHEDULE

The company's option plan will have been set up at formation, and stock option plans are all similar these days. Vesting is typically over four years with a one-year cliff. This means it takes four years to fully vest the option grant. A grantee has the right to exercise shares they have vested any time until the grant expires. The *cliff* means you don't vest any of your options the first year of employment, but at the one-year anniversary, you vest the first quarter of your grant; subsequently you vest 1/36 of the total grant each month. The one-year cliff is designed to keep people from hopping from one company to another so quickly that they don't have time to meaningfully contribute to the company.

EXPIRATION DATE

The expiration date is when options that have not been exercised (turned into shares or stock) go away. Expiration is usually far out in the future if you are employed by the company. If options expire, they are no longer available to the employee and revert to the company's pool of available options to be used for a future new hire.

STRIKE PRICE

The *strike price* is the price to the employee to exercise each option. Exercise means to turn an option into a real share that has value and can be sold later. The strike price is fixed at the time of the grant, and the lower that price is, the better. The idea is that the company will get more valuable over time, and consequently its stock price will rise, but the strike price the employee pays to own that share will remain fixed. As that happens, the employee sees their potential holdings in the company's stock become more valuable, whereas the cost to them to convert their options into stock is fixed at a relatively low price. This creates an incentive for employees to stay with the company because if they leave, all options they did not exercise go away. If they stay with the company and exercise every option available to them, when the company has a good exit, they have the potential to earn a significant amount of money on their stock. And no public tech company can offer anything close to that.

CHANGE OF CONTROL PROTECTION

Speaking of exit, *change of control protection*, usually only offered to the senior-most members of the company, stipulates that some percentage of their unvested options vest instantly upon an exit (acquisition or IPO). Because they have vested, the employee can exercise them and convert them to stock. The exit sets a price to be paid for all shares, which the employee is directly paid for. These numbers can be huge, which is a benefit unique to a startup.

Finally, the prospective employee may want to know what financings are expected between their option grant date and a potential exit. A financing will affect the percentage of ownership they retain in the company. The financing causes the company to create new shares to sell to the new investor, which increases the total number of shares in the company, which decreases or dilutes the ownership stake of the employee. Not a big deal if the value of the company goes up at that financing because what matters is the total value of their holdings.

These option benefits, along with a few other things you have in your bag of tricks, even the playing field with respect to the big tech companies. You should be able to hold your own and get that great future employee to accept your offer.

21.5   *The moral of this anecdote*

Once you have formed the company and gotten adequate financing to operate for long enough to prove something, you need to hire a team that can do the work those investors are counting on to build real value. And although hiring is an essential step for any founding team and their CEO, it is one of the most challenging pieces because it is not a science, it is an art. But hiring can become a lot less of a black art with a strong process imposed on it. For one thing, if the team is using their extensive networks of talented people (who may be engineers), that is helpful because the first order of business is usually building a product. After that, writing down the description of the jobs you need to fill and what they need to accomplish forms the blueprint for your next phase of hiring. Create a process for interviewing built around an interview team, and it starts to look a little more like a recipe that everyone can follow. You have some advantages against the Goliaths out there because of the benefits you can offer. Foremost, the stock options you provide can make the team you hire able to envision leaving a real legacy for their family.

Beyond foosball: Crafting a positive culture that retains your team

- Why does culture matter? And why does it matter more for a startup?
- How is culture formed and maintained?
- Is there a core set of principles that drives company culture?

Startup culture is related to *organizational culture*, an idea introduced in 1951 by Elliott Jaques in his book *The Changing Culture of a Factory*, where he submits that organizational culture incorporates a set of shared assumptions that guide the behaviors of its members. Shared assumptions will involve all aspects of your work life at a startup, such as how team members treat each other, how disputes are handled, how communications are delivered, how customers and partners are treated, how the company thinks about work–life balance, and many more that we will get into. These patterns of behaviors and assumptions are taught to new team members as they join the startup so they integrate well into the culture and the company. We sometimes joke about new additions to a startup becoming "assimilated," as if the startup is pretending to be the Borg from Star Trek. But that is not so far from the truth. Ultimately, startup culture will affect how much team members identify with the company. Put simply, if the culture is great, they will identify strongly with the company, and if it is poor, they are probably already looking for their next opportunity. Culture is that important!

DEFINITION *Culture* is a shared set of workplace beliefs, values, attitudes, standards, purposes, and behaviors. It reflects both the written and the unwritten rules that people in an organization follow. Your organization's culture is the sum of all that you and your colleagues think, say, and do as you work together.

22.1 Why culture matters deeply, especially at a startup

The overall experience at a startup, for it to be successful, needs to foster collaboration, cooperation, innovation, and good old-fashioned focused hard work. There just can't be negative forces at work, such as biases against minority groups, people widely viewed as not carrying their weight, arguments and dissension, or, worse, insults and yelling, or the resulting negative culture will quickly sink the startup. A positive culture is essential for employee job satisfaction, which means it will be a huge factor in your retention rate. I would surmise that if you have a high turnover rate (your retention rate is not close to 100%), you have a culture problem.

There are not many ways to compete with big tech companies, such as Apple, Meta, Google, Amazon, and Microsoft, in terms of salary and basic benefits like health insurance and vacation, but you have an unfair advantage over their big company culture. If a potential new hire is already leaning toward a startup but will take the best overall situation in terms of personal satisfaction, you should easily be able to get them to choose you. That is, assuming you have a welcoming culture that everyone on your team—including all the people interviewing this person—will gladly crow about. What's wonderful about a positive culture is that it is self-reinforcing. Each new best-in-class hire who is attracted to your culture will add to it and help attract more best-in-class people, each of whom will help continue to expand the strong, attractive culture just as you hope will happen.

22.2 How culture is formed and maintained

Culture flows from the CEO down—you cannot delegate this one. Sure, you need the full support of your entire team to create and maintain the culture you define and establish, but on all things relating to your startup's culture, *the buck stops here.*

Not only does culture start with the CEO, but it must also start on day one. If it starts off wrong, or even not at all, it is exceedingly difficult to change later. Why? Because culture is embodied in the people. To change it involves getting into the patterns of behavior and attitudes of everyone on the team. That just can't be done. Bottom line: right from the start, even when you want to be spending all of your and your team's time on product, market, sales, and messaging, you must spend time on culture first because it pays dividends in many ways. Let's talk about some of those ways.

22.2.1 Some big things that form a startup's culture

There are both big and not-so-big elements of the culture at a startup. It all begins by following a simple set of management philosophies. Keeping a flat organization makes sure people don't feel a big distance from the top management of the company. Communication is essential, and full transparency and honesty, even when there is bad news, go a long way toward building strong bonds between people. How people are treated further strengthens those bonds, making everyone feel like they are part of something good. The absence of politics is refreshing for anyone who has previously worked at a large organization, where politics apparently are inevitable. Let's examine each of these elements at the core of a positive culture.

MANAGEMENT PHILOSOPHIES

Management philosophies are first and foremost in this list. They matter a lot.

Four management philosophies I live by

1 Always assume the best.
2 Treat people like adults.
3 Trust (but verify).
4 Do unto others as you would have them do unto you (the Golden Rule).

Even if someone appears to be doing something that is not correct, avoid at all costs "jumping down their throat," ESPECIALLY IN ALL-CAPS EMAILS, because nothing destroys your relationship with your team quicker than that when it turns out they were doing nothing wrong. Often I misunderstand what is being done or said, but fortunately, I (almost always) assume the best and calmly find out what is really going on.

Treating people like adults should never even need to be mentioned, but unfortunately it does, especially with inexperienced managers and managers who feel they need to assert their authority. Again, being demeaning or patronizing to people will not create an environment in which they want to work hard or, perhaps, work at all.

Trust is a very big word. Well, it may seem like a small, five-letter word, but it carries a big weight, as if it were a 45-letter word like pneumonoultramicroscopicsilicovolcanoconiosis (a real word I just wanted to use somewhere in this book). You trusting your team makes them want to do more, to do better, to take on more responsibility, and to take on acceptable risks. Trust creates independent, autonomous team members who will grow quickly into more and more valuable employees. Sure, you must trust *but verify*, as Ronald Reagan famously said about the signing of the Soviet nuclear arms control treaty. But it's trust that comes first, and having your trust motivates your team.

The Golden Rule, "Do unto others as you would have them do unto you," is not just a management philosophy but a life philosophy. It's putting yourself in their shoes and seeing how this interaction you are having with them would feel if your roles were reversed. It is enlightening and sobering to think this way, and it will improve your interactions with everyone.

FLAT ORGANIZATION

Startups need to be extremely efficient with a very small staff. Thus it makes no sense to create a hierarchical organization—yet. Not only is a flat organization most efficient when the team is small, but it also fosters communication; makes it easier for people to "wear many hats"; makes it likely that people will naturally work across functional areas, avoiding stove piping—where activities and decisions in one group are made without consultation with other groups—and makes sure teams stay well aligned with each other. From your interns to the CEO and every level in between, be clear to the entire staff that everyone can and should reach out to and find support from absolutely anyone in the company.

TRANSPARENCY IN COMMUNICATION

You should strive for best-in-class communication that starts from the top down. Lots of transparency, even about challenges the company is facing, helps your team and cements them to you. Being open and transparent creates a sense of trust, and it makes people feel engaged in the company's journey. This is incredibly important at a startup because everyone is taking a risk to be there. Knowing there is open and honest communication makes everyone feel like they are at least taking that risk with their eyes wide open.

Have all-hands meetings frequently, as in every week. Keep them loose and fun. And don't do all the talking, so it is clear that your whole team is in on this. I have these meetings once a week with most of us standing up, which helps keep them short. I always kick them off but tap others throughout the organization to pitch in on topics they are best suited to talk about (and be recognized for). I always use these meetings to subtly, if not overtly, articulate the company values so the team is frequently reminded of them. Early on, because I love to bake, I decided to augment this meeting with a large basket of fresh muffins. The team loved that and would vote for their favorite flavors (winners included pumpkin chocolate chip and peach streusel). Food seems to make communication flow more easily. And with a limited muffin supply, it became, "If you feed them, they will come . . . on time!"

TREATMENT OF PEOPLE

Don't create a caste system. If there needs to be a pay cut, you take the first cut. If there is a travel policy, have it apply to everyone the same. If you have a large group of founders and you want that group to meet, do it offsite, or else everyone will know there is a founders' meeting and will feel like founders are more important. Sure, founders are important, but their importance comes from the (confidential financial) deal they got at formation and the fact that as founders, they have a natural leadership role that people respect.

Offer HR policies that make people feel supported; and in general, consider that you don't just have employees you are responsible for: you are responsible for your employees' entire families. If you can, offer flex time, vacation with no limits (and no accrual, which is good for the bottom line), generous parental leave (male and female), health benefits (I recommend that you cover 100% of employee premiums, and a portion of family premiums if you possibly can). You can't compete with the big tech companies in many areas, such as a matching 401(k), so these benefits are helpful in attracting the best people.

Depending on where you live, follow the adage of "hire slowly, fire quickly" if it is legal to do so. Regardless of your jurisdiction, you need to be as certain as you can that the person you are about to hire is a strong fit. Do that by having the right people on the interview team and by teaching them how to do effective interviewing (see anecdote 21, "Hire slowly—and correctly"). Thoroughly check references. Remember, interviewing is an unnatural act and does not simulate that person's behavior and performance at work, so you must do a lot to avoid costly hiring mistakes.

If your team tells you someone turns out to be a bad fit and is not working out, investigate quickly. If, as I put it, "The bozo bit has flipped," there is no turning back, and you must act fast. You need to be fair to the individual. If that means a performance improvement plan, put it in place immediately. After that step, following the laws of your country, if you can, let that person go quickly. Dealing with the situation right away sends a huge positive message to the team that you support them and hear them when something is getting in the way of their forward progress and productivity. Similarly, if someone on your team acts badly toward someone else, you must deal with it very quickly because if you don't, it can rapidly poison your culture.

Value diversity, make everyone feel welcome, and create a better company. It is still hard these days to find a lot of qualified women in engineering. You may need to use a talent firm to help hire a diverse workforce (which includes women in engineering).

ABSENCE OF POLITICS

The word *politics* in the context of company culture means two things. One use describes trying to get ahead, focusing only on yourself; this kind of politics is frequently held up as a key difference between big companies and startups. In my experience and that of every entrepreneur I know, a startup is allergic to this type of politics, and I rarely see it take hold. The other is the more common use of the word *politics*, which refers to political parties, candidates, their policies, and so forth.

Political conversations are very tricky right now in many countries, especially in the United States. Interestingly, in the United States, because political affiliation is not a protected class, there is no prohibition against asking "the question." My advice is to work this into your interviewing so as not to hire people from the opposite side of the spectrum. I know, you may think this exacerbates the divide and that it sounds inconsistent with the diversity goal. But I can't help it. Your company is small, and time is everything. You can't afford the disruption that comes when people are in close quarters, one person expresses their political views, and other people react negatively. This can become explosive very rapidly, and it absolutely destroys morale and productivity.

SUPPORTIVE ENVIRONMENT

In a startup, people need to wear multiple hats (it is what I love most about working at startups). Sometimes that takes us out of our comfort zone. But if you can set a tone where your team feels comfortable figuring things out together, even if sometimes it takes a try or two to get it right, they will be motivated to take acceptable risks and stretch themselves.

Foster growth in your people. Encourage them to expand their responsibilities. I have found that sometimes people don't believe they are able; but if it is clear that you believe in them, it gives them the confidence to try and, usually, succeed.

Fun ways to help maintain a positive culture

Here are some ideas of things you can do to keep your company's culture positive.

Food

An easy thing is to provide food. People want to graze in the kitchen. This is a small investment that keeps people in the office (if you use one) and happy. Another common food event that people like is pizza and beer on Friday afternoons. On an occasional basis, organizing a lunchtime potluck is popular, especially because we always try to include families. (Take any chance you get to include families, to recognize and thank the people behind the employees.) If the facility supports it, summer cookouts are great, again, especially when families can be included.

Games

Several of my startups liked to have a foosball table somewhere in the back of the office. It is a double-edged sword because others who could hear it did not like it—it did not help their productivity or morale. It also can grow into a major distraction from work if employees hold a tournament that takes up lots of time. Eventually a few rules had to be put in place to limit the hours the game was used, to minimize disruptions.

Hawaiian shirts

I have always been a Hawaiian-shirt-Friday kind of person since it was a thing in the 1980s in Silicon Valley. I've tried to make this a fun tradition. It was much harder to get it to catch on in Boston than in Silicon Valley. My theory is that Boston people hunker down during the long, cold winter, wearing lots of brown, gray, and black, and they just don't seem to be in the mood to wear bright colors or a short-sleeved shirt when it is 10 degrees outside. To help encourage them one year, I had our logo put onto Hawaiian shirts that we gave each employee. They still did not want to wear them, so I had to admit defeat. I was the only one consistently wearing a bright shirt every Friday, no matter what our New England winter had to offer.

Celebrating all "wins"

When the company gets a "win," whether it is a sale, closing a round of financing, a new hire, a patent filed or issued, or a successful webinar or conference, make it feel like every member of the team shares in that win. I got a real gong and put it in our common area, and whenever we were celebrating something, we banged the gong. I even got an MP3 file of a gong sound that we could play over Zoom when we were all remote during the pandemic.

Awards are a popular way to memorialize wins and mean a lot to people. This is also an opportunity to spread the love and recognize the people who have not invented a patent or made a big sale. I have seen some creative things done with awards. Boundless in Boston presented a "Cultural Achievement Award" to employees who had exemplified one of the four company values, represented by The Beast (the hardest worker), The Architect (the best strategist), Indiana Jones/Lara Croft (the dedicated adventurer looking for results), and The Most Interesting Person in the World (a well-rounded, funny, charismatic individual.

For more on this topic, I recommend Corey McAveeney, "How Do You Define Startup Culture?" *Wired*, September 2013, www.wired.com/insights/2013/09/how-do-you-define-startup-culture.

22.3 Aligning your teams

As I said in the introduction to this anecdote, startup culture will affect how much team members identify themselves with the company—and if teams are not aligned, people can feel disconnected from other teams and therefore from the rest of the company. This is why alignment is critical to maintaining a positive culture.

Alignment is having all the rowers in a long rowboat pulling in the same direction at the same time. That makes the boat track in a nice straight line. If one rower gets out of sync, it can not only send the boat off course but also screw up all the other rowers, so they become inefficient, confused, and upset. They are out of alignment, and if they are in a race, competitors who are aligned will beat them. In a company, alignment is about making sure that the individual functional teams know the strategy of the company (or their division, if it's a big company) and that they are doing all the things they need to do in their function to support achieving the company's strategic goals. I like BetterUp's definition of team alignment:

> DEFINITION *Team alignment* is the idea that each team and/or team member within the workforce collaborate to work toward a shared goal. When teams are aligned, communication, collaboration, productivity, and efficiency thrive.[1]

22.3.1 Why is alignment so important?

Small companies cannot afford to waste a single person's effort working on the wrong thing. Yet small companies will bob and weave (the predecessor term to *pivot*) as they learn from the market about the market, and they learn from customers, partners, and competition where their ideal positioning should be within their chosen market segment to maximize their chances of success. You absolutely must have each and every person—from the CEO to the chief architect to the marketing team to the test

---

[1] Madeline Miles, "5 Team Alignment Tactics to Boost Organizational Performance," BetterUp, October 6, 2022, https://www.betterup.com/blog/team-alignment.

and validation team and even to the HR department—all pulling in the same direction, aligned and working like a well-oiled machine toward precisely the same goal.

If the company is not aligned, it leads to unnecessary bobbing and weaving, strategy shifts, miscommunications, and wasted time. This is like trying to fix the bike while you are riding it. And it's yet another way startups fail.

22.3.2 *Achieving alignment*

What are some specific and actionable things the CEO and founders can do to achieve and maintain alignment? I have made the following five things part of my daily thought process and management style to create alignment.

1. COMMUNICATE COMPANY PURPOSE AND STRATEGY

Establish very clearly what the company's purpose and strategy are. Talk about it in your weekly all-hands meetings. Explain how everyone's contributions support this and help achieve the overall business objectives. Remember, every time you are forced to bob and weave, you must effectively communicate what the new strategy is, why it had to change, and how this impacts each function in the company. Change is hard, so you then must reinforce this over and over, not just top down in your all-hands meeting but in your walking around as well.

2. TEAM BUILD

Critical to having teams collaborate and work smoothly within the team and across teams is to make sure all your teams like, respect, and trust each other. Specifically, talk about how essential intra- and inter-team collaboration is, to put a fine point on both alignment within each team and alignment between teams. Highlight some critical inter-team dependencies. Getting to know people is essential to trust. Doing social things—barbeques, potlucks, picnics, theme parks, sports—outside of work goes a long way to achieving this. Also be sure to celebrate team wins, as this will reinforce how alignment is working.

3. MANAGEMENT BY WANDERING AROUND

Make "management by wandering around" how you and your senior team operate every day. Go find out if the individual contributors in IT, in HR, in software QA, doing hardware verification, and keeping the books understand the strategy and their roles in achieving it. Ask and explain if they are unclear. Repetition makes for understanding.

During COVID, we learned how this can work even when everyone is remote. The tools we used to make this easy were Google Meet and Slack. Each person created their own Meet link and published it so everyone had it at their fingertips. (If you send it to yourself in Slack, it is really handy.) If you want to "drop in" on someone or ask a quick question face-to-face and not in chat, you Slack them, and if their answer is yes, you meet on their Meet link in about 5 seconds. The other managers and I made sure the "wandering around" mantra stayed alive by doing this on a regular basis.

4. LISTEN

My saying "communicate, communicate, communicate" does not just mean you talk to all your employees; it's essential that you hear what message people are getting from you. You may not get the full picture from employees as you wander around. You may need to have a few "plants" to get it. I don't mean *plants* in any nefarious way. I mean people you trust who are out in the company, inside various functional teams, who hear what people are saying and can tell you. I always have a few of those, and they are invaluable in making sure your messaging is clear and precise and that people truly understand why you executed the most recent pivot.

5. INCLUSIVE PLANNING PROCESS

The need to change strategy, maybe a little, maybe a lot, is inevitable in an early-stage startup because you don't know what you don't know, and you are learning. But when it is clear that a change is needed, be sure the process of planning for the change in strategy is inclusive. I do not mean a committee. I mean when you have a clear sense of what is needed, start to meet with representatives of all the functional areas, explain what you are planning and why, and ask for their feedback. Getting them to understand builds trust and gives you emissaries who will help communicate your plan everywhere in the company.

Examples of misguided or just plain bad culture

A CEO who tries to force a harsh work ethic on a brand-new startup can create resentment. An example of this is the Silicon Valley startup where the CEO brought in a box of doughnuts on Saturday mornings and then counted how many were eaten to determine how many people were coming in on, ostensibly, a day off. People figured out they could just swing by, grab a doughnut, and get on with their non-company-related Saturday activities.

Another example, from a huge technology company, is of the worst culture I have ever experienced; it was a culture of screaming and demeaning people. There are many stories of important product meetings where a very senior VP would be presenting, and the CEO would scream at them that they were stupid. It got so bad that the CEO needed vocal nodule surgery not once but twice. I witnessed these scenes many times, and they were frightening. It made my friend, the senior VP, literally count the days until he was fully vested in his stock and could escape.

A final example is from a startup I founded. I stepped out of the CEO role to be CTO, and the replacement CEO's main management philosophy was fealty to him: unthinking loyalty with no discussion and no arguments—just get it done. Outside of the military and monarchy, blind loyalty does not equal high morale and does not foster high productivity or, because we all work with free will, longevity as an employee.

22.4   *Founders' pivotal role in maintaining culture*

Founders are natural role models from day one through when the startup is no longer a startup. They spend lots of time with team members, as many are also individual contributors. But they are human, and if they become disillusioned or unhappy, it can quickly destroy the company culture because not only are they role models but also they are thought of as canaries in the coal mine. Employees who see them go negative assume they know something. So although you do treat founders differently in some respects, you cannot let their negativity poison the culture, or you will have to make a really hard call.

I had to fire founders twice at two different companies, and those were two of the toughest decisions I have ever made. Although my normal philosophy is "hire slowly, fire quickly," I do not follow that when it comes to founders. I never fire founders quickly; doing so could completely break the company overnight. I try extremely hard to fix whatever is wrong, I exhibit extreme patience, and I spend huge amounts of time with the rest of the founders, trying to get everyone to help with the situation. Ultimately, it is only when the entire founder group agrees that the outlier is not fixable that I will make the move to have them depart, and then I work especially hard to explain what happened to the rest of the company to minimize the impact on the team.

Despite my best intentions, I have one trait that does not help create and maintain a great culture: excessive positivity. I frequently check in with my direct reports to see where I can improve, and one consistent theme is that although they appreciate my constant optimism, my *excessive* positivity can occasionally be a double-edged sword. There were times at some of my startups when things were sort of bleak, and people knew it, but I still spoke very positively—and the team later told me they knew I was not telling them how bad things really were. But at those times, I still thought I could pull off a miracle because so many times I had. On the other hand, there were a few times when I knew I shocked people with bad news. There's a fine line between sharing news too early and waiting too long. And frankly, I tend to err on the side of waiting too long.

Strangely, my team tempers their criticism by saying they do not want me to change this trait. In those bleak times, I was known even by the board and investors for being able to pull yet another rabbit out of the hat, and my team believed it was my ability to stay so positive that enabled me to work miracles so many times.

22.5   Driving company culture through a core set of principles

Many companies use a set of principles to establish and maintain their desired company culture. Jeff Bezos, in the early days of Amazon, famously established his principles describing what leaders should be.[2] Amazon job-seeking candidates are told that they need to not only memorize Bezos's 14 points but also have examples of each one that speak to them and that they will be asked about during their interview. Having interviewed at Amazon myself, I know that unfortunately, some interviewers turn them into cudgels to try to eliminate candidates as quickly as they can. That certainly did not indicate a positive culture to this potential employee.

---

[2] "Leadership Principles," Amazon, www.amazon.jobs/content/en/our-workplace/leadership-principles.

More relevant to us in this discussion about startup culture is a startup in the Boston area called Re:Build Manufacturing. It has a set of 16 principles that it mentions often, and each of its subsidiary companies hangs a poster with the principles printed on it so everyone sees them every day. When I speak to senior managers there, they say, "These are the core values of Re:Build, and they're not just words—they're really how we run the company."

Re:Build's 16 core values[3]

1. We care about our team members and put their safety before anything else.
2. Machiavelli was wrong! Winning at all costs is not winning at all. At Re:Build we want to be as proud of the path taken as the result achieved.
3. We recognize diversity as a source of value. We welcome and respect people from all walks of life. We encourage constructive dissent.
4. We protect the environment and devote significant resources to science-based sustainability programs.
5. We listen carefully and nondefensively to one another, customers, suppliers, and community members.
6. We are honest in all our dealings and seek mutually beneficial arrangements. We do not partake in zero-sum behaviors.
7. We are open in our communications, accountable for our actions, reject corrupt behaviors, and expect the same of other stakeholders.
8. We buy businesses to build them over the long term. We do not buy businesses with a plan to sell them.
9. We seek to improve the communities where Re:Build operates with a focus on apprentice programs and STEM education.
10. We use rigorous systems to ensure we hire and onboard team members who will be successful team members long term.
11. We provide long-term, meaningful opportunities for our team members to maximize both their contribution to Re:Build and their earning potential.
12. We provide forums for team members to share their knowledge and experience and refine their mental models. Re:Build is a learning organization.
13. We celebrate individual achievements but reserve the greatest accolades for team performance. The best ideas and solutions are rarely the product of a person working in isolation.
14. We focus on and measure inputs we control and expect excellent performance on input metrics to create long-term value.
15. We utilize Lean and continuous improvement as we strive for zero defects, lower cycle times, and minimal waste. We design quality into our products and systems.
16. We implement systems to ensure improvements last and identify and reward champions who propagate them across the company.

---

[3] "Our Moral Compass," Re:Build Manufacturing, https://rebuildmanufacturing.com/16-principles.

22.6   *The moral of this anecdote*

Culture is vitally important, and it must be established at the very instant of company formation. From then on, it must flow from the CEO and every person hired thereafter. A positive culture is self-perpetuating, attracts the best people, and allows you to retain them. There are a set of big things that work to create and maintain a great culture, including good management philosophies, having a flat organization, transparency in communications, consistently positive treatment of people, the absence of company politics, keeping teams aligned, and establishing a supportive environment. Founders play a pivotal role in maintaining a positive culture but can also play a potentially disastrous role if they lose faith. Some companies' approach to culture revolves around the establishment and consistent communication of a set of core principles. Whatever approach you take will be unique to you. This anecdote may provide some ideas for building the kind of culture you want to have in your startup.

Does a startup need
both a CEO and a COO?

- CEO versus COO—do you know the difference?
- Can you find a COO with complementary skills to the CEO to balance the latter's strengths?
- Co-CEOs or solo CEO+COO? Which leadership model will go the distance?

There are three anecdotes in this book about specific titles other than Chief Executive Officer (CEO). The titles that deserve their own anecdote are Chief Operations Officer (COO), Chief Marketing Officer (CMO), and head of sales. Why them and not others? Because these three have either controversy, special circumstances, or both surrounding them. The COO—the subject of this anecdote—is controversial because this role is rare for startups and sometimes is used to avoid having co-CEOs. The CMO (discussed in anecdote 24, "Marketing: Too often a startup's afterthought") is controversial because first, a lot of startups wait way too long to build a sufficient marketing team; and second, many startup CEOs do not fully understand the CMO role, and neither do other C-suite people, resulting in short tenures for CMOs. The head of sales (sometimes called the Chief Revenue Officer [CRO] and discussed in anecdote 25, "The right character for your sales leader—and when to hire them") is only controversial when hired too early. Sales leaders are definitely a different breed from other C-level executives and need to be treated differently.

Most companies have a CEO. In numerous situations, there is a COO as well. In rare circumstances, there are co-CEOs. I will discuss the rationale for one versus the other and walk through a set of questions you should consider in determining whether you should have, or be, a COO. What follows are those five reasons.

23.1   CEO vs. COO

Let's define the two roles to make sure we are in alignment on these two positions.

> **DEFINITION**   *CEO* is the top job in a company. They report to the board and are usually (at small companies) a member of the board. In most cases, they also hold the title of president, which, according to many states' business laws, is the formal title of the top decision-maker and the person responsible for all actions of the company. The team that reports to the CEO is mainly a set of other *chiefs* who make up what is referred to as the *C-suite*. In terms of the responsibilities of the CEO, they are responsible for determining the direction of the company, setting the strategy, and organizing and executing that strategy. The CEO is the final decision-maker and the owner of the company culture.

> **DEFINITION**   *COO* is defined mostly in terms of how this role best helps the CEO. It is safe to generalize that the COO is the number-two role in the company. They turn the strategy the CEO outlines (probably in close partnership with the COO) into processes and tactics that the COO must communicate to the teams that will execute them. The perfect COO is a generalist who, to be most effective, applies themselves where the need is the greatest. That need will move around as the company progresses. The COO is the CEO's most trusted advisor and, as such, sets out to squash problems before they become the CEO's problems. Sometimes they hold the title of president if the CEO doesn't. I have seen this happen when there are two equal founders, but they do not want a company run by co-CEOs, so they balance out their seniority by the COO being the president.

Let's be clear: most startups do not need a COO. The CEO can and should handle all the tasks the senior-most person in the company is responsible for. That includes all the things a COO might do. But for a variety of reasons I'll discuss, there are exceptions to this, and even I found myself being COO at one startup.

23.2   Five reasons for a startup to have a COO

Given that most startups don't need a COO, I have found five good reasons to have this role in a startup, depending on what the CEO needs most.

23.2.1 A mini-CEO

The CEO wants to focus on money. They will do the fundraising and have only the Chief Financial Officer (CFO) and COO as their direct reports. I've seen this when the CEO is not a good manager or has other outside responsibilities they cannot give up. The COO manages the entire rest of the C-suite as well as functional VPs and directors.

23.2.2 A super-CRO

Frequently, the CEO is not a sales and marketing expert, so they hire one as their COO. That person is effectively the CRO and maybe the CMO at the same time.

23.2.3 Head of operations

As the name says, COO is an operations role. Operations is somewhat vague because it means something different from company to company. But it can include responsibility for any of the following:

- *IT*—The operations of the network and computing systems and all the tools necessary for the development of the product or service
- *HR (if not under the CFO)*—The hiring operations of the company
- *Manufacturing*—The actual production of a hardware or biotech type of product
- *Facilities*—The buildings, equipment, and transportation as needed by the employees
- *Applied research and development*—The process of solving the open issues needed for the company to be successful

Small startups, especially software ones, don't usually need a head of operations. But this role is badly needed in industries such as pharma, biotech, hardware, robotics, medicine, and others where there is a large capital equipment need, where large staffs are employed, where the time scale to cash-flow break-even is very long, or where there are complex government regulations.

23.2.4 An untitled CEO

When coequal founders start a company, they sometimes propose being co-CEOs, but that rarely works. As President Truman's famous desk sign said, "The buck stops here." There can be only one person ultimately in charge; you can't have Truman's sign say "The buck stops here or over there." A more common approach for a working partnership is the CEO–COO plan. It might even work (if egos allow it and it is necessary, considering the two individuals' particular areas of expertise relative to the company's progression) to switch roles after 12 to 18 months.

23.2.5 A true partner (instead of a co-CEO)

As CEO, it's a good idea to have a tiny C-suite because you want to keep expenses very low. If you have a very capable, well-rounded "partner," you can make them a COO who is responsible for lots of areas, so you and they split responsibilities roughly 50–50. At the beginning, let's say you don't hire a head of sales or of marketing and maybe of engineering, then you can have the COO handle all that. Slowly, you fill those chairs, and the COO owns fewer functions as the company grows and becomes more complex.

23.3   Co-CEOs: A rare phenomenon

According to the *Harvard Business Review*, 87 US companies in the S&P Global 1200 and Russell 1000 have co-CEOs.[1] That's only 4%. The short answer to the question "Why so few?" is that it rarely works to have two people in a role where there is typically one decision-maker. This is especially true in fast-paced tech startups. Even tech giants find that co-CEOs don't work, as is true of Oracle, Salesforce, and SAP, all of which tried it and it failed.

Famous examples of co-CEOs

A few other big and famous companies you probably know have or had co-CEOs include

- *Research in Motion (BlackBerry)*—Jim Balsillie and Mike Lazaridis ran it as co-CEOs for 20 years before both resigned, after Apple had definitively crushed the company.
- *J. M. Smucker*—An old family business. Family members Timothy and Richard Smucker are co-CEOs.
- *Amway*—Also a family business. Steve Van Andel and Doug DeVos were co-CEOs for 16 years.
- *Whole Foods Market*—A public company. Cofounder John Mackey and long-time exec Walter Robb were co-CEOs from 2010 to 2016, when the company was bought by Amazon.
- *Netflix*—A public company founded by Reed Hastings. Ted Sarandos joined Reed as co-CEO in 2020; Greg Peters was COO. Then Reed became chairman in 2023, and the other two became co-CEOs.

23.4   Personal reflections on being CEO vs. COO

I was COO at GeoTrust because, as in the "mini-CEO" case, the CEO and I were coequal founders, and he wanted to focus exclusively on money and vision. Dave Chen was the CEO, and he wanted nothing to do with execution or daily operations such as IT, engineering, marketing, or sales, whereas my personality and experience were well suited to that side of things. Dave was also an investor, so focusing on financing the company made sense. He had the CFO (who also handled HR) and me reporting to him, although in practice, I reported to the board. Besides raising money, Dave, by nature and experience, had a solid vision for where the company should be heading (which unfortunately proved to be a case of being way too early to market). I ran IT, engineering (but the CTO, who reported to me, was tech lead and in practice guided engineering), marketing, and business development (that was sales for us). I was okay with this situation because I knew it was temporary. The plan from the start was for Dave to exit (remaining on the board) and for me to take over the CEO role.

---

[1] Marc A. Feigen, Michael Jenkins, and Anton Warendh, "Is It Time to Consider Co-CEOs?" *Harvard Business Review* (July–August 2022), https://hbr.org/2022/07/is-it-time-to-consider-co-ceos.

If the plan had always been for the situation to be permanent, I probably would not have accepted it.

At subsequent startups where I was CEO, there were several times I wished I'd had a COO. At Dover, I never created the title, but the VP of engineering took on all operational duties. He was sort of the CEO's dream come true. He handled all IT: he selected, negotiated, purchased, and managed the very expensive software tools and hardware engineering we used. He was involved in anything HR-related, and he was the resource marketing counted on for logistics for conferences. Only engineering formally reported to him, but because he was so well-liked and respected, he managed all the other teams through respect and competence. I had it great with a cofounder like that who did not have an oversized ego and just wanted to do whatever was needed for all of us to be successful. Having him in place, willing to be de facto COO, freed me to deal with the nonstop financing Dover ended up needing.

23.5   *The moral of this anecdote*

Let's be clear: the CEO is the top job in any company. But big company or small, there are situations when a COO is needed. In small companies, the decision-making around having a COO is about what is best for the CEO. If the CEO needs a partner, the COO should be a generalist who can go wherever there are problems needing senior attention. If the CEO is not able to manage sales and marketing, the COO should be CRO and CMO. If the CEO only wants to focus on financing and all things money, the COO needs to run the rest of the company. Try to avoid co-CEOs as a solution because it rarely works, despite some very famous counterexamples.

Marketing: Too often a startup's afterthought

- What are the functions of marketing? Are you underestimating this secret startup weapon?
- What is the optimal timing to bring in a chief marketing officer?
- Why is there friction between the CMO and other C-suiters and what can be done about it?

This anecdote focuses on who the chief marketing officer (CMO) is and what they do. I begin by diving into the role of marketing in any company, even an early-stage startup. Then we will walk through the evolution of the marketing function as the company evolves, perhaps growing into needing a CMO. The CMO, or VP of marketing, sits at the hub of many critical functions within the company, which makes them instrumental in defining minimum viable product (MVP), proving product-market fit (PMF), and driving the go-to-market (GTM) strategy—all activities essential to the startup's success. And yet many tech startups forget or marginalize marketing for far too long in the startup's evolution.

24.1 The role of marketing

Marketing is the center of a hub supporting most functions within the company, including engineering, sales, and CEO/CFO. They give all these functions information they need to interface with the outside world. They facilitate engineering people, especially founders and CTO, speaking at conferences to establish the bona fides of the company. They provide sales with leads to build the funnel that will generate revenues while setting up webinars so that sales can speak to large numbers of prospective customers and try to convert them into sales. They help HR show the company's talent brand to attract the best candidates. They provide the CEO/CFO with beautiful slide decks to present to investors to close financings while at the same time establishing the branding of the company to put it on the map. Generally, marketing in a startup has the goal of making the company seem larger than it is and demonstrating that it is stable, exciting, and winning.

I think of marketing as being divided into outbound and inbound marketing.

24.1.1 Outbound marketing

Outbound is marketing speaking to and influencing people outside the company. Here, marketing is telling the world about the company and its people, products, and services to get people to, at the very least, know about the brand and to become employees, partners, or customers. Outbound marketing includes many different types of communications, which are outlined in tables 24.1–24.4.

Table 24.1   Marketing communications

Website	The website needs to articulate the company's purpose, vision, and differentiation simply, quickly, impressively, and clearly. We always want the website to be the best place for people to go learn about the company so people who seem interested (and maybe want to apply for a job or download a white paper) are asked to register. They are put in a database for further marketing communications to keep "touching" them over time and keep them engaged and interested.
Hiring	Attracts people to apply for jobs, which involves a handoff to HR (under the CFO)
Collateral	To support sales, build the brand, and foster a sense of "thought leadership," marketing creates sales decks, brochures, and white papers.

Table 24.2   Corporate communications

Branding	Includes logos, trademarks, brochures, letterheads, business cards, and signage
PR	Includes press releases, handling media requests, getting executive interviews into magazines, blogs, podcasts, and other activities that promote the company's image and brand
Analysts	Companies beyond a certain size can afford to work with and subscribe to one or more appropriate analysts, such as Gartner, Forrester, and others. Startups can rarely afford their fees but wish they could.
Investor communications	Marketing supports the CEO/CFO for investor communications (e.g., investor and board pitch decks and board meeting materials).

Table 24.3   Demand generation

Go-to-market	Although GTM is a whole-company exercise designed to effectively engage with the market to generate sales, marketing must drive most of the steps in the creation of an effective GTM strategy (see anecdote 16, "Go-to-market: How to make your business viable and grow").
Events	Conferences, executive speaking engagements, and any other opportunities for team members to meet with potential customers and partners are managed by marketing.
Webinars	Web-based seminars are highly scripted and controlled opportunities to generate interest in the company and continue the branding and thought leadership work. Marketing constantly provides them with care and feeding.
Advertising	Placing well-crafted messages in places where prospective customers will see and engage with them is the art of advertising. Marketing creates the spots, pays for their placement, and measures their effectiveness.
Awards	Awards build credibility, increase awareness, and establish bona fides. To that end, marketing engages with the suppliers of the various awards, applies for them, and hopefully becomes the recipient of them.

Table 24.4   Research

Competition	It is essential to keep on top of who the competition is and carefully analyze what they have versus what you have, to check where the analysts think you stand, and to inform engineering about what is learned. Marketing may need an engineering resource (e.g., CTO) to complete the research. Competitive briefs for customers need to be created in a very attractive and easy-to-understand format.
Segments	Segmenting the vertical markets a company is engaging with is important to keep the sales and marketing efforts in those verticals as efficient as possible.
Market size	Understanding the size of a market the company is going after and how fast it is growing helps determine which markets are worth engaging with. Marketing needs to research the size and growth rate of each potential market.
Pricing	Product/service pricing is very tricky. It must match what customers expect and be reasonable from their perspective and yours. Pricing can have an enormous impact on the size and timing of revenues flowing into the company, which, in turn, relates to how sales personnel are compensated and affects the motivators for the sales team's behavior.

If you are thinking "Wow, that is a lot!" you are correct. What I find most amazing is the number of founders and CEOs who, at most tech firms being technologists, are frankly dismissive about the importance of marketing communications—the outbound marketing function. I believe this is because there has traditionally been an attitude among engineering-trained people that was immortalized in the movie *Field of Dreams:* "If we build it, they will come." It is just not true, as another famous adage of the tech industry expresses: the best technology does not always win. Sony Beta was considered a superior videotape standard to VHS, Segway is superior to electric scooters—the examples abound. People, of course, decide what they will adopt, but they are heavily influenced by what they know about and hear. This is why companies spend billions on advertising, which is marketing.

As the tables in this section show, outbound marketing's role is essential to a startup's success. However, the inbound marketing function is even more critical.

24.1.2 Inbound marketing

Many startups build marketing organizations that handle *only* the outbound functions we discussed in the last section, either because it is what most people think of first with regard to marketing or because outbound marketing (the communications function) is easier to build and staff and, for a limited time, can even be outsourced. However, the inbound marketing function is essential to company success, so it needs to reside somewhere either in marketing or (a common alternative) in engineering.

A synonym for inbound marketing is *product management*. In many tech companies, product managers are very senior and have important roles: it is their job to interact with the chosen vertical markets and bring back to the product development organization what features are needed in the product or service being offered, to be able to sell it. Often, a good product manager comes from the vertical market being targeted. This way, they already know the vocabulary this market uses. They know the environment where the product needs to work. They know the right partners needed to make the product successful. They probably also know many people in that vertical and can make introductions for sales. It is a fact that having a product manager from the market you are serving drastically reduces the friction for getting a foothold in that market.

> **DEFINITION** *Product management* works closely with prospective customers and the target market more broadly. It identifies the customer need and the larger business objectives that a product or feature will fulfill, articulates what success looks like for a product, and rallies the product team to turn that vision into a reality.

Any product manager needs a special set of skills that enables them to speak the customer's language to suss out what the customer needs. Equally, they need to speak the language of your engineers so the developers understand what needs to be built (and—also critical—what needs not to be built). Good product management is essential to achieve solid PMF; and as I discuss in anecdote 15, "Product–market fit: Making sure the dogs will eat your dog food," no company can succeed without proven PMF. This is why inbound marketing is essential to every early-stage startup.

24.2 Progression of marketing titles

As a startup progresses in size and accomplishments, it naturally goes through an evolution in the title, experience, and responsibilities of the person heading up marketing. From potentially no one other than the CEO or one of the other senior executives, to director of marketing, to VP of marketing, and ultimately to chief marketing officer, a succession of progressively more senior people may end up running marketing. To be clear, you do not *need* to have a CMO. You can go forever with a VP of marketing doing all the same things. But you might *have* to call the most senior marketing person CMO if you want to successfully hire them, because senior marketing people are now demanding a C-suite title to match their colleagues with CFO, CTO, and even CRO titles. The *chief-i-fying* of many roles previously called VP, such as chief revenue officer, chief people officer, chief strategy officer, and, yes, chief fun officer, happened 10 to 15 years ago, and chief among them (pun intended) was the creation of the CMO title. Here is how I think about the progression of roles up to and including CMO.

24.2.1 Director of marketing

This title is sufficient in the early days if product management is handled elsewhere, such as in engineering. This is someone with perhaps five years of experience in marketing organizations who understands all aspects of marketing communications and can manage a small team.

24.2.2 VP of marketing

Once multiple functions of marketing have senior people leading them through the natural growth of the company, an experienced, executive-level leader is needed. There may be a director of marketing communications, corporate communications, research and analyst relations, PR, and advertising. When this happens, it is time to have a VP. Why? Because this function is growing in importance as the company grows and therefore needs to be represented on the CEO's staff, aka the C-suite—and those roles are all VPs and above.

24.2.3 CMO

Once the company is cash-flow-positive, has proven PMF, and has its eyes on accelerating growth by expanding the number of markets it is serving, marketing needs a C-suite leader who reports to the CEO. The CMO must be part of strategy discussions, is an advisor to the CEO, takes on major account work, and is a leader in discussions about being acquired or going public. They probably have a cadre of directors reporting to them or maybe a couple of VPs.

The CEO needs to articulate the role of the CMO—and marketing in general—to the other execs and the company because most tech startups I know of have an endemic problem: the role of marketing is misunderstood, marginalized, or downright disparaged.

24.3 Friction between CMO and other senior execs

There is some natural friction between the CMO role and other equally senior execs. Engineering is largely driven by the product management portion of the CMO's responsibility. If the product definition coming in from product management changes based on market input, it whipsaws engineering, and they really don't like that. A change in definition could mean weeks or months of design changes, coding, testing, recoding, and more testing. It's essential for the CMO to understand that dynamic, keep changes to a minimum, and explain and justify them scrupulously.

Sales is looking for leads and revenue growth. If the CMO and team are off creating new products that sales can't sell yet, sales won't even pay attention; legitimately, sales only cares about products they can sell now, and they want the CMO to focus on their needs.

To illustrate, let me tell the story of my VPs of marketing and sales and the Sophie's Choice they forced me to make when I was trying to reinvent our company and take it into a new market. My VP of marketing (VPM) was not titled CMO because that title was not yet commonly used, but he was CMO by intellect and ability. He was responsible for driving the company to an entirely new market, new value proposition, new product, new branding—really, an entirely new direction. My VP of sales (VPS) was on the hook to bring in revenues, and, as is always the case, he needed help from marketing to do that. However, my VPM did not want to keep working on the old, dying business and preferred to put all his energy into the new direction. One day they came to me and said they could no longer work together, that they would stop talking to each other, and that I should choose only one of them to stay. I thought about this for 24 hours and ultimately made the wrong choice. I chose to keep my VPS because I believed we had to keep bringing in revenue on which we could build our new direction. But I should have chosen my VPM because there was no future without his ideas.

The CMO doesn't tend to last very long

The consulting firm Spencer Stuart found that average CMO tenure in 2022 was only 4.2 years, whereas CEO tenure was an average of 6.7 years.[1] The firm Raines International also studies the CMO role and found that CMOs are losing their influence and are not aligned with their CEOs, which is very bad for longevity.[2]

Here are a few worrying statistics from Raines:

- 4% of CEOs view their CMO as their most trusted team member.
- 34% of CEOs have great confidence in their CMO.
- 23% of CMOs are unsure whether their CEO understands what the CMO's job is.
- 21% of CMOs aren't sure they are aligned with their CEO on key performance metrics.

24.4 Why do CEOs sometimes undervalue their CMOs?

The question remains: why do CEOs very often not understand the importance of the CMO role? I think tech CEOs tend to focus on their product first and foremost and treat much of what marketing does as secondary in the early stages of the company. They or one of their other founders are probably driving PMF and dealing directly with

[1] "CMO Tenure Study: An Expanded View of CMO Tenure and Backgrounds," Spencer Stuart, May 2023, www.spencerstuart.com/research-and-insight/cmo-tenure-study-an-expanded-view-of-cmo-tenure-and-backgrounds.
[2] "The Wall Street Journal: Research and Advice for Chief Marketing Officers," Raines International, November 10, 2021, http://rainesinternational.com/the-wall-street-journal-research-and-advice-for-chief-marketing-officers/

prospective customers on that. Most tech startup CEOs are technically trained and have a natural affinity for other technologists, their CTO, and their engineering team. They may not have nearly as much common ground with their marketing leader.

By the time the company evolves to the point where a CMO is added, some of the relationships and alignment throughout the company may be set, and it takes an exceptional CMO to unwind those entrenched habits. An exceptional CEO will appreciate that growing the company, being attractive to an acquirer, and driving a world-class strategy for the whole company will take the full C-suite and especially the inputs of the CMO.

24.5   *The moral of this anecdote*

Marketing does essential work in two directions within the company: outbound and inbound. Inbound marketing is product management and is critical to establishing MVP and PMF. Outbound marketing is communications in all its forms, which is essential for establishing the company's existence, its brand, and its role and to start attracting notice and customers. Only when product management is covered elsewhere can startup companies begin with a director of marketing and graduate to VP and ultimately CMO. CMO is a truly strategic role reporting to the CEO and is part of strategy discussions and decisions (notably, including GTM), customer acquisition, partnerships, and ultimately company acquisition. But CMOs are strangely short-lived. Their role tends to put them in conflict with other C-suiters, and their role and true value are little understood even by the CEOs who hire and manage them. If this anecdote can change this perception and elevate the importance of marketing and its leaders, I will be gratified.

The right character for your sales leader— and when to hire them

- The sales function—do you really appreciate this startup superpower?
- The sales leader will be your revenue rockstar. But first, have you ensured that you have a sellable product?
- Managing sales superstars—and how do you snap them up?

In my experience, most tech founders do not have a shred of DNA for high-power relationship selling or for finding and hiring the best people who are the best at sales. I didn't. And I found it very hard to assess salespeople and be prepared to manage them. So, more than almost any other anecdote in this book, this is one I wish I'd had when I was struggling to build up a sales team for the first time.

This discussion is not about selling to consumers (B2C). This is about selling to businesses (B2B) and the salespeople who are superb at that. And this is not about the hugely oversimplistic idea some people have of sales as "get a prospect, contact them, pitch to them, close the deal, deliver the product, go on to the next." You can do everything else right and have a great startup in a great market with a great team and a great product and even have proven product-market fit (PMF), but if you don't have great salespeople, you won't get revenues, and you won't grow like you want and need to. This anecdote is about identifying and hiring star salespeople. Let's set the groundwork by talking first about the role of sales in a startup and when you will be ready to fire up the sales engine.

25.1 *The role of sales in a startup*

First and foremost, sales is responsible for generating revenue for the company and working to make that revenue stream grow. This is why, increasingly, we are seeing the head of sales have the title chief revenue officer (CRO) rather than the previously common title VP sales. To generate revenue and make it grow, they "fill the funnel" with new leads. That is, they identify and qualify new potential customers. Depending on the market and product, this can involve activities like cold calling, attending industry events, using referrals, content marketing, and similar activities. Because sales spends vast amounts of time with customers, they best understand customer needs. Their direct interactions with customers through discovery calls, demos, and conversations enables them to deeply understand what each customer is trying to achieve and how the startup's solution can address their needs. Frequently, these types of interactions establish strong customer relationships, ensuring high levels of customer satisfaction. Salespeople often become trusted advisors. Sales manages all interactions with prospects and customers in the company's customer relationship management (CRM) system, which requires constant attention to keep it up to date.

Sales is responsible for effectively conveying the core value proposition (created by marketing) of the product or service to prospects, and tailoring the messaging to resonate with each customer's specific needs and pain points. Once engaged with a prospect, sales goes through a process of overcoming objections: they address any doubts, concerns, or objections prospects have about the solution, pricing, implementation, or anything that might prevent them from committing to the purchase. The sales function is highly dependent on following a rigorous process. They must manage this process and move prospects through the sales funnel, converting them into paying customers. This includes activities like proposal generation and contract negotiations. Once a deal is closed, the goal for that customer—besides keeping them delighted—is to upsell additional products or services or, if applicable, move them to higher tiers of the product. Getting a satisfied customer to provide referrals to new prospects within the account is an approach commonly used by sales to increase revenues from each account.

Sales actively participates in the go-to-market (GTM) process and its implementation. They work closely with product management and engineering about what is needed in the product to close new deals and garner more revenues from current customers. Sales can quickly become a large team for a startup in a hot market with a product that fills a real need. Managing the building of such a team is critical to growing the revenue base for the company. Retaining a large, growing sales team is challenging; salespeople expect lucrative compensation packages. The team needs to be motivated and incentivized with high earning potential so they hit and exceed their quotas.

Sales has a critical role in reporting to the CEO, the board, and investors who all want to hear about where the company's revenues are headed. Typical reports are driven by tracking key sales metrics, identifying trends in customer segments, sales cycles, win rates, and more.

25.2 When to hire your sales team

Sales is not an area you fill on day one after founding your startup. That's worth repeating: you absolutely must *not* fill your sales roles too early—as in, before you have a product to sell. So, when do you need sales, and when is it too early?

It's too early when the product is not ready, such as when PMF is still uncertain. Salespeople become intensely frustrated if they have nothing to sell. If you hire them too early (if they even agree to stay), they tend to get thrown into the role of product management, gathering information from customers. That's a bad use of salespeople. They will wash out quickly because they are not doing what they love and are not making the kind of income they require, and you will have wasted your money.

You feel a sense of urgency because you need revenues badly—and building your sales team is the path to them. True, you and some of your C-suite can close a couple of early deals like some lighthouse customers. But that's not really sales; it's one-offs, and it's not scalable because you are not using the kind of tried-and-true process professional salespeople are great at. Sales and salespeople are vital to your company's success or even survival. Hiring your first salesperson is nothing like any other hiring you have done. They truly are a different breed and need to be treated as such.

The story of Ennea and the pain of not having PMF

A very good friend of mine had been CEO elsewhere when he was hired on as CEO of Ennea after its founder was moved into a technical role. The board realized they needed an experienced CEO who had a strong background in sales to accelerate the company's growth, and my friend fit that to a T. Once he was on board, he started looking at every aspect of his new company with a fine-tooth comb. That's when he made some startling discoveries.

Ennea had never proven PMF. Although the company had made a handful of sales, it was struggling to create a steady, growing steam of deals that would portend a growing company, which the new CEO absolutely had to achieve. In fact, he learned that the product didn't work as advertised. That message was not going to be easy to communicate to the board, but the CEO took the bull by the horns and explained what had to happen. To their credit, the board fully supported the radical plan he presented to them.

The CEO laid off all of sales and marketing and hunkered down with the engineering team to rebuild the product. He worked closely with the few customers Ennea had to use their feedback as product management inputs to the engineering team (he had started his career in product management). As the new product took shape, he recruited more lighthouse customers to gain additional feedback to further validate what the company was learning. And he kept at it and kept at it. As you can imagine,

(continued)

with a team hard at work, his cash burn meant he had to raise additional financing to support this all-engineering company with no sales and no revenues for the six months this process took.

When Ennea came out of this transformational retrenchment, everyone was confident that they had a product the market needed and that it would sell. Then the CEO rebuilt sales and marketing and reentered the market, revenues began flowing, and Ennea started to grow. He grew it quickly, merged with another company (which allowed him to accelerate that growth), and, after several years, sold Ennea to a large public company for over $2 billion.

The lesson is this: you can't hire sales too early; you can only hire them when you are certain you have a product they can sell to customers who really want and need it. If you do it wrong, you will have to retrench like this CEO did. He was lucky that he had a very supportive board and could raise money to support retrenching—that will not always be the case.

With the role of sales as the backdrop, let's delve into the characteristics of successful salespeople look.

25.3   *Characteristics of great salespeople*

A Harvard Business School (HBS) study from 2006 found that only about 1 in 10 people could be a top-producing salesperson. They developed a detailed questionnaire that they claim can suss out whether a person may be that one versus the nine flops. A few traits immediately disqualify someone from being a good salesperson, which we will get out of the way before we talk about the traits they need.

25.3.1 *Disqualifying traits*

The HBS survey highlighted disqualifying traits such as being rigid or opinionated or lacking empathy (that list got rid of me right away). Salespeople I've known don't have one particular trait—idealism—and this distinguishes them from what I look for in all other early employees. I mean idealism as in, "We have an idea that will change the world!" This is something I hear from every tech startup founder I have ever met. But not from salespeople. I believe it is because they are primarily motivated by something different: winning.

25.3.2 *Driven to win*

A skilled salesperson possesses an insatiable drive to win. They have a strong belief in themselves and their ability, and they are always sure they can blow past their quota. They are constantly driving to close that deal, get that customer, and bring in those revenues. They better have a strong ego because they experience a fair bit of rejection and must keep at it with unbridled enthusiasm.

Right behind winning is the fact that—and this is the uncharitable way to put it—they are *coin-operated*. The charitable way to put it is that they are the true business arm of your company. They are the source of the best kind of money you can get which is from customers (not investors), and that makes them feel like kings.

25.3.3 Relationship-builders

Great salespeople are highly relationship-oriented. They know the value of building long-term relationships, and they seek to make every successful sale a long-term relationship. As you would expect, this means they have strong interpersonal skills. They need to be engaging and personable. You can be sure they always look very professional with customers, too. In most tech startups, they are the only employees who routinely dress in business attire versus the T-shirt and flip-flops uniform of the rest of the team.

You will find that salespeople *own* the customer relationships they build. A way this manifests itself is that no one, not even the CEO, may call or interact with any customer without clearing it with sales first. They have good reason to demand this discipline. Only they know where the process is with that customer, so they must know about every interaction with the customer to make sure nothing upsets a pending decision.

> **DEFINITION** *Relationship selling* is when the sales team prioritizes building connections with customers and potential buyers to close sales. Rather than solely using price and other details to sell a product or service, the salesperson focuses on the interactions they have with their customers.

25.3.4 Detail-oriented

Salespeople are among the most detail-oriented employees in the company. They can never miss a meeting. They must execute thoughtful, well-crafted follow-ups after every meeting. And all the while, they need to close the current hot deal and add new prospects to the top of the sales funnel to keep the business moving forward.

I think we all prepare for important meetings. But a salesperson takes this preparation to a higher level. Sure, they update the standard deck they present from. But they include much more in their presentation that is unique to the target prospective customer. For that, the salesperson does extensive research on the firm and the people in it with whom they are going to meet. They know that to be successful, they must be extremely well prepared, or they will get a quick no. They want to know what drives a customer so they can align their pitch to the customer's needs and hot buttons. The salesperson must understand who makes the ultimate buying decision and who else, along the way, is what is called a *gatekeeper* and will need to give the nod to the buyer to get a sale approved. They will analyze how the product they are selling will save the prospect money, what competitive product it might displace, and how it is not duplicative with what the customer already has. Their financial analysis also includes some understanding of the prospect's budget so it is clear (because budgets tend to be fixed) that buying your product means something else in the budget is no longer needed and, at worst, it will be a zero-sum transaction.

25.3.5 Process driven

The heart of the process that salespeople follow is modeled as a funnel like the one shown in figure 25.1. It represents the set of states a prospective customer moves through, starting with the moment they become aware of your product and company. The process is shaped like a funnel because many more prospects enter the funnel than purchase the product, with dropouts occurring at each successive stage for a myriad of reasons.

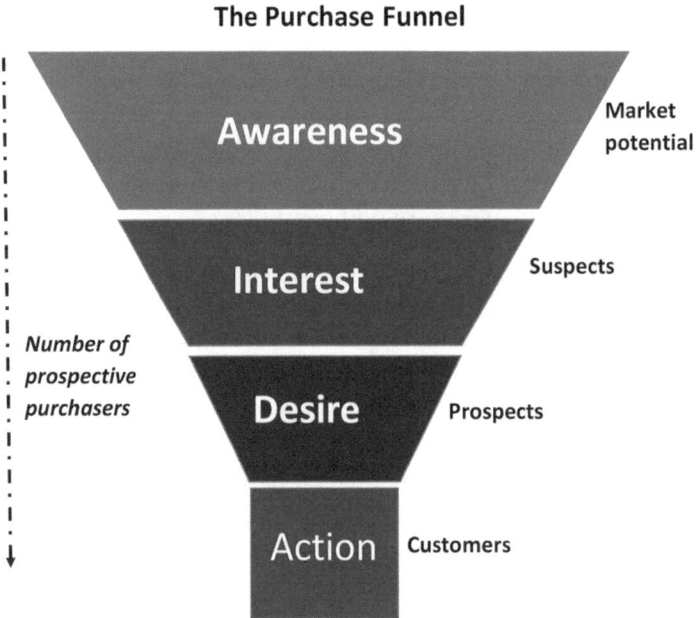

Figure 25.1   Diagram of a typical sales or purchase funnel. Original work by BronHiggs, based on a well-known concept. Licensed as CC by SA4.0.

The first order of business is for the salesperson to determine the right way to get a steady stream of people to the awareness stage so they become *leads*. This is where a strong intersection with marketing occurs. It is a prime directive of marketing to perform marketing activities (e.g., direct mail, advertising, webinars, conference presentations) that create awareness among potential buyers in the target markets, as determined by the company's GTM process. The salesperson engages in a well-defined set of activities to attempt to move the largest percentage of prospects they can from one stage of this funnel to the next until they are able to successfully close a sale. In addition to marketing, they will involve numerous teams, such as engineering, finance, and the CEO, to get to the finish line.

> **DEFINITION** *Customer relationship management* (CRM) is a technology for managing all your company's relationships and interactions with customers and potential customers. The goal is simple: improve business relationships. A CRM system helps companies stay connected to customers, streamline processes, and improve profitability.

The most important tool for salespeople is CRM software, the best-known example of which is Salesforce. Many smaller competitors are less expensive and still work well. Salespeople will have strong opinions about what software they want to use.

Every interaction with a prospective customer or partner is maintained in the CRM system. Sales and marketing enter into the system the target companies and the key people who work there. Marketing uses the names in the system to run awareness campaigns on a regular basis. The funnel is explicitly represented in the CRM system so that at a glance, anyone can see who is at what stage in the funnel, who the most likely ultimate sales are, and approximately when the sale could happen. By applying a percentage likelihood to each prospect, a salesperson can provide finance and the CEO with sales projections to make revenue forecasts to present to the board and investors.

25.3.6 Great listening skills

Salespeople must have excellent listening skills. To determine whether someone is really a prospect, and to learn what that prospect needs to see in the product and the proposed deal to move them all the way through the funnel to a sale, a salesperson asks a lot of *uncovering questions* about the prospect's needs.

The salesperson's goal, of course, is to get to yes. For that, they need to determine the big pain point the customer has and the fit the salesperson can make with the product they have to sell today (not the one a year from now). That takes uncovering questions, lots of listening, a high aptitude for problem-solving, and maybe some skills at talking to marketing and engineering to change the product to satisfy this prospect. This kind of product modification only happens when the product is still somewhat immature. A difficult dynamic can result: the salesperson wants to close the deal with this customer but needs engineering to make some changes in the product to do so. Engineering and senior leadership cannot afford to make unique changes for each customer and want to be certain these are changes that all customers will want. Product management must be called in to test this change with other prospects in the market to understand how to proceed.

What follows is the outline we followed in selling a hardware cybersecurity product to a semiconductor chip manufacturer. This is usually the first in-person meeting after several back-and-forth qualifying interactions but prior to a broader team meeting. The role of the person at the prospective buyer is a product owner, such as a business unit manager or a VP of hardware. A different product, market, and role can be easily substituted to make this approach work for you.

Sales process outline

Introductions

- Detail who you are, relevant experience, and why you are there.
- Tell them what you hope to achieve.
- Ask them what they hope to achieve.

Current situation

- What product is your team developing?
- For what market? For what target customers?
- What is your development timeline? Where are you currently in your development timeline?
- What is the projected market size for [your product]?
- How do your clients/customers think about [your category]?

Desired outcome

- What are your goals for this project? Market share? Units? Do you have stretch goals?
- How about your goals with respect to [your main feature]?
- What is the ideal outcome? Schedule? Market share?
- What are you looking to accomplish in terms of [value you add]?
- Can you charge more for this type of product?

Obstacles

- What has kept you from implementing a [your category] solution in the past?
- What is keeping you from executing on this ideal project?
- What else is holding you back?
- Keep asking "What else?" (It is important to get most/all of the obstacles out on the table.)

Next steps

- How do you typically evaluate [your type of product]?
- What specific aspects of [name of your product] are you interested in learning more about/evaluating?
- Would you like to see a demo?
- Would you like to schedule a technical deep-dive conversation?
- Who else will be involved in the decision process?
- Who else will be involved in the buying process?

As you can see, the salesperson spends most of their time listening and learning, not talking. And afterward, they have a lot of work to do!

25.3.7 *Empathy and patience*

While having these uncovering meetings and listening intently, the salesperson is exhibiting another critical trait they must have: empathy. They are putting themselves in the prospect's shoes and imagining the problem they are explaining. In this way, the salesperson can visualize how the product they are selling solves the problem. Their empathy extends to an ability to read people well—something they do during every meeting with prospects. I suspect that this ability makes them extremely good poker players—I was always way too smart to ever allow myself to get into a poker game with a salesperson.

Patience is also a virtue salespeople must possess, especially when tasked with selling major B2B products. These are large deals, and the time from first engagement to deal closure is measured in months—maybe even two-digit numbers of months. In the case of Dover, where we were selling a hardware product to a huge semiconductor company that had to manufacture a chip with Dover's product embedded in it, that sales cycle was on the order of 18 months. We had a very patient salesperson, despite how itchy he always was to win and win big.

25.4 *Unique compensation package*

A salesperson's compensation package is vastly different from anyone else's in the company. The basic tenet of sales compensation packages is that the bulk of their pay is based on commissions: a percentage of the value of the deals they close. That commission is added on top of a guaranteed base, but the base is small compared to others in the company. Just like everyone else, salespeople get an option component that is a long-term incentive based on the success of the company. The final component of the package is a temporary draw, which is cash on top of their base for the first few months; after that, they are expected to start closing deals and getting commissions. The length of time the draw is active is based on the market and type of product. In Dover's case, the draw had to run for a year.

Big companies tend to have very complex sales compensation plans, but at a startup where there is no hierarchy within sales, most CEOs keep it nice and simple.

> **Compensation breakdown**
>
> The salesperson's base should be approximately 40% of their total target cash compensation, and their quota (expected commission amount) should be 60% of their total. The percentage commission on gross sales should be 20%–30%, with no cap on how large their commission check can be. You can add a kicker to the percentage if they exceed quota. It's common for quota to be raised over time.

I love it when, instead of the rest of the team being jealous of the "no limit" cash compensation a very successful salesperson's salary can become, they root for the salesperson to make $1 million. They calculate correctly that if the salesperson makes $1 million, it means they brought $5 million in revenues to the company, and that is a good deal for everyone. Best of all, that salesperson is likely to stick around and try to keep winning.

25.5   *The moral of this anecdote*

When the startup is selling a product to another business (B2B sales) versus a consumer, the individual you need to hire is usually a relationship-oriented salesperson— a special breed. You can't hire them too early, or they will be frustrated. But when you have proven PMF, they are your gateway to revenues. The attributes of this kind of salesperson are different from those of almost everyone else in your company and only exist in 1 out of 10 people. They are driven to win, build long-term relationships with customers, tend to be detail-oriented, and drive their work through strict adherence to processes based on a sales funnel model. Personality traits they must have include great listening skills, empathy, and patience. They are also coin-operated and need a compensation package with a no-limits commission structure. They have to believe that if they are rock stars, they could make $1 million a year; you and everyone else in the company will be thrilled if they do.

Part 5

Management challenges

The final part of this book—apart from the last anecdote, which is about the joy of finally having that long-sought-after exit—is about some challenging management topics. The anecdotes in this part are as follows:

I begin this part with two anecdotes about startup boards. More of mine have been challenging than were smooth, easy sailing. I thought telling the stories of some of those more difficult boards might help you avoid the issues I had to deal with. Of course, every board is unique, so yours may be difficult in a different way from mine. Observers on boards are, in my opinion, always challenging. But it's still possible to minimize those challenges, as I discuss. Communicating well with your investors is important and can be very easy if you make it consistent and part of your routine.

Next come two anecdotes about very tough topics: layoffs and winding up a startup that has failed. But I close the book with the brightest and most cheerful topic you can have: an exit in the form of an acquisition (I don't talk much about IPOs because they are exceedingly rare these days). Hopefully it is big enough to provide a financial reward for you and your team, who have worked hard to get to this point. But even if you never get a ginormous exit, most of the time, being part of a startup is pure joy.

Startup boards: The good, (how to prevent) the bad, and the ugly

- What is the typical makeup of a startup board of directors?
- In the startup ecosystem, what is the board's role?
- How should you create meetings with perfect agenda, presentation, and post-meeting protocols?

If you are the CEO, the board is your boss. Regardless, the board is the ultimate authority on all decisions the company makes, whether explicitly or via proxy to the CEO. The board has huge responsibilities to protect investors' interests, approve senior hires, decide on compensation for the CEO and other senior managers, weigh in on financing and acquisitions, and handle a myriad of other things every company has to deal with. In this anecdote, you will learn how the board of directors compensates and manages the CEO. You will see how a board evolves, growing in size and the formality of its oversight, alongside the company as it too evolves. You will also see detailed suggestions on how to construct a board meeting presentation.

26.1   *Board of directors' role*

The board of directors has four primary roles in their official duties as the highest-level controlling entity for the company. They are a fiduciary protecting the value of the investor's holdings. They are the CEO's direct boss and have hiring and firing authority for that role. They, in conjunction with the CEO, determine the strategy for the company to be most successful. And they provide advice and counsel to the CEO and, indirectly, to the management team.

26.1.1   *Fiduciary*

The number-one thing the board is responsible for is taking fiduciary responsibility for the shareholders' stake in the company: they must protect the value of equity, whether granted to employees or sold to investors. They are legally bound to this responsibility, and this is why Directors and Officers Insurance is critical to protect board members, who are usually the focus of any shareholder lawsuits. While the company is pre-cash-flow-positive, the board will be focused very hard on cash: how much cash is in the bank, what the burn rate is, how long the runway is, and what the current cash-out date is. Once out of the woods and post-cash-flow-positive, their focus will be all about growth and making the company more valuable so the shareholders eventually get a good return on their investment. Of course, one or more of the board members is likely an investor, and they should all own some form of equity so they remain in alignment with investors looking for that great return.

26.1.2   *CEO's boss*

The board is who the CEO reports to. As the CEO's boss, the board and the chairman of the board need to coach and provide feedback almost continuously during the CEO's tenure. They also have the authority to fire them and hire a new CEO.

> **ADAGE**   "The board is 100% behind the CEO until they are 0% behind the CEO."

The board must be totally supportive of the CEO unless and until they want to fire the CEO. Anything less than 100% will show, and that will undermine the CEO and destroy their productivity—which will then force the board's hand and require them to let the CEO go. It should never happen that way. Any firing of the CEO must be planned, deliberate, and quick, with the replacement CEO already identified and standing by. That may not be possible if the CEO has truly done something wrong, in which case one of the board members or a member of the senior management team will need to move into the CEO role temporarily or permanently.

The compensation committee of the board (or the full board, if there is not yet a compensation committee) is responsible for the CEO's compensation and is advised by the CEO of their proposals for other senior management compensation. Setting the CEO's compensation directly is a critical way that the board cements its relationship with the CEO and, of course, attracts them to the company in the first place. Or if the CEO is a founder, it's how the board incentivizes and rewards the CEO as the company progresses.

> ### CEO compensation[1]
> Salary: $180,000 to $190,000, but varies by industry and geography
>
> My personal view is that it should be $200,000 in tech companies because the salaries of the CEO's team will otherwise push very hard against the ceiling that the CEO's salary creates.
>
> Equity: 5% to 10%
>
> If a founder, they will start with majority share but will quickly get diluted by other team members and initial financing rounds. After Series A, the founding CEO should be at 10%, and a nonfounding CEO who comes in later should be 5% or a bit more.
>
> Bonus: Totally discretionary but should be tied to overall growth or exit

26.1.3 Strategy

The role of the board of directors with respect to the management team (led by the CEO) is strategy. They are definitively not involved with operations—a mistake new VCs who land on portfolio company boards make regularly. That's because those new VCs are frequently from a startup of their own that did well, which got them a job at the VC that invested in them. Of course, the whole time they were building their company, they were mostly about operations, so continuing to apply their expertise where they feel most natural is what they want to do. But it's very bad for a board member to try to play in the operations arena. Operations requires not just day-to-day data ingestion and decisions but practically minute-by-minute focus, and no board member can afford to dedicate the necessary time to do that. Operations is not just their job—it is the CEO and his team's job and interference will upset everyone.

26.1.4 Advice and counsel

The board's third-most-important function is oversight and counsel of management, mostly through the CEO. Investors not directly represented on the board frequently want to know that the board sanctions things that management is doing. This simple fact can help avoid the not-so-infrequent legal actions that some investors are prone to take, known as shareholder suits. That leads to the next type of function the board fulfills: protection of management. Making sure things are formally discussed and approved through signed board consent can avoid a huge number of what some might call frivolous shareholder lawsuits. So, it is worth it to make sure everything major is papered up, goes to a vote, and has documentation of that approval process in case someone starts to rattle their saber.

---

[1] Kruze Consulting (https://kruzeconsulting.com using their AI bot).

26.2 Board of directors composition

The makeup of the board of a startup varies, but in general, major investors have board seats. Typically, each investor owns about a 20% stake in the company. That's assuming a snapshot of an early round, such as Series Seed or Series A, where the new investors, of which there are likely two, each owns 20% of the company. Both of those main investors will want to take a board seat so they have the necessary control to protect and grow their investment. Management—usually the CEO—has at least one seat. If the board is going to consist of only three people (which is typical at the seed stage), that is it. If it is later than seed or if an agreement was struck for a five-person board from the beginning, management might get two seats. The fifth seat, if management fights for it, can be an independent board member chosen by the CEO but approved by the rest of the board. Ideally this will be someone who can really help the company, perhaps because they come from the primary market the company will be selling to.

Also added to this three- or five-person voting board may be a few observers who typically come from small investors such as organized angel groups. Finally, at most board meetings, but certainly not voting, will be the senior-most members of management. I also always had my outside corporate counsel be appointed as the official secretary of the company; as such, they attended every meeting and were responsible for the meeting minutes. It is always nice to have your outside counsel at every meeting to be at your beck and call for critical in-the-moment questions. (They should never charge you for this time.)

26.3 Board of directors meetings

Most startup teams do not see or hear from their board members on a weekly or sometimes even monthly basis. So, the most involved interaction with the board is at board meetings. In this section, let's talk about those meetings, their frequency, how voting works, and what a board presentation should look like.

26.3.1 Meeting frequency

For a brand-new startup, once-a-month meetings make sense; this pace then slows to every other month for at most the first couple of years. In the beginning it's very helpful to treat your board almost as an extension of the senior team, solving all the initial issues that come up and establishing processes for the basic functions of a company. But then you will find that you are spending a week of every month preparing for the upcoming board meeting and spending only three weeks a month driving the company forward—and that's not sustainable for long. So, end this frequency as soon as it seems right to do so, and definitely after the first year. After that, and while the startup is still young, a nice cadence is every other month. That frequency doesn't feel like you are constantly preparing for the next board meeting, but even here, your goal should be to eventually meet once per quarter. That's the cadence public companies operate on.

Strangely, in my opinion, an awful lot of entrepreneurs go for completely ad hoc meetings with no schedule and only meet on the spur of the moment when the CEO calls a meeting. I'm surprised any board agrees to that. It's not good governance. It might even be risky for management if they make decisions without formal board approval that come back to bite them. I would avoid this approach.

26.3.2 *Voting: One dollar or one person per vote?*

Usually, voting on resolutions and consents works out fine and the way you expect. In fact, at my current startup, we have never had a non-unanimous vote in seven years. But sometimes, issues related to voting cause the "ugly" of a board to show its face.

A saying I like is "Prior to cash-flow positive, it is one dollar, one vote; post cash-flow positive, it is one person, one vote." This means although you are not cash-flow positive, you are totally beholden to your investors, and because one or more of them is a board member, you are beholden to those investor board members.

> **TIP** Until the company is cash-flow positive, the investor board members hold all the cards. For all intents and purposes, the votes of the other board members don't really matter.

If they don't agree with a vote, all they have to say is that if the vote does not go their way, they will refrain from any future investing. You are probably thinking that no one would be so petty, but you would be wrong. It may not even be in the category of petty: they really may not agree with the vote, and if it affects their attitude about the value and prospects of the company, they will vote no.

A story of the "ugly" in a board vote

To highlight the "one dollar, one vote" adage, here is a true story of an investor board member (let's pretend his name is Dick) who decided to exercise that ugly scenario in the hiring of a new CEO for a company I will disguise here and call BizIntel. The existing CEO (Stan) was the founder but did not have enough sales background to continue in the CEO role after about 18 months. He would move into the CTO role once the new CEO was hired.

The board was personally doing the CEO search and had narrowed it down to two candidates. The first, George, had extensive sales and marketing experience at startups. The other, Zero, had only worked at large companies, never startups; had no sales and marketing experience; and had never raised money. After the interviews were completed, the board met. The other investor board member and I wanted George, who we thought was great. But Dick said he would only support Zero—and if George got the job, Dick vowed to never invest in the company again. If BizIntel needed a round, it would have to raise it from insiders because it had not accomplished enough to attract a new investor. Having Dick's firm threaten to drop out was a death knell. Stan met with his cofounders, who had been part of the interview process, and they agreed that George was the guy they wanted. But the whole founders group saw the dilemma and decided it was best to lose this battle to live to fight another day. They all reluctantly, holding their noses, endorsed Dick's decision to support Zero. Zero got the job, was in way over his head, failed to watch the cash burn and runway, and literally ran out of money and had to shut down the company.

(continued)

Why did Dick refuse to support George? Because George was currently working for someone Dick had previously worked for, whom he considered an industry legend, but George was critical of this person, which Dick could not stomach. Because Dick was offended, he refused to allow George to become CEO. His vote was only one of three board members, but he won by using the threat of withholding an investment if he did not prevail.

26.3.3 *The problem with big boards*

A big board is anathema to a young startup and a real disaster for a brand-new CEO. Luckily, when you are part of a founding team starting from scratch, it is unheard of to have a large board. But coming into an existing company as a replacement CEO can land you with a big board, as happened to me my first time as the CEO. I inherited the CEO job when financing round F was coming up, meaning we had a lot of investors. There were 13 people, including observers, sitting around the table. This was a nightmare. Real board members numbered just five, but each small investor group along the way had insisted on having an observer seat. Those are not just requests, as in "Sure would be nice to be an observer"—part of each round of financing made them contractual.

A board meeting for this company was like a circus. Not only did we have input from the four board members other than me, but one of the observers refused to sit down. And he didn't just stand quietly on the other side of the room; he paced around, repeatedly circling the big table, including walking right behind me. He went around and around and around for the entire meeting. Not quietly, either; he spouted off about whatever the current topic was or things he just wanted discussed. I know what you are thinking: why the heck is it okay for an observer to speak up at all? Right you are. In fact, this is such a big issue that I have an entire anecdote about it: anecdote 27, "Board observers: Observe only, please." This was an impossible situation for a first-time CEO like me. I got a little help from the serious real board members, especially the chairman, but it was usually too little, too late.

26.4 *Presenting to the board of directors*

Small board or big board, being well-prepared with a solid presentation will help make the meetings go well. Eventually I learned how to structure the presentation and meeting to keep things on track and (mostly) avoid acrimony or drama. A good goal for a board meeting is to have it be totally boring. In this case, boring is good because it means no drama, no stress, and no tempers. Here is how I achieve that almost every time, even when things are not going fantastically (because going fantastically would result in it being nice and boring).

26.4.1 *Prep in advance, and socialize it*

Getting prepared well in advance of the meeting allows you to socialize it with your *real* board members—the ones who vote—and remove any controversies before you are in the meeting. The meeting may include observers who, in the face of any controversy, will not remain silent and will potentially derail the entire meeting.

Have a structure for your meetings with a template so you do not have to construct each presentation deck from scratch. Send it to your real board members, and schedule one-to-one time with each member. Not only does this give you time to hear their concerns, but it is also invaluable time spent with individuals of huge importance to you and your company in a mode where they are much likelier to have a substantive conversation with you.

Take all the feedback and work it into your final presentation. Then, at least 24 hours in advance (48 hours, if possible), send your board all the materials for the meeting, including previous meeting minutes and all consents (only the presentation goes to observers) so they get a chance to read ahead.

This process almost never fails unless something is very wrong with your company. The board meeting will seem perfunctory. It also means the "extra" topics, such as new messaging, a change of direction, a proposed acquisition, or a deep dive into one functional area of your company, will be the focus of all members, with no distractions.

Suggested board meeting agenda

Here is a suggestion for a two-hour agenda. Use these structural elements and customize them to fit your company.

I. Financials

Always the first thing—they are fiduciaries, after all. Be sure to cover cash on hand, cash flow, runway, and cash-out date! If there is a financing or acquisition on the horizon, talk about that here.

II. Sales activity

Always the second thing—you better have sales to get revenues and grow.

III. Current customers/partners

They have a lot of other things they are tending to, so they forget. Tell them who the big customers and partners are.

IV. [Something of import relative to revenues]

V. Rest of customer activity

VI. [Something new that they don't know yet]

I often include a team member spotlight here to do a deep dive into one functional area.

(continued)

VII. Company updates

This spot is for covering all the other functional areas more briefly.

VIII. Discussion

This is a placeholder in case needed discussions have not happened yet. This might be an executive session where observers and members of your team drop out.

IX. Board actions

Any voting is done here.

The last time I used this exact agenda, it expanded into 40+ slides. Keeping the meeting to two hours is always challenging.

I find that because tools like PowerPoint and Keynote are very one-dimensional and it can be hard for the audience to track where you are on an agenda like the one in this section, a simple trick in the slide format helps enormously. Using figure 26.1 as a template, I put the item from the agenda at top-right with an image or logo below it to indicate what is being covered. On the left two-thirds of the slide are the subtopic and bullets—but only three to five bullets, or you will lose your audience in a long meeting. (That dictum does not apply when you are looking at a spreadsheet or for slides from team members who are explaining presumably complex information.)

SALES ACTIVITY SUMMARY

- 3-5 bullets max

- 2nd point

- 3rd point

- 4th point

Figure 26.1   Example slide format that helps guide the flow of a board meeting

26.4.2 Post-meeting closure

After you say goodbye to the full board, the senior team should meet for a "post mortem." Don't leave them hanging. Those who were not in attendance, but especially those who were, will want to know the board's mood and whether any board member asked a leading question or was critical of anything. Most of them are not used to being at board meetings and will put a huge amount of weight on the least glance, eyebrow raise, or words spoken by anyone on the board.

26.5 The moral of this anecdote

The board is a critical element of your company, as the ultimate authority on all things the company and its leaders do; they are the fiduciary for shareholders and are required to protect the interests of those shareholders. The board is made up of investors, some management (including the CEO), perhaps an independent member, and some observers. If you are the CEO, they are your boss. They set your compensation, coach you, give feedback on your performance, and work with you on strategy, and they can fire you along the way.

Formal board meetings are how the CEO and their team keep the board appraised of everything the company is doing and plans to do. These meetings are where formal votes take place that determine whether certain things the CEO proposes are approved to be done. Votes are where some of the bad and ugly take place when board members do not act as they should. The CEO can make sure the meetings go well by planning extremely carefully for each meeting.

Board observers:
Observe only, please

- Why are there board observers, and how do they earn a seat at the table?
- How do some observers deviate from normalcy and end up disrupting the board meeting?
- Is there any way to remove problem board observers?

I'll be very honest up front: I have no love or tolerance for *board observers*. If you get one thing out of this anecdote, it will be to push back very hard whenever someone requests or even demands to add a board observer to your board. They are like pet pythons who have escaped or been dumped. They are now an invasive species in the Everglades, and no one is quite sure how to get rid of them. Let's explore what they are, how they get added to your board, and what you can do to avoid or remove this "species."

27.1   What is a board observer?

Here are a couple of helpful distinctions between a board director and a board observer:

- A *board director* has legal responsibilities to the company and has voting rights. They are permitted to speak at board meetings.

- A *board observer* has no legal responsibilities to the company. Their duty is to the organization that appointed them. The board observer has no voting rights. The board observer is not supposed to speak at board meetings.

My practical experience with board observers is that their existence is codified in terms of either an investment or a side letter coincident with an investment where they represent the interests of one of the investors who did not get an official board member assignment. In either case, their appointment is made contractual, and unless specifically stipulated in either of these contractual forms (investment terms or side letter), it is permanent—you are stuck with them indefinitely.

Pragmatically, board observers are invited to every board meeting and must be provided with the board meeting materials. They do not get to vote or attend executive sessions. But depending on who they are, they can still affect the overall tenor of a meeting and, in many cases, how the official members vote. Because most financing rounds contractually provide all major investors with the same information rights, investors who demand an observer seat are either small investors not provided those information rights or investors who worry that startups will not follow the letter of the law on those rights. Even with information rights, investors, depending on the management team at the startup, think that physically attending board meetings gives them more of an inside line than just reading all the information provided under the information rights clause in the financing documents.

> **DEFINITION** *Information rights* is a provision in the legal, binding, investment documents that outlines the information a company must deliver to investors beyond what state law requires. Generally this includes a commitment to deliver regular financial statements and a budget.

> **TIP** Considering the increase in shareholder lawsuits, some investors, especially smaller ones, want to avoid the liability of being voting board members and thus prefer being observers. They should not, however, think of an observer seat as being a proxy for a full board member with participation, but without voting rights, just to avoid the liability of being a board member. Be vigilant about this being the reason an investor chooses to demand an observer seat, and try to push back hard. Of course, if you need them as investors and they demand the seat in return, you may be stuck with them.

27.2 Stories of bad board observer behavior

Bottom line: it is the rare board observer who follows the observe-only implication of their title. And in more than a few cases, they become disruptive to the point of dominating a meeting or worse. I'll recount three examples of different types of observers—who never refrained from speaking—from my startups and what behaviors caused their stories to be told here.

27.2.1 *The loudmouth, undisciplined observer*

My first time as CEO, and therefore my first time leading a board meeting, I realized we had 13 people sitting around the table—actually, the table did not comfortably seat that many, so some of the observers sat in chairs against the walls. One of the observers never even sat down throughout the entire meeting. He continuously circled the table, walking in the space between the backs of the chairs of those seated at the table and those seated against the wall. On every topic I broached, he loudly proclaimed his "expert" view before I even got to explain why I was bringing up the subject. It appeared that no one—not the voting board members, the chairman, or the other observers—had the wherewithal to control this undisciplined person. Many board meetings later, I learned that this individual was the godfather of the child of the patriarch and largest investor on the board, so no one had any intention of reprimanding him unless the patriarch determined it was necessary—and he never deemed it so. I further learned that this godfather had invested $100,000 of his personal money without even the knowledge of his wife; I was installed as CEO because the company was in serious financial distress, and he was in a total panic from my first day forward. He ultimately lost every penny of that investment two years later when that same patriarch decided it was time to shut down the company because it had gone on too long for the lifespan of his firm's fund.

27.2.2 *The self-dealing observer*

Next is the observer representing a large angel fund who was a participating angel in that fund and therefore an investor in my brand-new startup. Not only did this observer completely fail to follow the dictates of "observe but don't speak," but what he said was always in the context of what was good for his investment, not what was good for his sponsoring angel group or the company. That was particularly glaring when we were discussing the creation of a convertible note to bridge the company while searching for a Series A round. The topic was the interest rate on such a note, and this observer wanted the interest rate high. That was not good for the company. That was good only if he purchased one of those notes and made money just for holding the note a while.

27.2.3 *The palace coup observer*

Saving the most egregious example of bad observer behavior for last, there is the observer who was the manager of a large, elite university alumni angel organization. Like many startups, mine got into some distress, and this observer decided he would roar into action to deal with the issues. He went to voting board members and secretly suggested to them that the CEO—me—be replaced, and he told them he had just the guy to take over. Without me knowing anything about that interaction, he came to me to suggest that I get to know this individual and "partner" with him to work on the challenging issues. I always welcome good, experienced advisors and took on faith that this was all the observer intended. I spent many hours getting this advisor up to speed on the technology, our business situation, and our go-to-market strategy. I liked the person. But then the observer came clean and let me know that he had the board's full support to install this advisor as the new CEO. That, of course, was patently false. He did not have the board's full support, but I had a lot of work to do to survive this incident because the observer had poisoned the well of other observers and small investors.

27.3 Can you get rid of observers?

At each successive round of financing, a new set of legal documents is created, reflecting the terms of that investment. These can include a wide variety of things that potentially modify the company bylaws and previous rounds of financing. Essentially, a new financing creates a clean slate. One thing that is almost always included in a new financing is the makeup of the board going forward. It may expand the board and allow new investors to occupy the newly expanded seats. But it can also specifically remove existing board members and replace them with ones acceptable to the new investors.

I have noticed that modifying the makeup of observers is frequently overlooked at that time, but it is the perfect opportunity to remove previous observers. If that step remains overlooked, you will be stuck with the previous observers, and potentially have some new ones added, until the next major financing. Don't miss the chance to wipe that slate clean as well.

> **TIP** The only practical way to get rid of observers is when you are closing a new round of financing. The new investor has an enormous amount of power over many things in the structure and operations of the company going forward, especially as relates to the board of directors. They will require a board seat, and they may expand the board or require changes to the existing membership. They should be your ally in changing the observer membership. The entity that has an observer seat from which the observer is being removed may protest, but they don't have much power, and they do not want to be the one who, by refusing to give up that spot, causes the new investor to walk away and potentially destroy the company.

27.4 The moral of this anecdote

Board observers are representatives of an investor who is not leading a financing round and does not warrant, want, or need full board representation but wants to be able to fully observe everything that transpires at board meetings. They never have voting privileges and typically are not supposed to speak—only listen and observe. Unfortunately, many do not follow the dictum against speaking, and some even become disruptive. Their right to attend board meetings is codified contractually through financing terms or a side letter. Removing a board observer is best done during the next round of financing, but it's not automatic. CEOs need to be attentive to the detailed terms of financing to make sure that if they want observers removed, the terms call that out explicitly.

Investor communications: They needn't be cod liver oil

28

- Why is communicating regularly with investors an absolute must?
- What should you do in bad times? It's even more important to keep lines of communication open.
- How should investor updates be structured for efficiency and effectiveness?
- Is there a special way to handle those extra-needy investors?

To be a world-class startup CEO, you must have outstanding communication habits with all stakeholders: your team, your board, your advisors, and, most importantly, your investors. In this anecdote, I focus on those all-important investor updates, including some ways to make them as painless as possible and nothing like taking cod liver oil. We begin with why communication is so important.

28.1 Why communicate with investors?

There are several reasons it is worth your time and effort to have consistent, excellent investor communication:

- *Positive culture*—As I have said in other anecdotes, communication is key to establishing and maintaining a positive, mutually supportive culture. It is critical to keeping your investors happy and supportive.
- *Money*—The most practical reason is that you probably will need another infusion of capital that will include the investors you got to invest previously. The easiest investment to get by far is from existing investors *if* they have been kept supportive and are behind you.
- *Legal requirements*—A legal reason to provide investor communication is to avoid them getting upset (lack of information always makes people think of the worst possible things that could be going on) and eventually opening yourself up to a shareholder lawsuit. The contract you agreed to in your previous financings typically includes *investor information rights*, so you are contractually bound to provide them with information about the company and its situation.

28.1.1 When times are good

Effective investor communication needs to be a habit and a priority when times are good; it is even more important when times are bad. If you successfully raised a round of financing, you have already proven that you are excellent with investor communications. You had to convince them that you are solving a compelling problem in a big market and that your approach was different and better than your competitors' ideas. You need to build on that carefully and establish a solid foundation of trust now, when times are good, that you can tap into if times get bad.

For at least the first couple of years—some might argue for always—you should communicate with your investors monthly. Some CEOs communicate more frequently, but investors may not appreciate that unless you are in an all-out crisis. Other CEOs communicate closer to quarterly, but in my opinion that's not often enough to really get investors on your side (especially the smaller, less sophisticated ones).

Surveys from experts in this area endorse these views. NFX, a seed investor and a serial blogger in support of founders, teaches founders how to do best-in-class investor updates. NFX found that 60% of founders communicate monthly, 21% do so weekly, 3% communicate daily, and 16% communicate quarterly. Daily is either when the crisis is extreme or the founder is excessively nervous.

I have always communicated with my investors monthly except during the pandemic, when things slowed down so much that there was no news, so I slowed my communications, too. In hindsight, I should not have slowed down because with all the uncertainty, they needed to hear from me more than ever. My decision backfired, and investors were no longer strongly supportive of me. You never want that to happen.

28.1.2 When times are bad

We are so immersed in our company and the day-to-day battles we're fighting that we can easily forget that our investors have many investments and possibly other major roles that occupy them day to day, so we are not going to be top of mind for them.

This means regular, efficient communication is the only way to keep you and your company top of mind, which will set you up to have investors' support when you need it most. We are all guilty to some extent—it's truly a weakness of mine—of wanting to relay the good news and downplay or avoid telling the bad news. But human nature causes our minds to drift toward the negative in a communication vacuum. Silence breeds negativity, and investors will start to wonder if something bad is happening. But if they hear from you regularly, even as you are dealing with major challenges, they can track those issues as things move along. Then, when you need them most, they will not be surprised by out-of-the-blue challenges; consequently, they will be likely to stand behind you through thick and thin.

Even worse than a regular surprise is a surprise that you sat on and failed to report to them. There is no better way to lose their trust permanently than to hide bad news. Let's just agree that they will get that news eventually, either from you or from someone else. That's a disaster, so don't do it.

At difficult times, it is important to remember that investors would much rather not walk away from the investment they made in your startup. If they see that you are facing tough challenges totally clear-eyed, you stand a good chance of keeping them in the boat with you. It is also useful to remind yourself that small investors who invested a small amount are no different from large investors who invested a large amount—both want to protect what they invested because the investment is proportional to what they can afford and to what they have in reserve to support you through a rough patch. My point is that investing in communications with an angel who invested only $25,000 is worth your effort because they could be *the one* ideally suited to help you. Besides, it's just as easy to communicate your basic update information with all investors.

28.2 *What to communicate*

My best starting-out advice is that just as it is beneficial to establish a template for an investor pitch (see anecdote 7, "The art of pitching to institutional investors") or a board update deck (see anecdote 26, "Startup boards: The good, (how to prevent) the bad, and the ugly"), you will want a template for your monthly investor updates, as well. This makes it relatively easy to get these out once a month; a fixed outline is much easier to start with than a blank page. In fact, use the previous update's data as the starting point for the new one because it will make sure you put the new information in the context of what they heard from you a month ago.

If you repeat yourself every month, that's bad. And if this month you contradict what you reported last month, that is worse. If you explicitly need to make changes, such as with plans or for some of your key performance indicators (KPIs), be sure to explicitly call that out so investors who compare a new update with the past few won't see the change and wonder what is going on.

Monthly investor update outline

Here's an outline of an investor update template that has worked well. The first section is short and formatted in bullet points. This way, it can be the only part the investor reads, and they can still get the basics of what they need to know. They can read more in section two if they desire. I include a final section, "Potential asks and thanks of investors," but I usually don't broadcast those to everyone; I target the specific individual(s) I want feedback from one to one.

Executive summary

   i Cash burn + runway (*most important info to always report*)
   ii Highlights, including anything generating revenue
  iii Lowlights
  iv Metrics (ideally only the most critical KPIs)

Monthly update details

   i Key performance indicators (KPIs)
     a The list of data you are measuring yourself on and regularly share with investors, comparing actual to predicted (e.g., burn rate, length of runway, expenses, team size)
   ii Accomplishments by functional area
     a Sales deals closed, new deals in the funnel, deals lost, overall sales forecast
     b Product accomplishments, if relevant
     c Marketing accomplishments (e.g., events, webinars)
     d Partner accomplishments
     e Staffing
  iii Challenges
     a A plan for how you are addressing each one
  iv Plans (including any new KPIs) for
     a Next month
     b Next quarter
     c Next year
   v Market updates, including changes in competition status or in the overall market(s) in which you operate
  vi Miscellaneous (*placeholder for anything you want to add to the template*)
 vii Forecasted next financing
viii Potential asks or thanks to investors

28.2.1 *Managing major events*

Major events that may occur will inevitably happen "off cycle" of your normal investor update cadence. Because these are things that could have a major impact on your investors, and because some investors may be very useful in dealing with them, it is prudent to quickly update all investors on the situation and to strategically recruit one or two to be part of the response to the event. Regardless of whether any investors can be useful, these events are major enough that your investors will hear about them elsewhere. They fall into the category of "better to hear from you than from others" and are worthy of an off-cycle update.

The types of events I am referring to include, but are certainly not limited to, the following:

- You need to rapidly downsize to cut your burn because a revenue deal you were counting on went away.
- You need to raise a bridge round of financing because your Series A round is not going to happen fast enough to cover your expenses.
- You just got a signed term sheet from a prospective lead investor, and the terms of the proposed financing will have an impact on all shareholders.
- A company has expressed strong interest in acquiring you.
- A key founder or member of management has decided to leave the company.

28.3   *Dealing with extra-needy investors*

It seems there are always a few very needy investors who can't wait for the next update. In my experience, this is common with small, non-institutional, nonprofessional investors and is very uncommon with the pros. A situation you'll respond to needy investors about is typically one of the following:

- Something happened in the market or economy, and they want your reaction.
- An event occurred that showed the importance of your product or service. Or maybe it's the opposite: it points to your product's seeming irrelevance.
- They read something about a company they think is a competitor, and they want your assessment of the threat.

The best defense against these happening is what we have been discussing all along: regular, specific, thorough investor updates. But updates won't eliminate random queries when something provokes one of your small investors to reach out to you and not wait for your next update. In that case, you need to answer it and add it to your next update because others probably will read the same thing. And if more than one writes to you, you had best use that as an excuse for an off-cycle communication that addresses just that question and does not follow your normal template.

Unfortunately, some of these questions—especially the one about a potential competitor—cause real work to have to be done, so they are distractions. On the other hand, when you are still young and small, you can't keep up with all the potential competitors, so you can think of these investors as canaries in the coal mine. If they think so-and-so is a competitor (even if they are not), that could mean your potential customers do too, and doing the detailed assessment of their product versus yours may end up being very useful.

28.4   *The moral of this anecdote*

Investor relations is part of the CEO job, and you must accept and embrace that. You need to become outstanding at it to be a world-class startup CEO. Investor updates should be done monthly using a template; then it's easy for you and your investors to keep track of your progress, and updates feel less like that spoonful of cod liver oil some mothers gave us. This is important during good times but essential during bad. Keeping your investors in your corner will pay dividends the next time you really need them, such as your next financing. Going silent is very bad and very dangerous because investors are human, and in an information vacuum, just like all of us, they will start to drift toward the negative and could turn on you. There will be very significant events that do not occur "on cycle" with your updates and will need to be addressed separately; you should do so because investors will hear elsewhere about whatever it is. You will likely also have some needy investors who don't wait for the next update and ask questions about market conditions or how a new company they read about may affect you. You must deal with them in real time and be sure to add whatever they asked about to your next regular update; then perhaps they will stop asking.

Heaven forbid if you must downsize

- Expenses are higher than revenues, and options to increase the top line have been explored. Now what?
- How do you go about executing layoffs with humanity and compliance?
- Is there a trick to delivering this bad news with empathy and still boosting the remaining team's morale?

You are watching your cash burn and the resulting runway, and you are losing sleep. The revenues you were sure your sales team would start bringing in are not coming. The dogs are not eating the dog food. What is wrong? Is it the product? The business model? The assumptions that led to your forecast? You must figure out the answers, and fast. Raising money at this moment may not always be possible, especially if the issue is the product and you need to rework it. Perhaps the problem is that you or your predecessor expanded too fast, and the burn rate is too high for the rate at which you can sell the product. In any case, there is a mismatch between your expenses and your income. You are rapidly heading for that cliff.

29.1 Heading for that cliff

Because at almost all tech startups the big driver of expense is people, it is critical that the staffing strategy is as tight and careful as possible so your expenses don't get ahead of your ability to execute your plan. But if, in spite of great care, you find that you are burning cash too fast, don't wait: act fast. You are, among other things, going to have to cut staff. That is called *layoffs*. You will not be the first. Nor are layoffs rare at startups. But it is likely the hardest thing you will ever do. You built a talented team, you've established a great culture, and now you must pick some members of this team—who have done nothing wrong and have worked hard—to be on a list of people who will no longer be working here. And it is not just them but also their families who have been betting on you. If they must depart before the end of their first year, they will get nothing in equity.

29.2 How to execute layoffs correctly

It is important that you do this next task very carefully. There are many landmines as you head down the layoffs path. In this section, I will describe what doing layoffs correctly looks like. I will examine the cause of the layoff, what form of layoff you will use, how you must communicate with the affected individual(s), and how you must communicate with the company that remains. I also add some examples of layoffs I have been part of in the last 30 years. First, let's talk about what is causing the need for a layoff.

> **NOTE** I am describing the layoff process in the United States. Things are very different in different countries, and readers outside the United States need to follow the laws and customs of their locale.

29.2.1 What is the cause of the layoff?

Which of several possibilities is the reason for the burn rate, and thus staffing levels, having to be cut?

1 You need to cut the burn rate, but you absolutely must keep the major functions you have.
2 The product is not selling, so the product needs to be reworked before you apply sales and marketing again.
3 You spent too much opening sales offices, and revenues did not follow the expansion as expected.
4 You are executing a significant pivot that changes what the company is going to do.

The first case is, I would say, rarer than the others. It also calls into question how and why the company got too big without a structural problem.

29.2.2 *The form of the layoff*

There are four common types of layoffs that take different forms depending on the situation that has led the company to this event: an across-the-board downsizing, a structural change necessitating some reductions in force, reducing or eliminating sales and marketing staff, and a pivot of the company to a new direction.

ACROSS THE BOARD

In the case where layoffs are across the board, you must look at a spreadsheet that shows your monthly expenses across the entire company and very carefully identify one person from each functional area. If that does not hit the new target burn rate, make another pass so you are smoothly and evenly bringing down the staff size across the company without burdening one functional area more than another—unless there really is a structural problem.

STRUCTURAL

In the case where the problem is structural, it clearly identifies the action to take: cut the functions you built up too early. They should either be cut completely or cut down to just one person who "holds down the fort" and represents that function in all planning while the structural problem is being addressed—except if the structural problem is a product not being ready,

SALES AND MARKETING

If the product is not ready (as in, you have failed to prove product–market fit), you have nothing for the salespeople to sell, and you need to cut sales completely until later when it is time to rebuild. In this case, you might cut marketing down to just one person who works closely with the engineering team as part of a product management effort to spend lots of time with customers and make sure the product being rebuilt is what the market wants and needs.

PIVOT AND REBUILD

In the fourth case, a major pivot, you need a full plan of what the adjusted company should look like in terms of market, product, and business model. Essentially, you're rebuilding the company from the ground up, at least on paper. See which of the team will stay (usually most of them) and what gaps you have that need to be hired anew, and you have your list of who you need to lay off.

29.2.3 *Communicating with those being laid off*

In all cases, what distinguishes how to do and how not to do layoffs is a rock-solid plan for the company going forward. That will lead you to the communications you need to convey to the company.

THE PACKET

For each person leaving the company, a packet needs to be developed. The packet contains the following, at a minimum:

- A letter explaining what is happening
- Information about their final paycheck
- Information about their stock options
- Information about career help
- Information about how to apply for unemployment
- Information about COBRA health insurance coverage

THE MEETING

Divvied up across you and your team, happening as close as possible to simultaneously, hold meetings where you sit with each person to explain that they are being let go and why. In each meeting, two people need to be present: the employee's functional manager and a person from HR. This is important to avoid any appearance of intimidation or accidental wandering into topics the HR person is trained to stop. The meetings are either in the manager's or in the HR person's office. The message to be delivered is clear, simple, and unemotional:

> *The company needs to make a change caused by X, and we need to cut expenses. Unfortunately, your role is being eliminated. This is not a performance-based action; we must eliminate your position for structural/financial reasons alone.*

They may ask all kinds of questions that can get you into dangerous territory. "Who else is being laid off?" "Was my performance poor?" "I thought we were doing great." "I got a good performance review, so why me?" Answer none of those, because who else is being laid off is a privacy issue: the company has to strictly adhere to "This layoff is about expenses being too high, so jobs have to be eliminated, not an action about poor performance." If necessary, repeat the same simple statement.

Quickly get into what happens next. Clearly lay out the steps and what the employee will receive. Do they get a two-week severance? Did you hire a firm that helps with transitions, such as getting them career help? Tell them the particulars of their stock options. In the United States, where there is no guaranteed health insurance, you need to talk about COBRA coverage, which is a program that extends company-sponsored health insurance. All of that is in their packet in writing because once you say "laid off," their hearing becomes "impaired" and they may not recall anything you say afterward. A final thing to answer preemptively is whether you will be willing to act as a reference.

Hopefully the employee will not be contentious, in which case you would have to walk them to the door. But you still want to get them out of the offices (if you have offices) somewhat quickly. You can offer them two hours to clean out their spaces and depart by N o'clock, or you can suggest that they come back the next day or the coming Saturday to finish. Even if you want to have them remain for a couple of weeks to transition work to an employee who will stay, you still need them to leave within two hours so that they can cool off and you can do the vital final step of this process, which I'll discuss shortly. They can come back the next workday to start the transition process.

TRANSITIONS

Transitions never take as long as people expect. The minute a team knows that Bobby is not going to be sticking around, the team (both consciously and unconsciously) moves Bobby to the side and starts to absorb Bobby's work into the remainder of the group. Sometimes I hear people offer four or six or more weeks of transition. No matter what the role is, it does not take that long. I promise you, even two weeks will seem long, and usually the person completes all the transition work in the first week and stops coming in the second week. This all assumes that the transition time is *before* a paid severance period, or they won't want to help you with the transition. The right thing to do is to give people at least two weeks of severance to find a new job. In most cases that will not be enough, and they may need to collect unemployment for a few additional weeks.

29.2.4 *Communicating with those remaining at the company*

Cutting expenses is the easy part. And although it is gut-wrenching, communicating with everyone affected is also relatively easy, compared to the last and most important step in the process: communicating with the new, smaller company *and* retaining all of them. Give the message in an essential all hands, *on the same day*, but after the last laid-off person has left the office:

> *Today we did a layoff of N of your coworkers. Here is why we needed to make this change. We are scaling back X / we are doing a pivot to Y because of Z. Your manager will tell you later today who in your group was affected and what the transition plan is for some of their tasks we need to continue to do.*

The critical part is the new strategy the company will employ. You and your whole team need to give a masterful performance. A serious amount of enthusiasm needs to come across. You and the management team made a mistake. But now it is time for a do-over, and it's essential that the new plan is believable and as exciting as the story you told all the people remaining with the company when you hired them. The test of the effectiveness of your communication here is going to be how many people are seriously spooked by the layoffs and get their résumé spruced up that afternoon. You won't know right away; the first shoe may take weeks to drop. When that first one drops, it sends another shock wave through the company, leaving everyone in its wake thinking "What do they know that I don't? If they have lost faith, should I be out there looking?"

My layoff experiences over 35 years

I have had more than my fair share of experience with layoffs over the 35 years since I started down the path of tech startups. Here are a few quick stories of two of those.

GeoTrust had several pivots and layoffs

GeoTrust was a frequent pivoter as it tried to find a strategy that would make it successful. Each pivot required downsizing through layoffs. One involved closing the office in Portland, Oregon, and only keeping the company's much smaller Wellesley, Massachusetts, office. To put it mildly, there was overt hostility as I announced the news to the Portland team. This was happening in conjunction with my hiring a new CEO as I slid into the CTO role to support him. The downsizing allowed the new CEO to hire his old team in Wellesley—people he knew well and trusted. This team was highly motivated, as it was their first time at a startup. They had a shared vision with the CEO, and that vision carried them to major success and a sale to Verisign for $125 million on sales of $25 million.

Dover had to lay off the entire company but didn't shut down

Dover Microsystems struggled mightily to sell hardware-based cybersecurity to huge semiconductor companies. Eventually, because I was unable to raise a Series A, we were headed for the running-out-of-cash cliff. Before we got there, I had no choice but to lay off the entire company except myself. But prior to that, although it still looked like there was a chance of closing Series A, I asked the entire company first to take a 20% pay cut and then, for the last couple of months, to go all the way down to minimum wage. Everyone agreed. Not a single person bailed and left the company—they all stayed to the bitter end. Ultimately, Dover survived, and I rebuilt it as a company selling to the US government, especially the military, using a different business model.

29.3 The moral of this anecdote

Layoffs are horrible. But running out of cash and closing down the company on *all* the employees is atrocious and must be avoided at all costs. When you see your runway shortening and you can't fix it with revenues, act fast and cut expenses. In a tech startup, that almost always means cutting staff. There is a correct way to do this, but there are lots of bad ways to do it. Be careful. Be thoughtful. This can be dangerous territory. Get some advice.

The most important thing for the company to survive is how you communicate after the layoffs: why everyone left should *believe* in your new strategy and should stay put and redouble their efforts to make the company successful. Although layoffs can be very damaging, they happen a lot, and many companies that go through it survive and wind up being very successful.

Heaven forbid if
you must wind it up

- What can you do when you see the end of the runway but there is nowhere to turn?
- If the shutdown is inevitable, what does a team-centric, timely windup of the company look like?
- Are there insider stories that could be helpful to prepare for (or avoid) the worst?

Let's suppose your company can't be saved. Either you have tried everything and it is just not working, or the investors have pulled the plug, and you have been ordered to shut down your startup. In this anecdote, we will talk about what you need to do, who can help you, what the process looks like, and how to finalize dissolution, put it behind you, and go on to your next thing. There is no shame in a startup failing. At the very least, you learn a lot—I sure did when it happened to me. The next one you do will be better because of what you learned this time.

30.1 Your startup is running out of runway

As you run out of runway and head toward that cliff, do not let your bank balance fall all the way to zero. Shutting down will cost some money. If you drive the cash down to zero, you have backed your investors into a corner, forcing them to put in enough money to have a clean shutdown. But they will not be happy about that.

252

I have seen situations where the investors told the CEO to keep running hard right up until the bank balance really was zero. They did this hoping that if the CEO was not distracted and stayed focused on closing some huge deal, they could pull off a miracle and save the investors' investments. In such a case, if they told you to run the cash all the way to zero, if you do not pull off that miracle, your investors will typically do a tiny raise of just enough money for a clean shutdown.

The first thing to decide is *how* you are going to shut it down. Investors do not like to file for bankruptcy for a startup. The process is too lengthy and too expensive. They don't want bankruptcies on their record of past investments, either. Bankruptcies are public and easily discoverable, but quiet windups are not. Bankruptcies might scare away limited partners and prospective entrepreneurs. They also don't want a bunch of creditors angry about being stiffed, as can happen in a bankruptcy that is a closure, not just a reorganization. These are small worlds we circulate in; the last thing investors want is to make enemies.

Instead of bankruptcy, you are headed toward winding up your company. More officially, it is called *assignment for the benefit of creditors*.

> **DEFINITION**   *Assignment for the benefit of creditors* is a way for a business to handle its debts without going through a formal bankruptcy process. Instead, the business transfers all the assets to a trust, which liquidates the assets and uses the money to pay off the business's debts. There are no courts involved, and everything is quicker and much cheaper.

You will need help with this. Like everything else in this world, there are experts at windup, and they have a process. You can hire a law firm that specializes in this "end-of-life" work. Or you can hire an independent consultant who is similarly experienced. I have done both.

In either case, before they will do one lick of work, you will pay them in the form of a retainer. They will draw down on that retainer as they expend time and money, and they will come back to you if things take more time than they estimated. As you can imagine, in their line of work, where they are dealing all day, every day with creditors, they don't want to add their name to that list. No, they get paid first, before any of the creditors waiting to get paid.

30.2   The goals

The goals of the windup are simple: sell off all assets, pay off all creditors, and file formal dissolution papers. And do these things without any lawsuits. Maybe there are no assets. Or maybe they didn't sell. For whatever reason, there may not be enough cash to pay off all creditors in full. Hence the need for someone who knows how to navigate these choppy waters.

Usually, by the time you get to this point, it is not possible to pay all creditors in full. After all, no one believes well in advance of running out of money that it is going to happen. And entrepreneurs tend to be risk-takers, so they wait until they've explored every alternative to shutting down, by which time the cash is too low to pay everyone in full. The windup experts are good at convincing creditors to take cents on the dollar and go away quietly. It may surprise you, but creditors are used to that. They don't want to enter a lawsuit if they can avoid it. Landlords have a stronger position than most because they are sitting on a legally binding contract, but I have found that even they are willing to take a hit on what is owed to them.

30.3   *The process*

In this section, we'll follow the roadmap for dissolution. We'll begin with the formal resolution from the board of directors. From there, we will look at the people involved, the documents needed, how assets are resolved, how debt is resolved, how all the important company relationships are cared for, and how the final step of dissolution happens.

30.3.1   *Formal resolution*

Before anyone can be hired or any steps in the process begin, the board needs to approve a formal resolution in which they go on record as saying that a windup must happen, how it is being paid for, and who from the startup is being asked to do the work.

> **TIP** You definitely want the board to authorize this step, not do this on your own volition. The board is the official fiduciary for the company and is highly protected by Directors and Officers insurance.

30.3.2   *People needed*

Let's be clear—you are perfectly within your rights to just walk out the door and have nothing to do with this process. And if the investors decided to shut it down against your advice, no one would blame you. But the whole thing works best if someone from the company remains behind and helps the windup firm understand what's what. This will also keep your reputation clean with the investors, with the creditors, and with important relationships the company has, especially customers. In addition to the CEO, the CFO is frequently needed. Whoever it is will require some compensation because they are putting off their next career move.

30.3.3   *Documents needed*

At a minimum, the following documents will be necessary:

- Fully executed board resolution authorizing the windup of the company
- Fully executed engagement letter from the windup firm
- Receipt from the windup firm showing that you paid their retainer
- Assets inventory description for all elements of all products, including hardware (if any), software, documentation, demonstrations, and patents

- Liquidation analysis, which includes, in the order they must be paid: taxes, payroll and benefits, windup costs, secured creditors, settlement reserves, general creditors
- Invitation to bid that sets the ground rules for a bidding process for the company's assets

30.3.4 Asset resolution

Once the windup team is engaged and the assets inventory has been created, establish the schedule parameters for the bidding process and create the invitation to bid. At the same time, in parallel, the target buyers list can be researched. Once both are in place, send out the invitation to bid to the target list and start the bidding clock. The bidding time includes room for potential bidders to request deep-dive meetings with the technical team (whoever you can get for this) to get answers to any of their questions. With no knowledge of what other bidders offer, each interested party submits their bid; and on the specified date, the bids are opened and a winner is determined. Assets are formally transferred to the winner, and their payment is received and added to the company's bank balance.

30.3.5 Debt resolution

While the bidding clock is running, negotiations with creditors can begin in parallel. Although the team does not know how much money the assets sale will bring, the company still needs to negotiate the creditors down to a reasonable amount to preserve whatever cash it has. The team starts calling all the creditors and making them offers. This is not my forte, but I do know that the windup firm let each creditor know that all other creditors are accepting *NN* cents on the dollar and that once the money is gone, the company is shutting down. It's a variant of the fear of missing out; a creditor is encouraged to hurry while there is still a company to pay them anything. They are also getting the message that there will be no one to sue if they wait. Leaseholders are different: a lease is a legally binding contract, unlike bills such as your internet provider or your credit card. But even leaseholders generally agree to some cutbacks.

I have watched in awe as this unfolded. The attorneys are very good at this, using just the right mixture of being tough and being empathetic.

30.3.6 Relationship care

Even a young startup has a lot of relationships tied to it. These include investors, customers, partners, advisors, and vendors who are not in the debt-resolution category (i.e., you don't owe them any money). All of these are very much worth your time and effort (and psychic discomfort) to arrange a personal call from the CEO, another founder, a board member, or someone else who represents the company, with an explanation of what brought this on and what is going to happen to the company and the team. You are almost guaranteed to run into many of these people over the years, and you want to smooth things over with them as much as you can.

30.3.7 *Final dissolution*

Two or three months after the start of the process, the windup will be complete, and dissolution papers can be filed with the secretary of state where the company is registered. That makes it complete and final. That company no longer exists.

Now lock the door and walk away. That is the end of that startup. What's your next idea that will change the world?

My windup experiences

FactPoint (formerly NovaSoft)

After the board decided to shut down FactPoint and I had laid off all the employees, the only ones who remained were the CFO and me. My next move was to hire Looney & Grossman, which had a department that did bankruptcies and liquidations and was ready to go the next day.

While the CFO went through piles of paperwork to settle things with employees and I began calling every customer, Looney & Grossman started to look at all assets and reach out to potential buyers. There was not much to sell: furniture, a few computers, and some patents that had potential. There were a couple of patents that I wanted to get as the basis for my next company which I had originally thought would cost me $1 million to purchase. Out of curiosity, I asked the attorney what she thought they should cost me. She said, "If you wait three weeks until our IP sale completion, I can offer you those patents for $65,000." The harrowing task of winding up FactPoint morphed into a new startup that a friend and I founded with that IP, which sold seven years later for $125 million.

A couple of attorneys, the CFO, and I worked every day for two months in offices that shortly before had housed 45 employees. We wrapped things up in a nice bow, made our final payments to ourselves, locked the door, and never looked back.

Dover Microsystems

Dover was not just running on fumes; it was running on severely borrowed time. Because I still held out hope that a very large deal I had been working on for a year with the Air Force Research Laboratory (AFRL) would still come through, I did not want to "prematurely" end Dover's life. I was stretching out all our creditors, racking up debt, and asking employees to take pay cuts, followed by all of us working for minimum wage, but finally I had to admit defeat. After laying off everyone, I remained as the sole employee to close things down. Instead of a law firm, I decided to hire a windup consultant, KallanderGroup, which had done hundreds of such shutdowns.

The only assets we had to generate cash were our patent filings; we had 15 of those, but none had yet issued as an official US patent. KallanderGroup was good at creating the fear of missing out through a blind bidding process. Potential buyers had three weeks to consider our proposal. We had two who showed a modicum interest and one who asked for multiple meetings, so it sure seemed like they were going to bid. But ultimately, we got no bids. At this point, I was almost numb from the torrent of bad news.

Before KallanderGroup could begin the next step of settling with our large pile of creditors, we finally got some good—no, great—news. The long-lost AFRL deal came in. I immediately did an about-face and asked KallanderGroup to stay on and instead help revive the company. The deal enabled us to pay all our creditors and to hire a CEO and CTO out of the Department of Defense market where Dover was heading, and I happily gave up the CEO role and became executive chairman instead. Dover just used up its second life, and I hope I don't have to find out whether, like a cat, it has seven more to go.

30.4   *The moral of this anecdote*

No sugarcoating: when the runway runs out or the investors pull the plug and the only thing left in this startup's life is to wind it up, that is a really bad, no good, horrible day. You just have to get through it and move on to whatever the next thing is. Some firms specialize in windups, and their help is invaluable, especially because parts of this process are extremely emotional. Prepare the documents that describe the assets and liabilities. Get the assets sold if you can. Let the windup professionals take care of negotiations with creditors—that's hard, and they are experts at it. You should focus on relationship care to keep from burning any bridges. Then it is over, and you move on. Hopefully you will get back on that horse.

31
Acquisition: Your financial dream come true

- What are the pros and cons of acquisition versus IPO?
- How do investors view an exit? It's all about liquidity and timing.
- What planning should be done well in advance of an acquisition? And how do you execute it?

Sad to say, most startups don't make it to an exit. Of those that do, most, by a large margin, are acquired. IPOs are few and far between these days. This anecdote is about acquisition. It is important to plan an acquisition from day one and keep it on the front burner as part of your strategy planning. An up-to-date ecosystem map is key to that strategy process. This map shows all potential competitors, partners, vendors, major customers, service providers, and any other types of companies your company may encounter during the course of business. It is also important to keep your investors' business model and timing in mind to understand what pressures are on them to get to liquidity. With multiple investors, you will need to make sure you understand who is most sensitive to time and who is most sensitive to price, and navigate that thin line. You will need to be deeply involved in the acquirer's due diligence process; and during that, you'll start planning how this will affect you, your team, your product, and your customers. Then, once the acquisition deal closes, you will be the point of the spear, working to keep your team happy and engaged. It's a lot, but it's what you most hope for, and it is (almost always) worth it.

31.1 Exit choices: Acquisition vs. IPO

It's not always a real choice between the two. Remember, as I discussed in anecdote 9, "Understand the VC business model: Raise money faster," there is an expiration date on a startup that raises money from venture capitalists. Those investors need to see a return within about seven years. Fewer is better, and 10 is the absolute max. They'll only stay that long if things are going well but there is no imminent offer, so they remain supportive. This timeline means the startup is driven by rapid growth, which is expensive and burns a lot of capital. Everything is poured into growth, so more capital is needed periodically to provide funds to run the company. Some startups have explosive growth. There, the investors begin to think of the company as being their "lead dog"—that it should be a public company that acquires other startups—but this is increasingly rare. Realistically, you should probably only be thinking about acquisition as your exit strategy.

In a rapidly growing startup—the desirable case—growth represents *future* revenues. This is why such a startup is valued at some multiple of current revenues (how big a multiple depends on the industry and business model). The most typical for a product company (versus a service company) is 5× revenues, but 15× is not unheard of. When my startup GeoTrust was seven years old, it got an offer from Verisign, the lead company in its space, for 5× its $25 million revenues. The other acquisition exit in my string of startups, Webspective, was an outlier. Due to the 1999–2000 internet bubble, it received an offer for $106 million on revenues of $2 million. No one then or ever expects 53× revenues!

31.1.1 Types of acquisition

Financially, there are two types of acquisition: *asset sale* and *equity sale*. An asset sale usually is not a positive event. This is what happens when the company has failed and, to pay off creditors, its assets are offered up for sale. It is not a going concern at this point and typically has lost all its employees, save for a small shutdown team. I talk a lot more about what happens when the company has failed in anecdote 30, "Heaven forbid if you must wind it up."

An equity sale is the desired and most common way a startup is acquired. A share price is offered for the company, and typically the acquirer purchases all shares. The company is and remains a going concern, and the acquirer is highly motivated to work very hard to retain most or all of the employees.

31.1.2 Benefits of acquisition vs. IPO

This anecdote is about acquisition, but first let's compare and contrast *initial public offering* (IPO) versus *acquisition* to highlight the benefits of each. First, the benefits of acquisition.

TRANSACTION SIMPLICITY

Acquisition is a *private* transaction—as opposed to an IPO—and can be kept so throughout the process. This makes negotiations easier because Wall Street is not even aware of it and can't interfere. And very little of the process is regulated (which would require lots of regulatory [e.g., SEC] reporting), making it dramatically simpler than an IPO.

FREEDOM TO EXIT THE COMPANY

Some (many) founders do not enjoy the prospect of going from founder and leader to becoming the acquirer's employee. IPOs usually involve a contractually binding *lock-up period* for founders during which they are not allowed to redeem or sell their shares. Given how much money they will make in an IPO, they tolerate this, but some prefer startups to public companies and want to get out and do other things professionally. An acquirer usually tries to retain founders for a while, and many get key roles in the new company and stay a long time. But they are *at-will* employees, and the acquirer is likely far from a startup and not what they are used to. In an acquisition, they can leave whenever they want to with no legal repercussions.

EXISTING INVESTORS WIN

Most acquisition offers are at a premium price that is higher than the current valuation. This will be true especially when there are competing bids, which the investment bank working with the acquiree will try to make happen. This higher price puts more money directly in the existing investors' hands, whereas in an IPO, they retain their ownership while the public is offered newly authorized shares. Sometime later, they can sell their shares on the public market and, of course, typically do very well.

31.1.3 *Benefits of an IPO vs. acquisition*

Now, let's consider the benefits of an IPO as compared to an acquisition.

MANAGEMENT STAYS

Usually, in an IPO, the management team stays in place initially due to a contractual lock-up. But remember, this is the same company: the one they founded. Because this is the team that knows the product, the market, the customers, and the strategy, they are the ones to keep the newly public entity going. If anything, the new institutional investors want to give that team more resources so they can do more. Supporting keeping management is the fact that the existing shareholders, who know and probably like this team, represent a significant share of voting stock, meaning they can protect management from a hostile public shareholder vote trying to displace them.

LIQUIDITY

The IPO process calls for new shares to be sold to the public. Going forward, it is much easier for a public company to issue new shares and sell them on the public market to raise capital as needed than it has been as a startup to raise money from private equity investors. If the acquirer in a straight acquisition is already a public company, that benefit accrues to the newly acquired startup.

IPO exits are very involved

An initial public offering is a complicated process. IPOs, heavily regulated by the Securities and Exchange Commission (SEC), require the filing of a registration statement with the SEC as well as the state securities regulating body. This registration statement is a very onerous document, which is why you engage an investment bank (also known as an *underwriter*) to run this process. Extensive disclosures about company operations, finances, and other data are required. Once the registration statement is accepted, the company must go on a road show to advertise the upcoming public sale of stock to help boost its price. This is essential so various entities and individuals who are influencers know about your company and will support a good price on the day of the IPO.

The company will authorize the creation of new shares for the public sale. Founders will have the option of selling some of their shares after a lock-up period. The investment bank will marshal institutional investors to consider buying the stock. All these activities must converge on the chosen go-public day. After the sale, the investment bank is paid a substantial fee via some cash and some discounted shares. With the IPO complete, the company has new capital it can use to expand or just to operate.

31.2 Planning for an acquisition

From day one, you need to be thinking about the eventual acquisition of your company. That does not mean you are just going to quickly build up your company and flip it as if it were a fixer-upper house. I doubt you could pull that off even if you wanted to.

The conscious acquisition plan for GeoTrust

GeoTrust's conscious acquisition plan to be acquired by Verisign was to take a point a month of market share away from the only competitor that mattered (Verisign) until it could not tolerate the pain any longer and would "fix" the problem by acquiring GeoTrust. We and Verisign were in the business of selling digital certificates to companies to keep their online transactions secure. Critical in this sale was knowing for sure what company was purchasing a digital certificate. Verisign had a totally manual process to authenticate the company, which took a service bureau full of people running a multistep process for a minimum of four days. GeoTrust automated the process down to 10 minutes.

GeoTrust went from 1% market share to 25% market share in two years. After a loss of 25% of its market share, Verisign seemingly had no choice but to acquire our company. GeoTrust's acquisition strategy was deliberate and effective.

31.2.1 Liquidity

As you may realize, because you are leading a startup and a startup is considered a highly risky investment, you cannot raise capital from banks. Banks make *loans*: the money they provide you must be secured against some sort of tangible asset, like a home or office building, that they can sell if you default on the loan. So that is not an option.

Instead, startups are funded ahead of having created any tangible assets, such as a product or service, much less customers who generate revenue when the product or service is sold. The investors who fund startups are using *risk capital* to fund you. This is very different from banks making loans, because the money they invest gets them an ownership stake (equity) in your company. These investors (angels, family offices, venture capitalists, and hedge funds) are called *private equity*. Because you cannot create a product, find your product-market fit (PMF), sell the product, and prove you will grow in a short period, they have to commit to a long enough time, like 7 to 10 years, for you to build a real, sustainable, growing business. This means your investors must be constantly thinking about when their investment in you can reach *liquidity*.

From day one, you may be thinking of changing the world, or at least how to build your product and get it to market, but not about liquidity. But you should. You must think like your investors, so I will try to convince you to consider liquidity from the beginning.

As I said, private equity needs a long time horizon (7–10 years), plus the riskiness of startups translates to many failures. Taken together, these two facts mean these types of investors require an enormous return of around 20%. Most funds with, say, 10 portfolio companies will see 5 fail, 3 do so-so (maybe with a return of invested capital), and just 1 or 2 be big wins; these must provide all the returns this fund will accrue. That's a lot of pressure. Luckily, most entrepreneurs never know if they are viewed as one of those two until they are looking at an exit.

Private equity investor math explaining the focus on liquidity

Let's examine the investor math on a 10-year fund's investment of $1 million in each of 10 companies. The standard compound interest formula is

$$A = P \cdot (1 + r/n)^{n \cdot t}$$

A = accrued amount (principal+interest)

P = starting principal

r = annual interest rate

n = number of compounding periods

t = duration time in years

Applying our values of P = $10 million starting principal, r = 20% rate of return per year, n = 12 monthly compounding periods per year, and t = 10-year duration to the compound interest formula,

$$A = \$10,000,000 \cdot (1 + 20\%/12)^{12 \cdot 10}$$
$$A = \$10,000,000 \cdot (1.0166667)^{120}$$
$$A = \$72,682,550 \text{ principal + interest}$$

This shows a return on the initial investment of $62,682,550, or 6× what was initially invested. Because likely only 2 of the 10 startups in this fund will end up winners, each has to provide liquidity of just over $30 million, which is 30× what was invested in them. You will hear people say that investors need at least a 10× return, but that is way off; it is 30× unless they do way better than 2 winners out of 10 in each of their funds.

31.2.2 Planning for liquidity

It should be clear that you need to be planning for liquidity from day one of formation. It is probably not what you wanted to hear, because perhaps you have idealistic goals to change the world (or at least a market) with a killer new concept. But because you went to investors to get capital to build and deliver that killer concept, you need to think like they do, and that means planning on liquidity. And as we have just discussed, the most likely way that will happen is an acquisition. As you think about the overall ecosystem you will be swimming in, the market(s) you will go after, your business model, your competitors, your potential partners, and everything else you already must think about to be successful, add thinking about who in this overall ecosystem might be an acquirer.

Five acquisition questions
1 How are you valued?
2 Who are likely acquirers?
3 Why would they acquire you?
4 How can you build this list up and keep it up to date?
5 When is the right time for this acquisition?

HOW ARE YOU VALUED?

Each market is a little different, so you have to get to know how acquirers in your market think. How do they value companies? Is it a multiple of revenues (common)? How is revenue defined (bookings, annually recurring revenue [ARR], lifetime value)? Consumer and Web properties measure active users and churn. In the health world, it is proof of efficacy, clinical trial progress, FDA approval, or Medicare reimbursement codes created.

The good news is that you had to do a lot of this anyway just to learn how your market operates, how to set your pricing, who is who, and so forth. Having information about how you are valued in your chosen markets is useful.

WHO ARE LIKELY ACQUIRERS?

One of the first things I do when I start a new company, or even when launching a new product, is build a detailed ecosystem map. In it, I list all the different types of partners, competitors, and suppliers relevant to our business. In this process, you will see potential acquirers jump out. Some may be competitors, and some may be partners. As you learn more and more and land a few customers and a few partners, your ideas about potential acquirers will morph and evolve, so keep your ecosystem map up to date. I put it in a prominent place like a big bare wall in our office so everyone sees it every day, reminding them where we sit in the markets we operate in so they can connect their daily work to the bigger picture.

For each potential acquirer, list the names of senior business development people and employees in the office of the CTO, as well as anyone in their ventures group, if they have one. You can get this list using ZoomInfo (www.zoominfo.com), or you can do a pretty fair job of it on LinkedIn by targeting a company and then searching for people by title. To get the best list, you will have to pay for LinkedIn Sales Navigator. Otherwise you cannot get contact information for anyone further removed from you than one level.

Talk to analysts who cover your target market. They will know who is acquisitive and what acquisitions have happened in the last 18 months. Talk to CEOs who have been acquired in your segment, and get their list of contacts. They may be willing to share because their acquisition is done and if they aren't helping a competitor to their acquirer, sharing won't hurt them. Besides, I have found over and over that CEOs like to help each other because everyone realizes it's an incredibly hard job and every way we can help each other can lessen that burden somewhat.

WHY WOULD THEY ACQUIRE YOU?

What's the business case for why each of the potential acquirers would buy you? Does it fill a product void? Maybe it provides accretive revenues. Maybe it adds to a product they are making. Maybe it adds your customers to theirs and expands their market share. Maybe it removes you as a thorn in their side. Maybe it helps them with a troublesome competitor. Or maybe it allows them to expand into a whole new market (yours).

HOW CAN YOU BUILD THIS LIST AND KEEP IT UP TO DATE?

Once you find a couple of these people using ZoomInfo, LinkedIn, analysts, or friendly introductions, talk to a couple and ask about what conferences they go to and what they read. Go to the conferences they go to. Be on panels, bump into them at the conferences, and get introduced to them. Write things for their chosen online magazines and blogs. All these things, of course, are exactly what you are doing for your customer development process; you are just adding some additional companies to that process.

WHAT IS THE RIGHT TIME FOR THIS ACQUISITION?

One path is to wait as long as possible so your revenues and growth are at their most impressive and you can attract a billion-dollar sale. But is your market really that hot? If it's not, you could be like many companies that wait too long—and the market goes away. At Service Integrity, the CEO who succeeded me waited too long: every competitor found a suitor, even though their CEOs all agreed that we had better technology and were flummoxed that they got buyers and Service Integrity never did. It was not acquired; it ignominiously shut down. You also don't want to be acquired too early, or your VCs may balk if the return is not good enough for their fund results (they can probably block a sale they don't like).

> **TIP** Liquidity is one of the few things you will be working on that you should keep mostly to yourself and not share with your employees. They don't want to be thinking that from day one, the company is for sale.

Even if your strategy is to build your company solely with the intent of being acquired, you have to tell everyone (including yourself), "We are building a real company." And you *should* be building a real company because if you cut corners by thinking, "I don't really need that [*person/thing/process*] anymore if we are going to be acquired soon," you could blow it. Acquirers want to buy a complete, healthy company, so never cut those corners.

The takeaway for you is that planning for an acquisition, even years out, is an important part of your strategic planning.

31.3 Executing the acquisition

When the prospective buyer has decided they want to make a formal offer and begins sharing deal terms with you, you will likely find deal terms that you want to change. However, negotiating leverage over who wins on major deal points is usually only available in a competitive bidding process. Otherwise, the acquirer has most of the negotiating leverage, up to the point where you decide to walk away. But the more you know about your acquirer and why they want this deal, the more you can influence decisions about a host of issues that won't jeopardize the deal. The list of points you can "win" on is typically large.

A really important point is how your company will be integrated after the acquisition. This integration depends on the structure of the acquisition with respect to the acquirer's products and customer base. The next section outlines the different structures.

31.3.1 The structure of the planned acquisition

There are five basic structures to acquisitions. The outcome for you and your team will mostly be good but will differ widely in these structures. It is vital that you understand which structure your acquisition falls into. They are differentiated by what your product and your customers do for your acquirer.

NEW MARKET: YOUR PRODUCT AND YOUR CUSTOMERS

The acquirer wants to expand their overall footprint in the market. They most likely view you and your product, as well as your customers, as adjacent to their current product, or they see you as representing their future and think you are a quick way to get there. This structure frequently leads to a new, independent business unit, which is what occurred when Oculus was acquired by Facebook, Android and Nest by Google, Mailchimp by Intuit, and Ring by Amazon. In this structure, the acquirer doesn't know anything about your product, and if you and they are not careful about your team's role, they could destroy it. So, an important goal to aim for is business-unit independence and maybe continuation of your brand, both of which could be essential to the acquisition being effective for both you and them.

NEW PRODUCT LINE: YOUR PRODUCT SOLD TO THEIR CUSTOMERS

As companies grow, they like to continuously expand their product and upsell new features to their customers, or at least continue to offer new features to hold on to the customers they have. It is a way to keep ahead of competitors and increase the revenue they are getting from each customer. A very fast way to expand their product is to acquire companies that have already built a product they can integrate into their offerings. Famous examples are YouTube being acquired by Google and Instagram being acquired by Facebook. Because this is such a frequent need of larger companies, this is the most common structure for acquisitions. And because this will be a tight integration of your product into their suite of products, they will want to quickly integrate you and your entire company into theirs. That is a good thing for you because you are essential to their strategy, which leads to success for both sides.

MARKET SHARE: YOUR CUSTOMERS BUT IN THE SAME PRODUCT CATEGORY AS THEIRS

You have built a successful product in the same market as your acquirer. They probably don't view you as a direct competitor because your customers are different than theirs. But they want to acquire you because they want to expand their customer base (market share) by bringing your product and customers into their orbit. Because you know your customers and they do not, remaining independent initially is good for maintaining your customers and easing them into the fold of the acquirer. When Marriott bought Starwood, and PayPal bought Venmo, it was this model.

DIRECT COMPETITOR: YOUR PRODUCT AND CUSTOMER BASE ARE THE SAME AS THEIRS

You are competing directly with them, so the acquirer wants your customer base and probably wants to completely remove you as a thorn in their side. There is no option to remain independent here; you are being assimilated by the (hopefully nice) Borg. They will fully integrate your product into theirs, and your customers will be quickly merged with theirs. They may not keep all of your team if some are duplicative with theirs, and those who are kept will be added to the appropriate teams and may not be kept together. This is what happened when Verisign acquired GeoTrust, Exxon acquired Mobil, AT&T acquired Time Warner, and Disney acquired Pixar.

ACQUIHIRE: THEY JUST WANT YOUR TEAM

This type of acquisition is incredibly common in the technology sector.

> **DEFINITION** *Acquihire* is a combination of the words *acquisition* and *hire*. This is when a company acquires a startup based on the team's skills rather than the product or service.

The scenario is that you built a stellar team, and hiring great people is hard. Your acquirer has discovered how great your team is and wants to grab them quickly before someone else finds out how good they are. It's typically not a barn-burner exit, for sure, but for the founders, it can be a very nice outcome. Facebook has done this a hundred times with companies like Drop.io, Hot Potato, Beluga, and FriendFeed. Google did it with Aardvark, Slide, Like.com, and reMail. And Twitter did it with Summize and Fluther. In all those cases, you will find that people from those startups ended up in very senior roles within the big acquirer.

31.3.2 Nuts-and-bolts issues to nail down for you and your team

Sure, you want to get a good valuation for your company, and you need to know what's going to happen with things like operating capital and indemnification. Typically, an escrow will be set up to deal with potential legal actions, such as from shareholders not happy with the deal or vendors that believe they are owed money. But it's the stuff with respect to you and your team that sets the tone for what happens to your company inside the new one over the long term: does it even exist inside after a couple of years? Don't trust what should happen to you, your team, and your technology once inside the acquirer to just happen, and don't forget to hammer out those eventualities in writing in *advance* of the transaction closing.

COMPENSATION

The salaries of everyone in your company, founders and management included, have been startup salaries because everyone accepted that a big part of their comp was in equity. Now all of your employees (not including senior managers and founders, who most likely have shares and not options) will (hopefully) reap the benefits of those options turning into cash as part of this acquisition (which was the point of their options in the first place). But they are going to be part of a bigger company, where presumably there won't be big payouts. They need a competitive, big-company salary. The best way to make that happen—because the acquirer may keep people's salaries the same—is for you to change their salary to that level *before* the acquisition. It's a trick most startups forget, to their team's detriment. You make this adjustment when you are sure the transaction is going through but not so close to the closing that it draws the ire of the transaction team. I have experienced the transaction team encouraging this because they know the wheels of HR inside their company move very slowly.

TITLES

Big companies typically have a very formal set of titles that map to levels of compensation and authority. However, titles like senior engineer, principal engineer, and director don't mean the same thing from one big company to another. You will have to get that mapping from the new HR department. Then it will be up to you to make the mapping for your team, advocate for your team to get the appropriate titles, and make sure their responsibilities, salaries, bonuses, and other compensation fit into the acquirer's rigid structure.

RETENTION

During their due diligence phase, an acquirer gets to know the team they will be inheriting. Part of this is to determine which people are key employees to retain. They will offer these key people extra incentives to stick around for a specified period. Try to make sure that amount of time is one year or at most two, not the three that some acquirers try for—three years for someone who had self-selected to be a startup person will feel like a very long time.

There is a secondary question about how to retain the people who want to take their equity earnings and leave right away. If that happens, it may make it difficult to accomplish what you need to for the acquirer to consider the acquisition successful. You can address attrition by negotiating a separate retention fund that you can use to try to retain people who don't care if they are key—they just don't want to stick around very long. Even retaining your whole staff for a short time could be very helpful in getting your product integrated into the new company.

HIRING

As someone who has also worked at very large companies, I know that controlling expenses through staffing constraints is their modus operandi. Again, if you get an up-front agreement before close regarding the hiring you will need to do to accomplish the goals you and the acquirer have mutually agreed to, hiring will be possible. If you don't get this agreement, hiring may not be possible because you'll find yourself in competition with senior managers who have been at the company a long time and know the ropes.

YOU

Where do you fit in the new organization? It is important that you know whom you report to. The more authority and seniority that person has, the better your life will be: they are your "overseer" or "caretaker," especially during the transition period, and you want them to have the clout to protect your interests. Remember, this is a big company, complete with tons of politics you may not be used to.

Be sure you report to only one person—many large companies these days are using matrix reporting structures.

> **DEFINITION**   *Matrix organizations* are structures where people have both a primary manager and a project manager.

This happens with engineering people all the time, but I've seen it for other functions as well. In my opinion, this kind of structure is a nightmare, especially if you are new and don't know how to manage big-company politics you have little experience with. If you are a standalone business unit, it sounds good, but the reporting structure can be really challenging. Some founders negotiate a board of senior leaders that they are part of to manage their new business unit.

EARNOUTS

This is a situation that is typically good for the buyers and bad for the startup team.

> **DEFINITION** *Earnouts* mean compensation for the management team of the startup being acquired is tied to hitting a set of milestones.

There are many unknowns—many more than the uncertainty you lived with while a startup—and the situation is fraught with risk to you. It may be off the table, but taking less money up front versus more money later that is tied to earnouts could be a good decision for you.

CULTURE

It is vital that you understand the acquirer's culture, or two years could end up feeling like an eternity. Your team needs to feel comfortable in the new culture, so make sure you dig into whether this company reflects the values you have been sharing as you built up your company. Talk to the people at the new parent company who form the acquisition team. This will be a cross-functional team, and they will be friendly because they are happy to be working on another acquisition. They will talk, probably openly. Also try to talk to any other employees you can find who previously were with small companies acquired by the parent company.

What happens if you find out the culture is bad? You can still cancel the deal if it's terrible. Or you continue but make sure the length of time your people have to commit to stay at the company to get their compensation is as short as possible.

31.3.3 The "day after" the acquisition

One critical question to ask before the close is about the acquirer's "day after" plan. These are the details of how they plan to execute the integration of your company into theirs, especially with respect to you, your employees, and your customers. No matter what, the integration process is always chaotic, stressful, and confusing. You will still feel like a team at first, and your employees will look to you for explanations of what is happening. Continue communicating steadily to keep them as comfortable as can be. Their roles may be changing, and yours certainly will. The culture almost certainly will be a change unless you are being acquired by another startup. They will have many systems and processes—probably a lot more processes than a startup is used to. That will feel stifling. And of course, there will be a lot of new people to get to know. An organization chart will be essential for you and your team. On the good side, the acquirer wants you and will be investing in you, and this means you may suddenly have more resources than you ever had as a startup.

But the thing I cannot stress enough is this: being acquired is the goal of an entrepreneur, and it is a rare and amazing accomplishment. When you're down in the details of the deal and the integration process, you may have trouble seeing the forest for the trees. But step back, celebrate this accomplishment, and patiently work hard to make the outcome for everyone the best you can.

31.4   *The moral of this anecdote*

IPOs are complex, long, difficult, and very rare. For every 10 startups, 5 fail, 3 just return the capital invested in them, and 2 are the big wins that will be the basis of the returns for an investor's fund. This means rather than the 10× revenues that most entrepreneurs think their company needs to return, it is 30×. An entrepreneur needs to be planning on an acquisition all the time, even when all you can think about is making payroll, getting revenues, and growing the business. Sure, some offers come in unsolicited, but most happen because you have cultivated a set of relationships.

When an offer comes in to acquire, it's at first a major gong-ringing moment. As always, the devil is in the details. It would be heavenly if there were multiple offers to choose between, but that is also rare. You have a lot to think about and plan for, starting with what type of structure the acquisition will take. Then there is the planning for your team and making sure points relative to the team are in the deal and not left to chance. In the end, despite the exhausting amount of work involved in being acquired, it is the outcome all entrepreneurs dream of, and the work is well worth it.

appendix

This appendix lists the answers I entered on the website Gust (http://gust.com) when applying for funding from angel groups. They are specific to my startup, Dover Microsystems, and are presented here because they may be useful for your company and situation.

A.1 Company Summary

Add an overview to help investors evaluate your startup. You might like to include your business model, structure, and products/services. 450 chars.

> Dover is a 16-person seed-stage silicon IP licensing business with a DARPA research pedigree and $28M in nondilutive financing. The product is CoreGuard, a hybrid HW and SW cybersecurity system that watches each instruction executed by the processor it is protecting determining if it is doing the correct thing or not. Contracts with NXP, Cadence, Air Force Research Lab through Centauri. Pipeline is healthy; 2020 revenues are projected to be $3M.

A.2 Management Team

Who are the members of your management team and how will their experience aid in your success? 450 chars.

> Jothy (CEO) is 9-time startup founder, 3 time CEO; held roles as CTO and COO. Did 2 HW startups, exits over $100M in 2 others. Two companies were cybersecurity. VPE managed HW and SW of a major RSA security product 12 yrs. CTO was lead processor architect at Microchip for 8 years. Sales was account exec at Mentor 17 years. CFO has done IPO, multiple acquisitions. Team has known each other for years creating strong mutual trust.

A.3   Customer Problem

What customer problem does your product and/or service solve? 450 chars.

> Annual cybercrime costs $6 trillion by '21. A business falls victim to ransomware every 11 seconds. Customers don't know what to do so they add layers of defensive software. Makes the problem worse: software has up to 50 bugs per 1000 lines of source. The cybersecurity problem must be addressed at the root cause—the attacker's ability to take over the processor by exploiting bugs. But processors are too simple to even know they are being attacked

A.4   Products & Services

Describe the product or service that you will sell and how it solves the customer problem, listing the main value proposition for each product/service. 450 chars.

> Our product is CoreGuard, a hybrid hardware and software solution. The HW is licensed silicon IP that protects host processor by monitoring every instruction. Ensures it complies with a set of security, safety, and privacy rules written in software accessible only by CG. CG comes with a base set of security rules and we license additional ones for customized levels of security, safety, privacy. Also provide services to write custom policies.

A.5   Target Market

Define the important geographic, demographic, and/or psychographic characteristics of the market within which your customer segments exist. 450 chars.

> We target the world's embedded devices—98% of all processors. IoT is expanding this by 30B. SoC builders for these devices are potential customers. This includes device manufacturers in vertical segments, large semiconductor manufacturers, automotive, medical, and mobile. Our Serviceable Addressable Market is calculated by taking the number of devices or parts created in each market times the expected value to Dover and comes to $8.5B annually.

A.6   Business Model

What strategy will you employ to build, deliver, and retain company value (e.g., profits)? 450 chars.

> Dover is a cash-efficient high-margin IP licensing company with five main revenue streams. 1. Discover license: $150-250K for paid evaluation. 2. Design license: $1.0-3.0M paid up front to design CoreGuard into their SoC design. 3. Deploy license: per chip royalty averaging 1.5% of ASP of part being protected. 4. Custom policy development tools and services: $TBD. 5. Monetization of CoreGuard's highly accurate real-time attack detection data.

A.7   Customer Segments

Outline your targeted customer segments. These are the specific subsets of your target market that you will focus on to gain traction. 450 chars.

> We primarily focus on two verticals at a time until we have a beachhead. Verticals are chosen based on who is being attacked and has proven willingness to pay for security. Secondary target is large semiconductors. We sell the full package to customers making ASICs. For customers who already use a chip with CoreGuard, we sell software and services around policies We have and seek highly leveraged partnerships: SiFive, Andes, Cadence, Synopsys.

A.8   Sales & Marketing Strategy

What is your customer acquisition and retention strategy? Detail how you will promote, sell and create customer loyalty for your products and services. 450 chars.

> Demand generation programs aimed at device manufacturers in selected verticals. Build on top of thought leadership and publicized market traction to attract decision makers. Direct sales to semi manufacturers. Leverage investors and advisors to get high level warm introductions. Once design win achieved, lock-in occurs because of long HW design cycles. Build leveraged partner channel who we sell through. Have Cadence already, Synopsys is goal.

A.9   Competitors

Describe the competitive landscape and your competitors' strengths and weaknesses. If direct competitors don't exist, describe the existing alternatives. 450 chars.

> Categories: security software, encryption hardware, memory safety hardware. Security software can't compete because SW can be attacked over the network. Encryption vital for data-in-motion. It's not what we do, but the market is confused and views it as competition. Vendors are adding memory protection hardware to their processors (Arm, SiFive). Their solutions only overlap with us a small amount (we block 95% of all attacks).

A.10   Competitive Advantage

What is your company's competitive or unfair advantage? This can include patents, first mover advantage, unique expertise, or proprietary processes/technology. 450 chars.

> A gap in the security stack is called APPLICATION SELF-PROTECTION. Nothing above this, including compartmentalization, kernel, encryption, and application are protected without CoreGuard's enforcement of instruction-level correctness. We uniquely immunize processors against attacks. Initial customers view CoreGuard as disruptive and a competitive advantage; market traction is our first barrier to entry. 2nd is IP moat: 60 patents filed 10 issued.

index

RELATED MANNING TITLES

Think Like a CTO
by Alan Williamson
Foreword by Ankit Mathur

ISBN 9781617298851
320 pages, $49.99
February 2023

Skills of a Successful Software Engineer
by Fernando Doglio

ISBN 9781617299704
192 pages, $49.99
June 2022

Succeeding with AI
by Veljko Krunic

ISBN 9781617296932
288 pages, $49.99
March 2020

Street Coder
by Sedat Kapanoglu

ISBN 9781617298370
272 pages, $49.99
December 2021

For ordering information, go to www.manning.com

 **MANNING**

The Manning Early Access Program

Don't wait to start learning! In MEAP, the Manning Early Access Program, you can read books as they're being created and long before they're available in stores.

Here's how MEAP works.

- **Start now.** Buy a MEAP and you'll get all available chapters in PDF, ePub, Kindle, and liveBook formats.

- **Regular updates.** New chapters are released as soon as they're written. We'll let you know when fresh content is available.

- **Finish faster.** MEAP customers are the first to get final versions of all books! Pre-order the print book, and it'll ship as soon as it's off the press.

- **Contribute to the process.** The feedback you share with authors makes the end product better.

- **No risk.** You get a full refund or exchange if we ever have to cancel a MEAP.

Explore dozens of titles in MEAP at www.manning.com.